D1276443

La America

La America   La America

לה אמיריקה

THE ORIENTAL PRINTING & PUBLISHING CO.

'LA AMERICA' ORIENTAL SPANISH-JEWISH JOURNAL

National, Literary, Political and Commercial Weekly Paper

Subscription Rates

United States   Foreign
One Year .... $1.50   10 Francs
Six Months 0.75   5

Payable in Advance

Director-Propietor: M. S. GADOL

New York

PRICE THREE CENTS   FRIDAY 23 FEBRUARY 1912   Vol. II. No. 31.

איל אדיטור דיל זורנאל

קונגריגאסיון ספרדית שארית
ישראל ד׳ ניו־יורק

La America

The Sephardic Experience in the United States

MARC D. ANGEL

PHILADELPHIA 5742 | 1982
THE JEWISH PUBLICATION SOCIETY OF AMERICA

Designed by Adrianne Onderdonk Dudden

Library of Congress Cataloging in Publication Data
Angel, Marc.
    La America: the Sephardic experience in the United States
    Bibliography: p.
    Includes index.
    1. Sephardim—New York (N.Y.)—History—20th century. 2. Gadol, Moise S.
3. Sephardim—New York (N.Y.)—Biography. 4. Amerikah. 5. New York
(N.Y.)—Ethnic relations.   I. Title.
F128.9.J5A53   974.7'1004924   81–20923
ISBN 0–8276–0205–7   AACR2

FRONTISPIECE: Page one of *La America*, February 23, 1912, with a picture of
Moise Gadol.

3993

This book is dedicated to the memory of my grandparents
BOHOR YEHUDAH *and* BULISSA ESTHER ANGEL
and
MARCO *and* SULTANA ROMEY
pioneers in the generation of La America

Contents

Acknowledgments   ix

1   The Story of This Book   3
2   In the Beginning   9
3   Organizations and Disorganization   19
4   A Hispano-Levantine Community   39
5   Toward a Unified Community   61
6   Old and New Sephardim Meet   88
7   The Struggles of La America   106
8   Zionism among the Sephardim   129
9   Economic Life   138
10   The Sephardic Diaspora in the U.S.   148
11   The Next Generations   164
12   Epilogue   177

Notes   185
Bibliography   209
Index   213

Illustrations follow page   60

Acknowledgments

It is with pleasure that I acknowledge the assistance I received in the preparation of this book. I owe my knowledge and love of the Judeo-Spanish language and culture to my maternal grandparents, of blessed memory, Marco and Sultana Romey; to my parents, Victor and Rachel Angel; and to my relatives and friends in the Sephardic community of Seattle, Washington. Had I not been raised in this environment, I would never have pursued this research with so much love and excitement.

I thank the staff of the Jewish Division of the New York Public Library, where much of the research for this book was undertaken. Victor Tarry and Joseph Tarica, of Congregation Shearith Israel, greatly assisted me in making available the many archival materials in the possession of their congregation. My thanks must go to all those individuals who provided me with personal information about Moise Gadol and helped to clarify my understanding of the man and his times.

Yosef Hayim Yerushalmi read through the entire manuscript and offered perceptive and useful suggestions. Maier Deshell, of the Jewish Publication Society of America, has been encouraging and helpful in many ways. Salena Rapp Kern provided valuable editorial advice. Most of the photographs that illustrate this book were made available through the courtesy of Victor Tarry, Louis N.

Levy, and Joel Halio. I thank them and everyone else who allowed me to use their photographs.

A special word of thanks goes to Hennie Imberman, who typed the many drafts of this manuscript. Her assistance and encouragement have been immeasurable; she truly has been a participant in the creation of this book.

I express my deep gratitude to my wife, Gilda, and to our children, Jeffrey, Ronda, and Elana, for their sacrifices on behalf of this book. Words are inadequate to convey my love and respect for them.

La America

1

The Story of This Book

Friday, June 13, 1941, was a gray, rainy day. A group of Sephardic Jews braved the downpour to attend a funeral at the Zion Memorial Chapel, at 41 Canal Street in the Lower East Side of New York. The deceased was Moise Gadol.

Gadol's wife had died in 1933; they had had no children. Several nephews and nieces, some acquaintances from the past, and a curious onlooker or two paid their last respects to Moise Gadol. The eulogy was delivered by the chief rabbi of the Central Sephardic Jewish Community of America, the distinguished scholar and author, Rabbi Nissim Ovadia. He spoke briefly, indicating that he had hardly known the deceased but that he was sure Gadol had done various good deeds during his lifetime.

The burial was at Mt. Zion cemetery in Queens. It was not possible to arrange for Gadol to be buried next to his wife, so he was interred in a family plot belonging to relatives. The grave was not part of a Sephardic section of the cemetery—nearly all the graves in the area were of Ashkenazic Jews.

Until his death, Gadol had lived alone in very poor conditions. During the last eight years of his life, following the death of his wife, he was melancholy, dyspeptic, and subject to fits of madness. Some questioned his sanity. A Sephardic woman who had operated a restaurant that Gadol frequented recalls that the customers used to ridicule Gadol. He would sit alone at a table, eating okra and meat or some other Sephardic dish, and would be taunted for his "crazy" ideas. During his last years he was bent on proving that Christopher Columbus was Jewish and that America owed its very existence to Jews and therefore should be especially kind to the Jewish people. "I pitied him, pitied him so much," said the restaurant owner. "Why did he care if Columbus was Jewish? Why did he argue with them? They only laughed and mocked him. I was so sad for him."

On Tuesday, June 3, 1941, Gadol became ill and was taken to Kings County Hospital. On Wednesday, June 11, at 11 A.M., he breathed his last. Gadol was sixty-seven years old when he died. As there was no immediate relative or friend to look after him, plans were made to bury him in potter's field.

Albert Torres, publisher of *La Vara,* the national Judeo-Spanish weekly newspaper, learned of the problem and personally undertook funeral arrangements for Moise Gadol. Several Sephardim paid all the expenses involved. Gadol, who had dedicated his life selflessly to the Sephardic community, at least received that ultimate reward from the Sephardim: a Jewish funeral.

In researching an article about the Sephardim of the United States, which appeared in the *American Jewish Year Book* of 1973, I scanned through a number of issues of *La America,* beginning in 1910. As I quickly reeled through the microfilms of the newspaper at the New York Public Library, I recognized at once that there was a brilliant, vibrant mind behind them. The issues were still exciting and thought-provoking so many years after they had been written. I took copious notes and made up my mind to come back to study *La America* when I could read the papers more leisurely and study the contents more carefully.

In 1979, I obtained a set of the microfilms of *La America* and spent many hours each day reading and copying. The work consumed me. Moise Gadol was editor of *La America,* the first Judeo-Spanish newspaper published in the United States, and as I read his writings that had appeared from November 1910 until July 1925 I felt I was coming to know the man personally. The newspapers recorded his activities and thoughts weekly: his struggles and achievements, failures and frustrations were becoming part of my life. I searched for—and found—people who still remembered him. I visited the Sephardic Home for the Aged in Brooklyn to spend some time with Rachel Pilosoff, the restaurant owner, and Joseph and Lily Varsano; Joseph Varsano had been a partner in the printing office of *La America* in the 1920s. I spoke with Gadol's nephew, now living in California. I received written recollections about Gadol from Albert J. Amateau, now in his nineties; Amateau and Gadol had been protagonists in many a communal battle. I visited Gadol's neighborhoods in the Lower East Side and Harlem. The images of Gadol that emerged in my mind captivated me.

Between 1880 and 1925, millions of immigrants poured into the United States, primarily from Russia and eastern Europe. With the passing years, this migration movement intensified. During the period from 1899 to 1910, more than one million Jews arrived at the Port of New York to begin their lives in the New World. Many had come in search of opportunity and wealth; others had fled from persecution in their native lands. Many came alone; others arrived with their families. Many planned to settle here permanently; others intended to remain only as long as it took to make their fortune.

The crowded, tenement-lined streets of the Lower East Side of New York, where hundreds of thousands of these immigrants settled, became a unique human experiment, testing the ability of different groups to coexist while maintaining their own identity. But this enormous experiment—which took place to a lesser degree in other immigrant ghettos in cities throughout the country—was not merely a test of groups. Each immigrant was involved in a personal battle, a fight to survive in a new and difficult social context. The immigrant brought the language and culture of his native land to New York. He had been used to a different kind of life; now he was confronted with an English-speaking American culture as well as with a variety of subcultures different from his own, all represented on the streets of the Lower East Side.

This human experiment produced many successes and many failures. The harsh realities of immigrant life pushed each person's abilities to the limit. From this milieu emerged a large number of intellectuals, industrialists, labor leaders, politicians, and folk heroes. No doubt many immigrants who did not achieve fame but remained part of the nameless masses lived noble and courageous lives. To survive in such a difficult setting is its own tribute.

Along with the immigrants who succeeded in rising above their environment were those who were crushed and ruined by it. The newspapers of the period record suicides of people who no longer could face life as it was. Poverty, miserable working conditions, and rampant disease all took their toll. The world of concrete and brick wrecked many lives. As an experiment in human civilization, the Lower East Side succeeded and failed.

Irving Howe draws a thoughtful portrait of these immigrants in his book, *World of Our Fathers*. Howe views the immigrants in light of their original cultural background and describes their adjustment to the new realities of America. The language of these immigrants was Yiddish, and the local Jewish organizations involved in helping immigrants used Yiddish as the vehicle of communication. *World of Our Fathers* is a monument to the life of the Yiddish-speaking immigrants, who were to have a profound influence on Jewish life as well as on American society.

Because the overwhelming number of Jewish immigrants spoke Yiddish, the relatively small number of non-Yiddish-speaking Jews was overlooked almost completely by the people of that time as well as by later historians. During the period from 1890 to 1924, about thirty thousand Jews from Levantine countries had come to the United States, and most had settled in New York City. The majority of these Jews came from Turkey and the Balkan countries and their mother tongue was Judeo-Spanish. However, there were also Greek-speaking Jews from Greece, as well as Arabic-speaking Jews, primarily from Syria. The members of these groups found themselves in an even more difficult position than that of other immigrants. Not only did they have all the usual problems of people who have come to a new land, but they had additional conflicts stemming from the fact that the existing Jewish organizations hardly recognized them as Jews. In the Yiddish-speaking world of the Lower East Side, there was little time to deal with small pockets of Spanish-, Greek-, or Arabic-speaking Jews. Although few in number, the Sephardim, as these Jews are known, needed to establish their own synagogues, schools, and communal self-help organizations, since they could not easily fit into the existing Jewish institutions.

It was in May 1910 that Moise Salomon Gadol came to New York from his native Bulgaria in order to visit relatives. Gadol was then thirty-six years old. He was a successful businessman and his commercial dealings had given him the opportunity to travel throughout Europe. In the process of his studies and travels, he had mastered eleven languages.

When Gadol arrived in New York, he was shocked to see the conditions in which people lived on the Lower East Side. In particular, he was troubled by the plight of the Sephardic Jews, then numbering perhaps ten thousand. The Sephardic immigrants were receiving no assistance or guidance from any organization and had little idea of what services or opportunities were available to them. Unemployment was widespread. Visiting some of the Sephardic coffee shops and restaurants, Gadol found young men and women who idled their time away, not knowing where to find work nor how they might integrate themselves into the society they now found themselves in.

Moise Gadol decided to abandon his commercial endeavors in Europe and settle in New York in order to devote himself to helping the Sephardim of the United States, particularly those living on the Lower East Side. On November 11, 1910, he published the first issue of a Judeo-Spanish weekly newspaper, *La America,* feeling that a newspaper would be the most effective means of educating the Sephardim.

Gadol invested his time and money selflessly in order to make the newspaper survive. In spite of his efforts and financial sacrifices, he had to stop publication during several intervals, and was finally forced to terminate the newspaper altogether in July of 1925.

Moise Gadol was perhaps the greatest voice of the immigrant Sephardic community during the years in which *La America* appeared. He was a heroic figure, although seldom appreciated by many of his contemporaries. And he was a tragic hero. The harsh conditions of immigrant life in New York brought out his greatness; but they ultimately destroyed him.

This book is primarily a study of the Judeo-Spanish-speaking

Sephardim of New York from 1910 until 1925 as seen through the eyes of Moise Gadol and his newspaper, *La America*. On its pages we can see firsthand the struggles of the Sephardim to adapt to a new way of life. This is the story of a people and of one man, the description of a sliver of history with ramifications that transcend time.

2

In the Beginning

Albert Amateau reminisces about his first encounter with Moise Gadol: "I can see it as in a dream, but I have to close my eyes to recapture the scene. It was midafternoon of an unseasonably cold day in September 1910. My unheated tenement room on Forsyth Street on the East Side in lower Manhattan compelled me to seek comfort in A. Levy's coffeehouse a block away on Chrystie Street. The place was almost full of fellow Sephardic immigrants seated around tables playing cards, dominoes, or backgammon and sipping Turkish coffee or tea. The doors were closed to keep in whatever heat was emitted by the gas heater in the center of the large room.

"The few nonplayers like myself sat watching through the large plate-glass windows the parade of people walking carefully in the snow from the storm of the night before. A man who was wearing a heavy overcoat with an Astrakhan collar and a Russian-type calpac on his head pulled over his ears, and carrying a black, silver-headed stick in his gloved hand, stopped in front of the coffeehouse, peered through the window, hesitated a moment, and then slowly opened the door and came in. The sudden draft of cold air caused everyone to look to the door. Instant suspicion was stamped on every face. He was an *ajenou*—a stranger—whom no one recognized. He spoke in a strangely accented Judeo-Spanish:

'Mi yamou Moise Gadol. Vengou di Bulgaria' (My name is Moise Gadol. I come from Bulgaria).

"He was swarthy, rather long-faced, five feet seven or eight in height, a bit rotund. His black hair and his moustache were sprinkled with a few threads of white. His small hands indicated that he was not a manual worker. His small feet were shod in black, high-necked leather shoes buttoned on the side, with rubber overshoes."

Gadol was surprised to see so many men in the coffeehouse in the middle of the day. Why weren't they at work? Amateau explained that many of the men were night workers in movie theaters, hotels, and night clubs. Were they organized into a community? Gadol inquired. Amateau responded that they were not, but there were various self-help societies comprised of members from cities in Turkey. Gadol was disappointed to learn of the difficult conditions and the general communal disorganization plaguing the Sephardim.

Why had these people come to New York? Why had they left communities in Turkey, Greece, the Balkan countries, and Syria, where their ancestors had lived for over four centuries? During the latter half of the nineteenth century, a small but powerful social and intellectual revolution was taking place within many of the Sephardic communities in the Levant. After centuries of cultural isolation, Western ideas began to reach the masses. Many of the changing attitudes derived from the network of schools established by the Alliance Israélite Universelle, a Jewish organization based in Paris. A goal of the Alliance was to bring modern French education to the young Sephardim of the Levant. The schools raised the academic level of the students, provided poor children with a better education, and brought Western thinking to the seemingly backward world of the Orient.

The Western education provided by these schools gradually alienated some students from their indigenous environment. Young Sephardim came to believe that it was possible to create new lives for themselves and their families by seeking out opportunities for economic and social advancement. The old way of life, perpetuated over the centuries, provided nothing but a future of hard manual labor and poverty while the idea of America, with its reputed wealth and industry, began to capture their imagination.

As young people became intoxicated with the modern spirit of progress they were willing to risk migrating from their cities and villages to search out new circumstances in other lands. Since the economic and intellectual possibilities in the communities of the Levant were quite limited for the most part, ambitious Sephardic Jews planned to migrate. Some intended to return; others left knowing they were leaving forever. Though some Sephardim migrated to various places in Europe, Palestine, Africa, and South America, the greatest number came to the United States.

As the first Sephardic immigrants—mostly young men—left their native towns to begin new lives in America, the long period of Sephardic cultural isolation was beginning to end. These young Sephardim in search of fortune and adventure were the pioneers of a demographic and ideological revolution. As these immigrants resettled in new cities, they would send back money to their relatives in the old country. In time, they would also send transportation fare for wives, relatives, and friends. To the Sephardim in the Levant, the image of America as a land of gold was fueled by the letters and money sent from the Sephardic immigrants in the United States.

But the migration movement started slowly. According to figures derived from the records of the United States commissioner general of immigration, only 2,738 Levantine Sephardim came to the United States between 1890 and 1907. The figure reported by the Hebrew Sheltering and Immigrant Aid Society (later to be known as the Hebrew Immigrant Aid Society, or HIAS) was somewhat higher but it is clear that there was no mass migration of Sephardim to the United States in this early period.

Conditions in Turkey and the Balkan countries, however, were soon to stimulate the migration movement. In 1908 the revolt of the Young Turks, which aimed at securing a constitutional government in Turkey, created hardships for many Jews. Compulsory military service was instituted, and for the first time Jews were included in the military draft. Many young men of draft age chose to leave.

Indeed, Moise Gadol, writing in March 1912, believed that the main reason for the step-up in migration from Turkey among Jews was the army. Under the so-called constitutional government of Turkey, one could pay a certain sum of money to avoid military conscription. Each time a person was called up for maneuvers or war, he would have to buy an exemption or enter the military. As a result, many individuals were perpetually paying money to the government. If a man between the ages of twenty and forty-five was not able to pay just one time, he would be taken as a soldier. Hence, the wealthy were able to pay their way out of military service while the poor had to serve. It was not surprising therefore that many young men—Jewish, Armenian, Greek, and even Moslem—chose to migrate to America.

Life in Turkey and the Balkan countries was very difficult at this time. Aside from its own political problems, Turkey was embroiled in a war with Italy in 1911–12 and had been struck with a number of natural disasters—fires and earthquakes—which had severely damaged some of its cities. During the Balkan wars, 1912–13, there was widespread violence in the warring countries, and the Sephardic communities were ravaged.

The situation of the Levantine Jews was desperate following these catastrophic wars and natural disasters. Constantinople (Istanbul, Turkey) and Salonika (Thessaloníki, Greece) were overcrowded with refugees from the war zone, and major cities of Sephardic settlement, such as Monastir (now Bitola, Yugoslavia), Janina (now Ioánnina, Greece), Kastoría, Greece, Kavála, Greece, and Adrianople (now Edirne, Turkey), had been severely damaged. The Jews of Bulgaria found it necessary to appeal to European and American Jews for assistance. It was estimated that two hundred thousand Jews in European Turkey were living in dire poverty. And the troubles were far from over. In 1914 the First World War broke out and with it came more suffering and misery to the people of the Levant.

In contrast to these terrible political, economic, and military conditions, the idealized picture of America was quite enticing. The pages of La America told of the boundless opportunities that existed in the United States: industry and commerce were booming there; one was not subject to the draft prior to becoming a citizen, and then, one got paid for serving in the armed forces—America was indeed "the land of the dollars." In addition to financial considerations, the public school system in the United States gave everyone the opportunity to advance. The availability of electricity, transportation, and machinery eased everyday life. There were strong incentives for women, too. Women were allowed to work for pay in the United States and they did not have to provide dowries before marriage. Girls received an education, attended public meetings, and went to parties. As one man said, "For an Oriental father of many children, America is his salvation." The impact of this propaganda on the suffering Sephardim can be measured in the tremendous upsurge in emigration.

It was estimated that more than ten thousand Sephardic Jews entered the United States between 1908 and 1914. Although immigration lessened during World War I, an additional ten thousand Sephardim arrived between 1920 and 1924. David de Sola Pool, writing in the 1913–14 volume of *The American Jewish Year Book*, states that 80 to 90 percent of the Sephardic immigrants had settled in New York City, mostly on the Lower East Side.

Although the number of Sephardic immigrants was large in relation to the communities from which they originated, they represented only a trickle in the wave of Jewish immigration. HIAS reported, for example, that in 1912 there were 64,738 Jews who arrived at the Port of New York. Of these 1,911 were from Turkey. Of the 130,237 Jewish immigrants who entered between January and November 1913, HIAS reported 2,344 Sephardim (1,421 men and 923 women).

The Sephardic immigrants, like all immigrants, faced the trauma of leaving family and friends and setting off for an unknown future in a new land. As they crossed the ocean, they no doubt spent much time thinking about what they had left behind. But, they also wondered about what would happen to them when they reached their destination, New York. They all had at least some vague knowledge that they would have to go through the American Immigration Office at Ellis Island and that they would have to answer questions. They probably knew that some individuals were refused admittance to the United States because they had certain diseases.

A lead article in *La America* (June 9, 1911) complained that the Turkish Jews were experiencing particular difficulties at Ellis Island because they did not know enough about American immigration laws. They were reluctant to answer some questions put to them by the American officials, not knowing what the officials wanted to hear. Some were detained for weeks and a few were actually sent back to Turkey. Gadol tried to assist by translating American immigration laws into Judeo-Spanish so that the Sephardim abroad could read them before arriving in New York.

Jewish organizations existed to help guide Jewish immigrants through the immigration process. Notably, HIAS was very much involved in this process. However, the workers of HIAS could not easily recognize Sephardim as being Jews since they did not have "Jewish" names, did not speak Yiddish, and physically appeared to be Greeks, Turks, or Italians. Consequently, Sephardic immigrants in the early years received practically no assistance from the organized Jewish community. Well-intentioned Sephardim who already were living in New York would go to Ellis Island to meet their friends or relatives who were arriving. More often than not, these good-hearted individuals would cause the immigrants even more problems: they interfered with the immigration officials, answered questions that were directed to the immigrants, and offered unnecessary advice to the newcomers. *La America* (April 5, 1912) urged Sephardim not to go to Ellis Island on their own, as the new arrivals were more easily able to get through immigration when no friends or relatives were there to greet them.

Recognizing the difficult and sometimes heartbreaking circumstances confronting the Sephardic immigrants on their arrival at Ellis Island, Moise Gadol determined to help alleviate the situation. He approached the leaders of HIAS and convinced them to establish a special agency whose established purpose would be to serve the needs of the incoming Sephardic Jews. Gadol himself served as the first secretary of the Oriental Bureau, which started its operation in the latter part of 1911. Gadol initially took no pay for his service. He not only provided assistance to incoming immigrants on their arrival at Ellis Island, but also set up regular hours for the Oriental Bureau in the building of HIAS to deal with other problems that the immigrants might have once they were settled in New York. On Monday and Wednesday evenings, Gadol assisted Sephardim in filling out citizenship papers. He also provided employment guidance. The pages of *La America* publicized the work of the Oriental Bureau and of HIAS at every opportunity. Apparently, the work on behalf of the Sephardic immigrants was quite successful. The chief rabbi of Turkey, Rabbi Hayyim Nahoum, wrote a letter to Gadol praising the work of HIAS, and in particular the labors of the Oriental Bureau (*La America,* March 29, 1912). In reporting about this letter, *La America* stated that Gadol "is the only one, thanks to his knowledge of so many languages, who can for now fill this post [secretary of the Oriental Bureau], for which he expects or wants no thanks from anyone. He is content with not receiving bad treatment in return for so much good work."

As the work of the Oriental Bureau expanded, Gadol found himself overwhelmed by the responsibilities. He was the sole staff member of the Oriental Bureau while trying to issue a weekly Judeo-Spanish newspaper. His problems were aggravated by the fact that *La America* was in poor financial condition and was steadily losing money. Since he had invested his own funds into the newspaper and since he had little other means of livelihood—giving whatever spare time he had to the Oriental Bureau—Gadol found himself in a precarious financial situation.

In June 1912 HIAS voted to pay five hundred dollars per year to the secretary of the Oriental Bureau. Gadol thought that ten dollars a week was hardly adequate compensation for the work he was doing, but he believed too much in his work to walk away from the task. He encouraged the Sephardim to contribute to the Oriental Bureau: "Our Turkinos, seeing the good of the Oriental Bureau, give thousands of praises and many promises of help; but do not come through. Some say: 'Let the rich Ashkenazim pay the bills'" (*La America,* June 21, 1912). Gadol suggested that if each Sephardic society contributed fifty dollars per year, the secretary could be compensated properly for his services. But the presidents of a number of the societies indicated that this expense was beyond their capacity.

Because Gadol's economic condition had deteriorated so much, he realized that he could no longer spend so many hours working at the Oriental Bureau. He therefore recommended a fellow Bulgarian Jew, Jack Farhi, to the post of secretary. Farhi was well known to the Sephardic colony in New York and had a knowledge of all the necessary languages. He had been a Hebrew teacher in Turkey after having studied for some time in the land of Israel. He came to the

United States in 1909 and had become active in Sephardic community life. He took over the responsibilities of the Oriental Bureau with energy and devotion.

But the task proved too much for one person to handle alone. Gadol believed that HIAS should have one Sephardic Jew at Ellis Island and another at the Oriental Bureau in order to best serve the needs of the Sephardic immigrants and that each should be paid at least one thousand dollars per year. Since HIAS had already voted five hundred dollars for the Oriental Bureau, Gadol pleaded with the Sephardic community to raise the additional fifteen hundred dollars. Sephardim did indeed contribute to the cause, but not to the extent that Gadol felt was satisfactory. By October 1915 the Oriental Bureau had been closed. HIAS stated that it simply could not afford to keep a special person on the payroll for the Sephardim, but indicated that it would continue to help all Jewish immigrants of whatever origin and would establish an information office especially for Sephardim. HIAS also volunteered its facilities to Sephardic societies. Even with the Oriental Bureau closed, HIAS believed Sephardim could still benefit from its services. But the existing staff of HIAS was not equipped linguistically or culturally to provide adequate service to the Sephardim and the Oriental Bureau was reopened in August 1916.

Another Jewish organization of importance to newly arrived immigrants was the Industrial Removal Office, which was supported by the Baron de Hirsch Fund. This organization attempted to divert Jewish immigration from New York on the theory that more opportunities were available in smaller, less congested communities. In 1907 the Industrial Removal Office sent contingents of Levantine Sephardim to Seattle, Gary, Cincinnati, Toledo, Columbus, and Cleveland. In 1912 Albert Amateau was appointed special assistant of the Industrial Removal Office at the urging of various Sephardic leaders, who recognized that the Office required an individual who knew the Sephardic languages.

Organizations dedicated to helping Jewish immigrants were overwhelmed with work during the first two decades of the twentieth century. In spite of various proposals in the U.S. Congress to limit immigration, no law passed that significantly limited Jewish immigration. Whenever a bill in favor of quotas was before Congress, mass protest rallies would be called. Gadol himself was involved in organizing rallies against proposed laws to limit immigration. He wrote numerous articles in *La America* to warn the Sephardic masses of the contents of these proposed laws and he wrote letters to government officials, including the president of the United States.

But the era of mass immigration was not to last forever. In 1921 Congress passed a law limiting the number of immigrants to three hundred thousand per year. Each region was limited to a percentage of the number of its immigrants in 1910. Prior to this law, about one-half million immigrants arrived annually. The new law had particular impact on countries that had had small immigration figures in 1910. The new law limited the number of immigrants from the following countries as follows:

Greece	3,286
Bulgaria	307
Albania	287
Yugoslavia	6,405
Romania	7,414

These numbers, of course, included both Jews and non-Jews. Following passage of this law, *La America* reported a number of instances where immigrants were detained at Ellis Island. In the issue of July 29, 1921, Gadol reported that boats full of immigrants were not allowed to enter New York. In the issue of September 23, 1921, he reported on the front page that Turkey had reached its quota for the year and that a ship carrying Turkish immigrants had been sent back. Gadol wrote that the Jews in Turkey who were contemplating coming to the United States should not come until matters improved.

As bad as things were, they were to become even worse. In 1924, another law was passed that limited immigration to 2 percent of the 1890 figure. It stated that the maximum total immigration could be 159,083. The quota system was slanted heavily in favor of England and Germany, and heavily against the countries of the Levant, Russia, and Poland. This law allowed the following number of immigrants from these countries:

Turkey	123
Greece	135
Bulgaria	200
England	62,558
Germany	45,229
Italy	4,689
Russia	1,892
Poland	8,972

The 1924 law almost completely eliminated the possibility of Sephardic immigration. Yet the situation of Jews in Turkey and Greece was becoming worse and many wanted to emigrate. Since so few could come to the United States, Sephardim found new homes in France, Spain, Argentina, Cuba, Mexico, and Palestine.

In *La America*, October 17, 1924, Gadol wrote in an article entitled "A New Chapter in the Sephardic History of America" that the immigration quotas would greatly affect the Sephardic community by almost entirely cutting off the immigration from the Levant. The major responsibilities in the future would have to be directed not to helping new immigrants but to organizing and strengthening the existing Sephardic community already in the United States. The American Sephardim would now be dependent on themselves.

3

Organizations and Disorganization

"We live in New York! In an oven of fire, in the midst of dirt and filth. We live in dark and narrow dwellings which inspire disgust." So wrote Jack Farhi in the summer of 1912, describing the situation of the Sephardic Jews of the Lower East Side. "We work from morning to night without giving ourselves even one day a week for rest. We sleep badly, eat badly, dress ourselves badly. Our economic condition is so bad that we cannot afford to spend several weeks in the country to get away from the oppressive heat of the New York summer. We are very frugal, saving our money to send to our relatives in the old country or just hoarding it away for a rainy day. We are losing the best days of our lives, the time of our youth. . . ."

The strange and hostile world that the Sephardic immigrants discovered on the Lower East Side was not at all what they had expected when they left Turkey or the other countries of the Levant. They had hoped to find streets paved with gold, to become wealthy easily and quickly. Instead of finding a paradise, they found the Lower East Side.

As Sephardic immigrants poured into the area, they naturally gravitated to the streets already inhabited by Sephardim. The new immigrants tended to seek out other Jews who had come from their own native cities in the belief that their common geographic origin created a deeper kinship and sense of responsibility for each other. By living in Sephardic enclaves, they could feel as though their social context had not been completely uprooted, that they were still living among their own people. In particular, they moved into the area of Chrystie, Forsyth, Allen, Broome, Orchard, and Eldridge streets.

The newcomers perpetuated their way of life from the old country by eating the same foods and enjoying the same pastimes as they had in Turkey and the Balkan countries. They sang the old Turkish and Judeo-Spanish songs, frequented the *cavanes* (Turkish-style cafés), and spoke in their native languages. These Jews of New York might just as well have been living on the other side of the ocean. Upon their arrival, many found rooms as boarders in the apartments of fellow Sephardim, and, in some cases, of Ashkenazim. The Sephardic immigrants would rent rooms on the highest floors of walk-up buildings because of the low rents. They lived meagerly on small incomes.

Because the setting of their lives was so dismal and strange, Sephardim looked for opportunities to meet their coreligionists in order to reminisce, to make plans for the future, or just to pass the time of day. The Sephardic coffeehouses and restaurants became the centers of the communities. The coffeehouses served not only the recreational needs of the Sephardim but also their intellectual and political needs. Any cause or movement that wanted to win adherents would seek them in the coffeehouses. Orators would speak and publicists would post their flyers and circulars on the walls.

Although the coffeehouses reflected the creative impulses for progress within the community, they also mirrored the problems within the community. They became centers for the unemployed, many of whom had become despondent. In addition, the Turkish cafés were also frequented by hard-working people who had short tempers and little patience, and fistfights were not uncommon. The pages of *La America* indicate such violent fights that people had to be hospitalized and arrested.

The Sephardic restaurants, like the coffeehouses, were centers of Sephardic social life on the Lower East Side. The restaurants provided foods to the taste of the Turkish immigrants—primarily a

Mediterranean cuisine. The proprietors felt they had to keep prices low because of their poor clientele and as a result the meals were sometimes criticized for being less than good. *La America* (August 9, 1912) suggested that it would be better if the proprietors served better food and charged the customers somewhat higher prices.

The "Turkino" cafés and restaurants witnessed "a dangerous epidemic" of card playing and gambling. Moise Gadol wrote (*La America*, January 23, 1914) that Sephardim gambled their money away, losing what they had spent much time earning. Many wives of gambling husbands came crying to the editorial office of *La America* pleading for advice. Although Gadol did not want to call in the police, he indicated that he would keep a list of the names of those who were mentioned in complaints. If these men did not stop gambling, he would give their names to the police department for prosecution.

The immigrant Sephardic community was also confronted by the other vices of the Lower East Side: alcoholism, prostitution, rape, wife abandonment, adultery. There were instances of brides having being sent for from the old country only to be abused and left stranded in New York.

Along with the social distress, the Lower East Side had more than its share of actual physical maladies. Various epidemics invaded the area from time to time. An article in *La America* (September 27, 1912) indicated that Turkinos got sick and died of diseases more frequently than the general population. An explanation was given for this phenomenon: Sephardim bought used clothing and these old garments were the spreaders of disease. *La America* urged the public not to buy used clothes, not to make such economies that could end up costing one's life.

The Sephardim were faced with a variety of problems that threatened their security and the stability of their neighborhoods. Chrystie Street, where many of them lived and worked, had become dangerous. Italians living on the street intimidated the Jews and there were several instances of bombs exploding in front of Jewish apartments. *La America* of December 20, 1912, reported that dynamite went off at 224 Chrystie Street causing significant damage. Anonymous letters were sent to the residents of the building telling them to move out if they wished to save their lives.

Jack Farhi (*La America*, August 16, 1912) complained about the crimes and bombs plaguing the neighborhood of the Lower East Side. Italian hoodlums were harassing the Sephardim, using bad language, throwing rubbish at them during the summer and snowballs during the winter. Farhi foresaw the day when there would be a real battle between the Italians and the Turkinos and recommended that the Sephardim move to an area where apartments were larger, cheaper, and cleaner. However, as long as the Sephardic candy stores, restaurants, and cafés were located on Chrystie Street, the Sephardim felt that they did not want to move to new apartments. Farhi therefore suggested that the Sephardic proprietors find new quarters for their businesses not in the midst of the Italian neighborhood. Although some Sephardim did move away from Chrystie Street, many others remained.

New immigrants, especially those who did not know the language of the land, were easy targets for con experts. Sephardic immigrants were victimized by quick-talking, well-dressed sharpsters who convinced the newcomers to part with their money, often with the promise that their investment would bring them much fortune or good luck. To alert Sephardim to the hazard, Gadol described the methods of these con artists. For example, *La America* reported an incident that occurred in August 1913. One man went into a Sephardic restaurant and said he knew of a place looking for three waiters. Three Sephardim got up to go with him. The man then told the three that they must each pay him four dollars before he brought them to the boss. They gave him the money. He led them to a certain place and instructed them to wait until he returned. Of course, he did not return. Gadol exhorted: "Brothers! For the last time I warn you to be careful, to open your eyes, read always our newspaper and listen to our advice."

Moise Gadol gave his best efforts and sacrificed his own financial well-being in order to help the Sephardim. The office of *La America* became a clearinghouse for the Sephardic community. People turned to Gadol for advice in business, on how to become American citizens, for immigration procedures, on how to find missing friends or relatives. He was ready to answer all questions and to give as much time as was necessary in order to help each individual solve his or her problem. He soon realized that it would be impossible for him to deal with everyone's problems and still manage to run his own newspaper and personal life. In the July 5, 1912, issue of *La America,* Gadol indicated that he would provide whatever information was requested concerning immigration laws, citizenship, and other issues free of charge only to those who were subscribing to the newspaper. He would no longer give his time freely to those who did not even support *La America* through their subscriptions.

Gadol frequently spoke to groups of Sephardim, to Sephardic societies, and to Jewish organizations that could be helpful to the Sephardic colony in New York. He was a Sephardic spokesman to the Ashkenazic and non-Jewish world. It was Gadol who organized mass meetings, who encouraged Sephardim to join labor unions, who urged the Union of Orthodox Jewish Congregations of America to take a greater interest in Sephardim, and who negotiated with the New York Kehillah, HIAS, and many other organizations.

In reading the texts of some of his speeches in the pages of *La America,* one finds an exciting, vibrant, and almost prophetic style. Yet, Gadol was not known as a good speaker. Joseph Varsano recalls that Gadol's voice was high-pitched and that he did not speak forcefully. Albert Amateau recalls that Gadol's speeches were long and rambling. Maír José Benardete, who worked for Gadol for a short time, remembers that Gadol's Judeo-Spanish pronunciation and use of words was somewhat strange. Being a Bulgarian, his language usage was a bit different from that of the Sephardim from Turkey. Yet, the fact remains that Gadol's intensity and sincerity helped make up for his lack of oratorical skill. While his style may not have captivated his audiences, his words and ideas were powerful and influential. Perhaps through his writings more than through his speeches, Gadol was to be a major voice of the Sephardic community between 1910 and 1925.

Another individual who gained prominence among the Oriental Jews was Joseph Gedelecia, who had come to the United States from Constantinople. However, he was an Ashkenazic Jew and did not know Judeo-Spanish. In spite of this limitation, he was able to become a recognized spokesman of the predominantly Spanish-speaking Sephardic colony. When the Federation of Oriental Jews was founded in 1912 Gedelecia was elected president. When efforts were made to establish a central Sephardic community, Gedelecia was elected president. He was the manager of the Bureau for the Placement of Handicapped of the Jewish community, and in this office he was particularly helpful to the Sephardim because he was able to extend the definition of "handicapped" to include a lack of industrial skills and an ignorance of English.

At a conference of social workers held in June 1914, it was Gedelecia, the Ashkenazic Jew, who spoke on behalf of the Sephardic community. He boasted of the accomplishments of the New York Sephardic community and told the social workers that if these Sephardim were posing a problem to the American Jewish establishment "it is a problem you do not understand. When the Yiddish Jews go to Turkey, they, too, are a serious problem there."

But Gedelecia was not universally loved. One of his major antagonists was none other than Moise Gadol who resented an Ashkenazic Jew, who could speak no Spanish, serving as president of the major Sephardic organization. Gadol's campaign against Gedelecia continued for several years until the good-hearted, but non-Sephardic leader faded out of community activities.

Albert Amateau had come to New York in August 1909. Originally from the island of Rhodes, he had studied in an American college in Turkey. He had graduated from the law school of the University of Istanbul and migrated from Turkey in order to escape military service. Soon after his arrival, he helped organize the Brotherhood of Rhodes, a self-help society. He was recognized as a young, progressive leader. Amateau was secretary of the Federation of Oriental Jews, under the presidency of Joseph Gedelecia. In *La America,* Amateau described how he came to New York and decided to give his best efforts in order to assist the advancement of the Sephardic Jews (November 29, 1912). "But I found myself isolated on all sides and it was impossible for me to work against this apathy alone, without help from anywhere." Amateau visited the Sephardic coffeehouses on Chrystie Street frequented by the young Sephardim. He spoke to them about the importance of education but his advice went unheeded. He was ridiculed and some suspected he was attempting to deceive them for personal gain. Amateau generously admitted that he could not blame the young people for their skepticism. They had not received a proper education in the old country either and did not understand its value.

But Amateau was successful in finding a number of isolated young Sephardim who were trying to improve their situations. "The malady [of the Sephardim] was ignorance, and it was against this that I directed my attack." He began an English class in a small dark room in back of a candy store, which was attended by twenty young people. Amateau visited the cafés daily, talking and lecturing on politics, geography, health, and cleanliness. His zeal provoked some of the Sephardim he was attempting to help. Some believed he was trying to make the young people turn away from religion. Soon, Amateau had become a controversial personality. Among those who supported him at that time were Gedelecia and Gadol. Amateau praised *La America* for having helped bring the message of the importance of education to the Sephardic people. He believed that it was necessary for Sephardim to leave many of the old bad habits behind and aggressively assume the challenges of a new life in America.

Perhaps the one figure who was universally respected by the Sephardic immigrants was Nessim Behar. Born in 1848 in Jerusalem, Behar devoted his life to the education of Sephardim through the Alliance Israélite Universelle. When he came to the United States, he was already in his fifties. Behar's tireless work was recognized and appreciated. He visited the various synagogues of the Sephardim on the Lower East Side and in Harlem in order to persuade his people of the need for education. He was a significant voice in the Sephardic community, urging the immigrants to learn English and to attend evening classes sponsored by the government and by various charitable institutions.

Maír José Benardete, who was then a young man, admired Behar's strength of character and joined him in his visits to the tenements where the Sephardic Jews were living. "We went up and down the malodorous tenements, knocking at the doors of those humble, temporary homes of the new arrivals at the very hour when the men were having their supper after working long hours at very unhealthy and unremunerative jobs. Nessim Behar, the apostle, expected these bodies, whose energies had been squeezed out of them, to have enough physical stamina to respond to the appeal of the spirit. Some, overcome by shame, others, out of respect for the venerable, diminutive old man, made a big sacrifice in the name of culture and the future; heeding the call, they attended special classes organized exclusively for them at the school of their neighborhood."

Benardete saw in Behar a fine example of a human being and also a classic Sephardic symbol. Influenced by the French culture of the Alliance, profoundly imbued with the spirit of Israel, the land of his birth, Nessim Behar spoke to the masses in Judeo-Spanish. In the slums of New York, this educated and noble man provided guidance and hope to a people desperately in need of such leadership.

Aside from these outstanding men, there were a number of individuals who had been involved in the formation of Sephardic self-help societies. There were others who gave their time and money to establish religious schools for the children. To be sure, some of these people were petty, uneducated, and self-serving. There were those who sought to found societies only so that they could become president and thereby gain some type of community power and honor. Yet, there were so many others—many of whose names are now long forgotten—who made great sacrifices to help their people. They would not accept the conditions in which the Sephardim found themselves; they worked to change the course of history and direct their community to a better life.

During the first decades of the twentieth century, when Sephardic immigration was adding thousands of people to New York, there was a proliferation of Sephardic societies, almost all of which were established on the basis of geographic origin in the old world. These societies played an important role in the lives of the masses of Sephardic immigrants, providing them with a sense of belonging to a community. In a new milieu, especially one so chaotic as that of the Lower East Side, this feeling was vital for their emotional and psychological well-being. On a practical level, the societies provided for a number of necessities, including cemetery plots and synagogue services for the High Holy Days. Some societies also provided free medical service for their members; some had a committee that visited sick members; most offered financial assistance to members who were temporarily unemployed or who had suffered a severe financial setback. Members were expected to pay a minimal sum, usually fifty cents a month, in order to be entitled to these privileges.

In January 1912 *La America* reported the existence of a number of New York societies comprised of Oriental Jews. The oldest and most prestigious Sephardic society was the Union and Peace Society, founded and incorporated in 1899. It was reported to have about two hundred members in 1912, most of whom came from Turkey, with a few members from Morocco and elsewhere. The official language of this group was English. Among its members were the illustrious Shinasi brothers, the multimillionaires who had made their fortune in the tobacco industry. Many of the members of the Union and Peace Society worshiped at Shearith Israel, the Spanish and Portuguese Synagogue of New York City. This group was known as the wealthiest and most assimilated society of the immigrant Sephardic community.

The Oriental Progressive Society, founded in 1904, had about sixty members in 1912, nearly all of whom were Ashkenazim from Turkey. Their members spoke either Yiddish or English. This society established a Judeo-Spanish club in April 1911 to assist the Sephardim. The club had the backing of the New York Kehillah and was to serve as a literary society and provide English classes. David de Sola Pool, then the assistant rabbi of Congregation Shearith Israel, addressed the club at one of its early meetings to encourage the cultural progress of its members. Individuals were required to pay twenty-five cents per month to be in this club. Apparently, however, it was a short-lived venture.

A group of Greek-speaking Jews, primarily from the city of Janina, formed the Hebra Ahava Ve-Ahvah Janina (Love and Brotherhood Society of Janina) on July 12, 1907. The group was led initially by Leon Colchamiro and Zeharia Levi. In November 1910 it was reported to have about two hundred members, own cemetery space in Brooklyn, and meet for religious services on the Sabbath and festivals at 277 Allen Street. This society engaged a doctor to serve the members gratis and employed a secretary to conduct the society's business. To belong to this society cost ten cents per week and anyone who did not pay dues on time was not allowed to vote on any society matters.

With the arrival of many Jews from Kastoría, a number of

those who belonged to the Janina group seceded and formed a new society of Kastoríalis, under the name Hesed Ve-Emet (Mercy and Truth). The reason for this break was mainly a matter of language: the Janina Jews were Greek-speaking while the Jews from Kastoría spoke Spanish. In November 1910 the Kastoría group claimed a membership of about eighty to ninety. It met for religious services at 109–11 Grand Street.

Hesed Ve-Emet attempted to provide its members with better services than any other group. Very early in its existence it established a subcommittee called Ozer Dalim (Helper of the Poor), whose main purpose was to assist the needy. The Ozer Dalim was directed initially by Delicia Eliyahu, who was praised for being able to inculcate humanitarian sentiments in the hearts of her coreligionists. However, in May 1912 she left for Salonika in order to be married there, but the work of the Ozer Dalim continued. This society also included a committee known as the Bikur Holim, whose purpose it was to visit the sick and care for them while they were hospitalized or ill at home. The Bikur Holim was headed by Hannah Mayo.

Another Greek-speaking society, the Tikvah Tovah (Good Hope), was founded on September 14, 1907, and incorporated on September 22, 1908. It included a number of Jews from Janina as well as some from Smyrna (now Izmir, Turkey), Salonika, Kastoría, and elsewhere. This society cooperated with the Janina society, Ahava Ve-Ahvah. In December 1910 Tikvah Tovah claimed a membership of about one hundred and twenty-five.

Ahavath Shalom (Love of Peace) of Monastir was founded in 1907 and incorporated in 1910. In February 1911 it had approximately one hundred and twenty members. The group met at 197 Chrystie Street. The Monastir Jews were a significant entity within the Judeo-Spanish-speaking community. There was a strong Jewish tradition upheld among its membership and it established a Talmud Torah as well as a regular synagogue. In *La America* (April 14, 1911) there is a description of the great ceremony of bringing a new Torah scroll to the synagogue of the Monastir Jews, comparing the festivities to the coronation of a king—music played, crowds of people danced in the streets, and American, Turkish, and Jewish flags were displayed in their glory. Ahavath Shalom invited Jews of all backgrounds to participate and sought the support of the entire community.

During 1912 and thereafter, Sephardic societies proliferated in the New York area. As before, membership was commonly based on the city of origin. The Jews from the Island of Rhodes founded the Yeshuah Verahamim (Salvation and Mercy). Turkish and Syrian Jews founded the Rodefei Tsedek (Seekers of Justice). This society had about eighty members, most of whom were Arabic-speaking, and met at 87 Eldridge Street on the third floor.

A large segment of the Spanish-speaking Sephardim were from Salonika. Shelomo Alvo, a Salonikan Jew, wrote an impassioned article in *La America* (April 19, 1912) urging his compatriots to form their own society. He wrote, "We need to unite. We should not be discouraged by the difficulties of the task; we can succeed." A month later the Ez Hahayyim (Tree of Life) Salonika was formed. The leadership of this new society was thankful to Gadol for his support in *La America*. The society, meeting at 168 Chrystie Street, elected its first officers: David Carasso, president; Moise Gadol, vice-president. Gadol urged the society to drop "Salonika" from its title and be open to all Sephardic Jews. This society stressed loyalty among its ranks and members were encouraged to wear badges that identified them as belonging to it. In 1913 the Ez Hahayyim announced that it was the first society in New York authorized to conduct weddings according to the prescribed Oriental Sephardic custom.

Also in 1912 Vitale Naon, in *La America*, called on Sephardim from Rodosto (now Tekirdag, Turkey) and Churlu (Turkey) to form a society. "Shall we have to depend on others? Is this to our honor?" he asked. He called a meeting at the home of Binyamin Ouziel, at 167 Chrystie Street, to organize both a synagogue for the High Holy Days and a society.

Another society was comprised of Spanish-speaking Sephardim from Dardanelles (Çanakkale), Turkey. This society, the Mekor Hayyim (Source of Life), had a membership of 122 in 1913. It held a Purim celebration in 1914, attracting more than 400 people. Gadol, who was present, attributed the success of the party to the fact that the celebrants had paid to attend. "All are happy because they eat and drink from their own money and not from charity." In

1915 the Dardanelles Social Club was established to provide its membership with a comfortable place to socialize. However, card playing was strictly forbidden.

In 1915 Sephardim from Silivria, Turkey, established the Ahim Mevorakhim Society (Blessed Brothers). In the same year, the Haskalah (Enlightenment) Club was formed by Sephardim who were mainly from Gallipoli. Gadol praised it for not identifying itself with its native city in its title and for reaching out to serve the entire community. In 1916 the Gallipoli Progressive Club was established with forty-three members. It sponsored lectures and conferences of interest to young people. Gadol, while pleased with its aims, urged it to drop "Gallipoli" from its name.

One group, the Salonika Brotherhood, changed its name in hopes of reaching the larger community. It became the Sephardic Brotherhood in 1921 and wished to establish a large center for all Sephardim.

The Ahduth Benei Israel's thirty-five members were from Palestine. The Angora Union Club was comprised of Sephardim from Angora (Ankara), Turkey. Its president was Louie Rousso.

A few new societies emerged that sought a diverse membership. The Oriental Hebrew Association was formed in 1914 of "our most intellectual people." Its purpose was to espouse social and political ideas to the Sephardic community. All members had to be U.S. citizens. It held a successful Purim ball, which more than five hundred people attended, among whom were Ottoman government officials.

A group affiliated with the United States Socialist Party was founded in 1914. It was called the Oriental Federation and Socialist Educational Society and it planned to improve both the moral and material state of the Sephardim. It sponsored classes in English, sociology, and civics. Morris Nissim and Moise Soulam directed its activities.

The sixty-five members of the Oriental American Civic Club, under the leadership of Salvadore Malakh, who was from Salonika, met at 16 West 115th Street. It claimed its membership was "the most enlightened" of the Sephardim in New York City. The Independent Voters Political and Social Club, with headquarters at 108 East Twelfth Street, was comprised of Sephardim living in New York's Twenty-sixth District.

A Sephardic Democratic Club was founded by Albert Amateau in 1924. It was to function as part of the Democratic Party organization and its members had to be U.S. citizens.

A number of societies were formed to bring young Sephardim together for social and cultural activities. The Young Men's Sepharedim Association began in 1916 with twenty-five members and with Albert Crudo as president. The Sepharedim Social Club was organized by young men from lower Manhattan; its headquarters were at 173 Eldridge Street.

La Luz, which functioned from 1916 to 1918, offered English and Spanish classes to young Sephardim. It also intended to establish a gymnastics group and a musical band. The Filo Center Club, established in 1921, served young Sephardim in the Harlem area. Its goals were to own a building that would have meeting rooms and classrooms and to offer a general program of cultural assistance to its members.

The Sephardic Liberty Loan Committee was established in 1918 to encourage the purchase of Liberty Bonds among the members of the Sephardic community.

The Sephardic Union of New Lots, in Brooklyn, was established in 1922 to assist the approximately fifty families that had moved to this area. By 1925 it had organized a synagogue, a Talmud Torah, and a social and literary club as well.

The Beit Hinukh Sephardi (Sephardic Education House) in Harlem attempted, in 1923, to coordinate all the religious educational endeavors of the Sephardim in Harlem.

The Sephardic community apparently did not suffer from a shortage of societies and organizations. Aside from the groups mentioned, there was a variety of other groups established under the aegis of the Spanish and Portuguese Synagogue of New York. There were also a number of Sephardic Zionist societies, youth groups, neighborhood groups, and so on. Yet, if the Sephardim were so organized, why were they so disorganized?

The reality was that the masses of Sephardim were concerned mostly with earning a living and sending money back to their relatives in the old country. Most immigrants could understand the need for self-help societies, but found it difficult to pay their dues regularly and on time. *La America* (October 4, 1912) reported that all the Sephardic societies suffered because their members simply did not pay their dues or pledges. As it was impossible for voluntary officers to pursue each member and collect what was owed, Moise Gadol suggested that a paid collector was needed to collect the dues and pledges for all of the Sephardic societies as well as for subscriptions for *La America*. He suggested that the societies pay such a person ten dollars a week plus carfare, and a commission of 10 percent of all funds collected. Gadol even invited individuals to apply for the position in *La America*. However, the societies found it difficult to part with any of their limited funds and would not agree to go along with this idea.

In spite of the fact that so many societies existed, many Sephardim remained unaffiliated. Gadol felt that individuals often could not tell which society would be most beneficial. Each of the societies was so preoccupied with its own constituents that it did not make clear to the general public what benefits it offered. Moreover, Gadol believed that the societies needed to be democratic, having uniform entrance requirements and fees and officers who were answerable for the use of funds and for other major decisions.

The host of small societies tended to be introverted. Each group was so concerned with its own problems that it seldom thought about general community problems. Pride among the Sephardim was an ingrained social characteristic. A Jew from one town would have strong loyalty to others from his same town but would not necessarily feel any special responsibility for those from another locality.

Moise Gadol used the pages of *La America* to urge the various Sephardic societies to merge into several large groups. These pleas usually occurred during the season prior to the High Holy Days when each society was busy renting a hall and selling tickets for religious services. In an article of June 27, 1913, Gadol urged the small societies to unite for services on the High Holy Days. He suggested that *La America* participate in organizing a mass meeting that might convince the Sephardic population of the need to unite. This effort was in vain. In September 1915 *La America* reported that there were more than twenty Sephardic services going on in New York City for the High Holy Days.

Not one of the Sephardic societies had its own separate synagogue building. The few that held regular services did so in rented quarters. The majority, however, simply rented halls for Rosh Hashanah and Yom Kippur, since these were the only holidays when all the members wanted to have services. Gadol argued that the Sephardim had to establish "real" synagogues. On September 24, 1920, he reported that the Sephardim of New York held thirty different services for the High Holy Days. Instead of coming closer together, there was even more disunion. In the October 14, 1921, issue of *La America,* he counted even more services. Gadol felt it was time for the societies to stop striving for preeminence. He urged them to unite and use the money raised by the Sephardim to the advantage of the entire community, rather than in the interests of the distinct societies.

Gadol felt the Sephardim should conduct one or two dignified services and employ professional cantors. He recommended that the Sephardic community of New York have its own chief rabbi, preferably a man from Turkey, who would not only be a learned sage but a good singer. He wished that such an individual be relatively young and be English-speaking, or have a facility for learning new languages quickly. The responsibilities of the position would include teaching the children and forming a youth choir. Gadol exhorted: "We must show the Portuguese Jews and the Ashkenazic Jews that we Sephardim of the Orient are descendants of the Spanish-Jewish greats and we are capable of united action." The disunity apparent in Sephardic communal and synagogue life was also apparent in the area of religious education for the youth. Rather than working together to establish several large Talmud Torah schools, the Sephardic societies tended to support their own religious schools and some simply did not bother with this need at all.

La America of December 13, 1912, ran an article describing "the brilliant success of the Sephardic Talmud Torah." On Sunday, December 8, exams had been given to students in the Allen Street Religious School, which then had an enrollment of over one hundred students. The room was filled with men and women who came to witness the examinations. Among those present were David de Sola Pool, Alice Menken, Ephraim Benguiat—all of Shearith Israel—Nessim Behar, and other prominent individuals. At a public exami-

nation of the Talmud Torah children from the downtown religious
school in March 1913, Moise Gadol himself served as one of the
examiners. The children did well. Congregation Shearith Israel sent
several boxes of candies for the children as rewards and donated
books as prizes for the two best pupils.

In a report of January 28, 1914, Joseph Benyunes, the leader of
the Orchard Street Synagogue and Religious School sponsored by
the Sisterhood of the Spanish and Portuguese Synagogue, noted
that their Talmud Torah had an enrollment of 107 boys and girls.
This downtown Talmud Torah continued to grow so that by
March 9, 1914, the enrollment was up to 130 students. By January
24, 1916, it was reported that it was necessary to divide the
students into split sessions rather than have them all attend school
at the same time.

Yet the fact was that most of the Sephardic children in the area
were attending other smaller schools, or no religious school at all.
Nessim Behar and several other leaders headed an effort to establish a unified Sephardic Talmud Torah in 1915. It was announced
that the Alliance Israélite Universelle would give financial support
to this school if the American Zionist Federation and the New York
Kehillah would contribute. Unfortunately, this was not fruitful.

On February 4, 1917, at 186 Chrystie Street a mass meeting of
one hundred people met to discuss a Talmud Torah in the downtown area, since the previous communal school had failed. Nessim
Behar, in opening the meeting, suggested that the Sephardic community work with the Sisterhood of the Spanish and Portuguese
Synagogue, thereby gaining widespread support for the project.
This speech was followed by a lively discussion. Morris Nissim
criticized Behar's suggestion, asserting that the Portuguese Jews
were antidemocratic. Jack Farhi disagreed. Joseph Gedelecia stated
that the Portuguese Jews did not contribute anything from their
own treasury to help the Sephardic immigrants. Eliah Crespi felt the
Sephardim should not seek help from Portuguese or Ashkenazic
Jews. Following the discussion, a committee of twelve was appointed to approach the various societies to win their support for
the organization of a new Talmud Torah. This effort failed.

Meanwhile, the society of Sephardim of Angora established its
own Talmud Torah at 184 Eldridge Street. *La America* (September

6, 1918) reported that this Talmud Torah had a celebration at which the thirty students of the school were dressed in American military uniforms. This was apparently intended to show the seriousness of the school. In the issue of November 15, 1918, *La America* reported that the society of Sephardim from Monastir was raising funds in order to open its own Talmud Torah at 105–7 Eldridge Street. Some people claimed that the Monastir group was forced to start this school because the Talmud Torah of the Sisterhood of the Spanish and Portuguese Synagogue was not tolerant of children whose parents were not members of Berith Shalom, the synagogue of the Sisterhood's settlement house. This appears not to have been the case, since of the 170 students then enrolled in the Sisterhood's Talmud Torah, seventy came from families who were not members of Berith Shalom. The reason some children were turned away was not due to intolerance but simply to a lack of space. In any case, the Talmud Torah of the Ahavath Shalom Monastir made great progress and by December 1919 had an enrollment of 150 students.

Gadol believed that one committee should be in charge of the Sephardic Talmud Torah schools and should be responsible for both the Talmud Torah of the Angora group and that of the Monastir group. He also suggested there be a communal Talmud Torah on the Lower East Side, as the existing ones were not big enough to accommodate all the children.

Efforts to establish a Talmud Torah in Harlem also ran into difficulties. In November 1916 there had been a mass meeting sponsored by the Young Men's Sepharedim Association, which aimed to establish a Talmud Torah. Approximately one hundred men and women attended the meeting. Gadol was invited to speak and he argued eloquently for the need of a permanent Talmud Torah that would be open to the entire community without distinction of geographic origin. He stated that the name of the school should not include the name of any society. Other meetings also took place with the intention of establishing a unified Talmud Torah, but none was successful.

In February 1917 almost one thousand people attended a ball in order to raise funds to establish an uptown Talmud Torah. The school was finally opened at 18 West 114th Street on Sunday, July

22, 1917. More than forty students registered for the first classes of the school. Even Ashkenazim wanted to send their children to the school, since it was believed that it would be of high quality. The dedication of the Talmud Torah took place on August 5, 1917, and gratitude was expressed in the pages of *La America* to the Young Men's Sepharedim Association for their efforts in making this school a reality. By May 1918 it was reported that about one hundred children attended the school and more had to be turned away for lack of space. The students of the Talmud Torah formed a Hebrew Sephardi Club of Harlem to foster the Hebrew language. Yet, while things seemed to be progressing, communal tensions didn't cease.

Aside from the communal and financial problems of the Talmud Torah schools, the academic situation in the schools left much to be desired. It was not easy to find competent teachers who would work for very low pay. It was difficult for teachers to keep control of their students and few were sophisticated enough to develop a substantial curriculum. One teacher in the uptown Talmud Torah was accused by a parent of inflicting corporal punishment on a child: the Sisterhood's Oriental Committee, which was responsible for the school, ordered the teacher not to carry a cane or a ruler in school.

In April 1925 an attempt was made to organize Sephardic teachers in New York both to enhance the profession and to stimulate better school programs. Albert Levy served as president and Albert Matarasso as secretary. Writing in 1926, Louis Hacker commented on the Sephardic community of New York: "There is no vital religious life in the community, with the result that the synagogues languish and the younger generation is being frightened off." Hacker stated that there were only two communal Talmud Torah schools worthy of the name and one was in constant financial trouble. The total enrollment of these schools was only four hundred children. Three hundred fifty other children attended five Talmud Torahs sponsored by individual groups.

Disorganization and disunion, then, characterized Sephardic communal life in the early years of the twentieth century. People aware of the disunity offered solutions to the problem and analyses of the Sephardic temperament.

Joseph Gedelecia, as president of the Federation of Oriental Jews, wrote a letter to the editor of *La America,* which appeared in the issue of October 1, 1913. He agreed with Gadol that the Levantine community in New York needed a competent and learned rabbi as spiritual head of the colony, a man who could unify the community's religious and educational institutions. A major hindrance seemed to be a lack of money with which to pay a rabbi's salary. Gedelecia suggested that the topic of a chief rabbi be discussed in all the synagogue services during the High Holy Days and that each society raise at least $75 for the purpose of hiring a chief rabbi. The New York Kehillah had agreed to pay $750 a year for three years in order to help obtain the services of a religious leader. David de Sola Pool himself agreed to contribute $100 a year toward this goal. Yet this project too was doomed to failure. Each year there would be calls for unity, for a chief rabbi; each year people would nod their heads and agree, and each year things would continue as before.

Aharon Ben Eliyahu, in an article in *La America* (October 23, 1914) offered his analysis as to why the Oriental Jews were impotent in public affairs, organizations, secular institutions, and communal groups. He bluntly stated: "The Judeo-Spanish organism is really sick." He felt the problems stemmed from the attitudes of the Jews in the Levant, where they were impassive, waiting for things to happen, seldom bothering to take the initiative themselves. The Oriental Jews in the United States expected others to pay for their schools, institutions, and societies.

In the following issue of *La America,* there was a reply to Eliyahu, in an article signed "a lover of truth." This more sympathetic Sephardic person wrote that it was indeed true that the Sephardim in New York lacked a general sense of organization. But this was not the case with their coreligionists in Turkey who did not rely solely on others. On the contrary, he wrote, many communities in the Levant sustained themselves admirably, in particular, Salonika and Alexandria. The problem was not an innate sense of disorganization. Rather it derived from the fact that the Sephardic masses were very poor and did not have the time to think of lofty ideals. He thought it was up to the leaders to inspire the masses to organize the community.

Maír José Benardete, the first Sephardic Jew from Turkey to become a public-school teacher in the United States, wrote an article in *La America* (January 12, 1917) that offered another insight into the Sephardic problem. He stated that Sephardic Jews used the word *impossible* too often. Whenever confronted with a challenge, the response would be "impossible." He felt this pessimism was due to inexperience, ignorance, and a lack of perseverance. Most of the Sephardim had immigrated when they were young and had not had the chance to be leaders in their native cities. They came in search of economic opportunity, not having the least idea of how to organize a community. They needed to learn by experience.

Benardete reminded the Sephardim that great discoveries were made by people who defied the "impossible." By shaping one's destiny, rather than by accepting one's fate, even the "impossible" could be achieved.

While the Sephardim suffered from their proliferation of societies and Talmud Torah schools, progressive voices continually prodded them to unity and organization. These voices, though few and generally ignored, did have some influence on their coreligionists. Even more important, they signified the cultural and communal forces latent among the Sephardim. There was heroism and vision even in the midst of the chaos and pettiness.

4

A Hispano-Levantine Community

Early this century, Spanish senator Angel Pulido visited numerous Sephardic communities throughout Turkey and the Balkan countries. He was amazed to find people who were of Hispanic culture and character, who spoke a medieval-sounding Spanish, who sang medieval Spanish folk songs—and yet had never been in Spain. Their families had not lived in a Spanish-speaking country since the expulsion of Jews from Spain in 1492. Pulido referred to the Sephardim as *españoles sin patria*, Spaniards without a country. He urged the government of Spain to use its influence to reestablish relations with Sephardic Jews and reclaim the Sephardim as a legitimate segment of Spanish society. The mystery of the survival of Sephardic Jews as a distinctively Hispanic group caught the imagination of many Spanish intellectuals. There was a burst of academic and literary activity in Spain dealing with this living remnant of the past.

The Sephardim of Turkey and the Balkan countries were the descendants of Spanish Jews who had fled from persecution in the Iberian peninsula to the Ottoman Empire during the fourteenth and fifteenth centuries. Proud and confident, the Spanish Jews had transplanted themselves in their new setting and had succeeded in large measure in maintaining their Hispanic character. They created a vibrant Jewish life in Constantinople, Salonika, Smyrna, and many other cities and villages of the empire. They produced a vast rabbinic literature in Hebrew, as well as a voluminous literature in Judeo-Spanish. The Spanish Jews came to dominate Jewish life in the Ottoman Empire, and their culture absorbed most of the native Greek-speaking Jews as well as many of the Ashkenazic Jews.

The Spanish language used by these Jews in their daily life as their mother tongue was isolated from the developments of the language in Spain. The Sephardim retained many pronunciations of medieval Spanish and also added to their language numerous Hebrew words as well as other words and phrases borrowed from the languages of the countries where they lived. The result was a curious Hispanic language, now referred to as Judeo-Spanish. The correct name of the Hispanic language spoken by Sephardim has been the subject of confusion and debate. In some communities, for example, Sephardim simply referred to the language as "español." The term *Ladino* applied to the literature of the language, especially translations of the Bible and prayer book. The word *judezmo,* meaning Judaism, was seldom used as an appellation for the language. *Judeo-Spanish* is a modern term, which takes into account the fact that the Sephardim thought of their language as being Spanish yet also indicates that the language was specifically developed by Jews.

During the course of the centuries, the Ottoman Empire suffered a serious decline, both militarily and economically. The Jews of the empire, as could be expected, suffered along with the rest of the populace. By the eighteenth century many of the Sephardic communities had become impoverished. A small group of the intellectual elite maintained a tradition of rabbinic scholarship but the masses were not able to maintain the high intellectual levels of preceding generations.

The Sephardic communities were almost entirely autonomous, having their own schools, courts, and communal institutions. They governed themselves and were even responsible for collecting the taxes that had to be turned over to the Ottoman government. The communities followed religious law and were generally well organized and efficiently administered.

The Sephardic Jewish communities were islands in the midst of the Ottoman Empire. Although they were strongly influenced by the surrounding culture, the Sephardim retained their Hispanic Jewish identity. As one Turkish Jew has said: "We were *in* the empire but not *of* the empire."

The Sephardic Jewish communities of Turkey and the Balkan countries were isolated from the overwhelming masses of Ashkenazic Jews living in eastern Europe, Russia, and the United States. And Ashkenazic Jews had little or no knowledge of the existence of Sephardic communities in the Levant.

The Sephardic communities, therefore, formed a culturally independent world of their own, sharing a common history and culture. Insulated to a certain degree from the non-Jewish society of the Ottoman Empire, separated from the rest of world Jewry, the Sephardim of Turkey and the Balkan countries had to rely on their own religious and cultural resources. But the terrible economic conditions stifled significant progress in education. In 1835, an American described the Sephardic Jews of Constantinople in the following terms: "I think it will hardly be denied that the Jewish nation in Turkey is in a complete state of indigence, as is sufficiently shown by the mean and vile employments to which individuals devote themselves." Leon Semach, the first director of the Alliance Israélite Universelle School for boys on the Island of Rhodes, noted, in a letter dated August 13, 1903, that nearly all of the Jews of Rhodes were in pain or misery. The poverty in the community was frightening. Some children attended school barefoot, dressed in rags; a large number of students required full-tuition scholarships; many were so poor that their lunch consisted of only a piece of dry bread. Children were often required to leave school and go to work to help support the family. Needless to say, such terrible economic conditions tend to hinder intellectual progress.

While some Jews in the Levant engaged in import and export trade, in banking, or in other large-scale commerical ventures, the overwhelming majority of the people worked as unskilled laborers, trying to find whatever work might be available just in order to survive. The Sephardic masses, however, did not view themselves as members of the lower classes; rather, they saw themselves as members of an aristocratic group that had been temporarily impoverished. A Judeo-Spanish proverb, *Basta mi nombre que es Abravanel* (My name is enough; it is Abravanel), suggests that the Sephardim felt that regardless of the present circumstances, one's noble Sephardic name and its great historical associations were enough to maintain one's dignity.

Arriving in New York, the Spanish-speaking Sephardim, whose families had been living in Turkey and the Balkan countries in relative isolation over the centuries, now found themselves in a very different setting. Whereas the mother tongue of the Jewish communities in their native lands was Judeo-Spanish, the language of the Lower East Side was Yiddish or English. Whereas the communities in the Levant were organized and had a chief rabbi at the head, the community in New York was disorganized and had no single recognized and authoritative religious leader. Indeed, the Sephardim came from strong, closely knit communities to a society that was fragmented. It is inaccurate to speak of *a* Jewish community in New York during the first decades of this century. There really were a variety of subcommunities, each going in its own direction and following its own leaders. Even the effort to unite all New York Jews into a Kehillah, a unified community, which began in 1911 under the leadership of Judah Magnes, was far from successful. In spite of its various achievements, it could not possibly bring together hundreds of thousands of Jews of diverse backgrounds, religious persuasions, languages, and world views. In the midst of the general chaos and confusion of the Lower East Side, the Spanish-speaking Sephardim were bewildered.

There were certain cultural features that set the Sephardim of the Levant off from all other groups. For one thing, they had a strong sense of pride, bordering on stubbornness. They resented charity and were offended by any person or group trying to help them in a conspicuous manner. Cyrus Adler, speaking at a meeting of the Sisterhood of the Spanish and Portuguese Synagogue on November 27, 1916, noted: "The Oriental Jews unless they be decrepit, blind or maimed ask and take no charity, and to maintain themselves no work is too hard." Louis Hacker, a perceptive observer of Sephardic life, indicated in 1926 that the Sephardim "considered themselves a people apart; they are 'Spanish Jews' with a distinct historical consciousness and, often, an inordinate pride."

Although the Sephardic community was a great mystery to outsiders, the Sephardim followed social patterns that were quite understandable to themselves. Their language, not understood by outsiders, was *their* language and they used it not only in the coffeehouses and synagogues but in their businesses. There were Spanish phrases and proverbs for every occasion. Aside from the publication of Judeo-Spanish newspapers, the community had quite a few other Judeo-Spanish works available for their entertainment and enlightenment. There were frequent productions of dramatic presentations in Judeo-Spanish, which were enjoyed thoroughly by large audiences of Sephardim. The constitutions and bylaws of most of the early Sephardic societies were published in Judeo-Spanish. Meetings were conducted in that language and the minutes were recorded in it also.

Obviously, the role of language in a people's culture is very significant. Judeo-Spanish was a strong force linking the Sephardim in America with their relatives and their own cultural history in their former homes. Yet, the American experience had its influence on the language of newly arrived immigrants. Sephardim Hispanicized and incorporated English words into their normal conversation. A Ladino-English dictionary, compiled by Sam Maimon of Seattle, Washington (published in 1980), includes a number of words that the Sephardim had adapted from English. Thus *abechar,* from the English slang phrase *I betcha,* became a verb in Judeo-Spanish parlance. *Drivear* became a verb from *drive.* Other English words were borrowed either in their regular form or as corruptions of English words. An example of the latter is the word *mopitch,* derived from *moving picture.* Consciously or not, Sephardim made changes in their language, incorporating in it the dominant language of their new land.

Another factor in the Sephardic mentality was their loyalty and attachment to their native lands. They felt a general patriotism for Turkey and demonstrated a keen interest in the welfare of the Jews of the Levant. Reflective of this concern, Gadol urged the American government not to draft Turkish people in the United States into the American army during World War I. He believed it was unjust for Turks to have to fight against Turkey. His primary concern, of course, was for the Sephardim of Turkish background.

The Sephardic Jews in the United States often came to the aid of their coreligionists in the Levant. Local committees of Sephardim would raise funds to help alleviate the suffering of Sephardim abroad. A Sephardic relief committee was formed in order to help victims of the great fire in Salonika in 1918. Gadol was one of a committee of three that presented the needs of the Sephardim to the Joint Distribution Committee. In 1923, a Smyrna relief society was founded in order to help suffering Sephardim in that city. Other similar committees existed in Sephardic communities throughout the United States.

One of the great events sponsored by the Federation of Oriental Jews was a reception, held on April 23, 1916, in honor of Henry Morgenthau, the American ambassador to Turkey. More than three thousand people attended. Among the speakers were Joseph Gedelecia, Jack Farhi, Nessim Behar, and Ambassador Morgenthau. There were also speeches in Arabic and Greek, and a presentation of music by a Sephardic musical society. It was clear that the Sephardic Jews in the new world were still emotionally and culturally attached to Turkey.

The Sephardim ate different foods than the Ashkenazic Jews. These customs did not change with their arrival in the United States. A number of restaurants and cafés catered exclusively to Sephardic tastes, serving the typical dishes that had been enjoyed in the old country. Grocery stores and candy stores featured favorite Sephardic items. Sephardim enjoyed foods made with zucchini, eggplant, okra, fava beans, spinach, leeks, and other vegetables used in Mediterranean cooking. They loved Turkish delicacies such as *loukoum,* baklava, *tispishti,* and marzipan. And the men enjoyed a glass of *raki.*

Traditional Sephardic foods were served on the Sabbath and holidays. *Borekas* (a type of pastry stuffed with potatoes and cheese, or eggplant), *boulemas* (delicious pastries stuffed with spinach and cheese or eggplant filling), *filas* (pastries made with paper-thin fila dough) were among the specialties. Of notable importance were the *huevos haminados,* hard-boiled eggs cooked for a long time in water, oil, and onionskins, until they take on a dark brown color. After boiling the eggs, they are baked in an oven to give them a very special texture and flavor. Various cheeses, sliced tomatoes, Greek olives, and a variety of other appetizers were also served at Sephardic meals.

These were Jews who had never heard of gefilte fish. On Friday nights, they enjoyed *pescado con tomat,* fish baked in a sweet and sour tomato sauce; or *pescado con huevo y limon,* fish cooked with a special egg and lemon sauce *(avgolemono).* The Sephardim knew nothing of chopped liver or *tzimmes* or *kreplach,* the dishes common among Ashkenazic Jews. Nor did they cook with chicken fat. My mother remembers that during her childhood in the Sephardic community of Seattle, Ashkenazim would taunt Sephardim by calling them "mazola." This was due to the fact that the Sephardim cooked with vegetable oils (such as Mazola), which the Ashkenazim considered strange. In response, the Sephardim would shout back at the Ashkenazim: "schmaltz" (chicken fat), a staple in Ashkenazic cooking.

A major feature of Sephardic cultural life was the theater. Plays were presented in Judeo-Spanish to capacity audiences. The plays, some written by Sephardim in the United States, others in Turkey, and some translations of French plays, usually dealt with Jewish themes. After each production *La America* would praise the actors and actresses. Although the Sephardic community never developed a professional theater, its amateur performances were noteworthy for the sincerity of the efforts and for the creative outlet they offered to the actors and the diversion they offered to the audience.

The Sephardic culture of the Levant could also be observed in the structure of the family life. There was a definite hierarchy of authority, with the father holding the supreme power. Children were taught from infancy to respect their parents, especially their father, and to be respectful of elders. A number of Sephardic customs reflected the closeness and deep ties that bound Sephardic families together (and reflect the differences from the Ashkenazim). For example, children were usually named after living relatives. Normally, the first-born son and daughter would be named after the father's parents, while the second son and daughter would be named after the mother's parents. Subsequent children were also named after relatives, alternating between the two sides of the family.

One of the benefits of this custom was that grandparents had the opportunity of seeing grandchildren who bore their own names.

They could experience a profound sense of family continuity, as well as a sense of personal immortality. On the other hand, grandchildren could immediately develop role models and feel deep respect for their grandparents after whom they were named. In large extended families, it was not uncommon for a number of children—all named for the same grandparent—to have the same name. Thus, cousins would grow up cognizant of the family ties that bound them to each other as well as to their common grandparent.

Another popular custom among Sephardim was that when a parent, grandparent, or any other relative was called to the Torah during synagogue services, the younger relatives would stand up in respect. They remained standing while the one called to the Torah recited the blessings, and oftentimes they remained standing during the entire reading of the Torah portion. This practice taught respect for and loyalty to older family members. It also created a bond among all of the relatives who rose. Since everyone else in the synagogue was seated, the individuals who stood up immediately recognized the uniqueness of their own family. (I remember vividly when my own grandfather, of blessed memory, would be called to the Torah in Seattle. He was blessed with many children and grandchildren, and all of us would stand up for him. We could not help but feel respect for him and pride in our entire family, so many of whom were in the synagogue together. We felt that our "clan" was important and honorable.)

Another custom was the kissing of the hand of a parent or grandparent in return for a blessing. Whether on Friday night at home or in the synagogue on Sabbath, children would kiss the hand of a parent or grandparent as a sign of respect and affection. When a number of children were involved, they would form a line in order of age, eldest first. The patriarch or matriarch would recite a blessing by holding a hand over the child's head. Receiving these blessings from their elders was a special joy for a Sephardic child and left many valuable memories.

The structure of family life and the general status of women were greatly influenced by the social setting in the Levant. In that male-dominated world, women were clearly expected to be subservient to men. Although the forces of modernism already were beginning to expand the role of women, the overwhelming weight of traditionalism limited women in many ways. The Sephardic immigrants brought to the New World the mentality that was prevalent in Turkey and the Balkan countries. The pages of *La America* reflected the old and the new attitudes toward women. Gadol himself rejoiced in the fact that girls were able to receive the same education as boys in the public schools of the United States and he was generally sympathetic to the idea of allowing women more freedom.

Gadol printed several articles signed by "a suffragette" that argued in favor of women's suffrage. The articles, which appeared in April 1911, condemned discrimination based on sex, and stated that men and women needed to work together for the betterment of both groups. The articles discussed the Oriental stereotypes of women, which cast women as the agents of mischief, and discussed the traditional antifemale prejudices, which enslaved all who were influenced by them.

In the issue of February 7, 1913, the formation of the Oriental Jewish Young Women's Social Club was announced. This was the first such women's organization among the Oriental Jews. Its goal was to improve the moral and material state of Sephardic women. Stella Maimon was elected president. A mass meeting of the club was held on February 9 at 186 Chrystie Street with more than two hundred women attending. Most were of Spanish-speaking background, but there were also others of Greek-, Arabic-, and even Yiddish-speaking backgrounds. One of the speakers spoke in favor of women joining labor unions. Gadol felt that influential Jewish women should become involved in this new organization. He suggested that the group establish three sections: one to raise money for the needy, a second to operate classes in English and Yiddish, and a third to serve the needs of working women by giving them an opportunity to discuss their problems and learn how to improve their situations. The group began with enthusiasm, but was not to last. In *La America* of March 28, 1913, Stella Maimon complained of poor attendance at meetings and urged young women to become more involved in the society. It seems that the young women, like many men, were so tired from the long hours they put in at their jobs that they had little energy left for organizational meetings. It should be noted, though, that a number of the Sephardic societies did have women's divisions, and that women actively participated in them.

Articles in *La America* indicated the deep-seated desire of Sephardim to maintain the virtue and morality of their daughters. In the issue of June 21, 1912, a letter from the chief rabbi of Turkey, Hayyim Nahoum, urged parents to watch their daughters more carefully and not to let them marry a man whose background had not been checked. He asked parents not to accept marriage proposals for their daughters without first checking that the groom was clear of past problems and had a good reputation, as bad marriages would cause problems that would last a lifetime. It appears there must have been men without honor or conscience who wished to take advantage of Sephardic young women.

An article of June 19, 1914, reported that Turkino fathers did not like the idea of letting their daughters go out with men without a chaperon. But strong-willed daughters did not appreciate this arrangement. Some fathers, seeing that their daughters were going on dates unchaperoned, insisted that the daughter and her boyfriend go to City Hall and get a marriage license. Then, since the government recognized them as being married, the father would permit them to go out alone. What the fathers did not realize was that if things did not work out between the two, the couple would need to get a civil divorce. The legal and financial problems involved seem not to have concerned them. Gadol urged fathers not to urge their daughters to get marriage licenses in this way. He cautioned that no couple should get a marriage license until the Jewish marriage ceremony was arranged.

The steady concern for morality and proper behavior was emphasized in articles encouraging parents to educate their children properly. Fathers who had daughters who worked in factories were urged to explain to their daughters that they should not become corrupted by the other people who worked in the factories. Since the goal of parents was to have their children get married, they were anxious that their children associate with good and upright young people. Whereas in the old days parents often would negotiate marriages for their children, in the United States the young people wanted to make their own choices. In February 1922 Bohor Hanna founded a Sephardic marriage agency with the goal of arranging marriages and helping Sephardim who were having family problems. He named his organization the Jewish Business Agency in order to give it a general title, so that no one would feel self-conscious in coming to him for help. The agency was located at 22 West 115th Street.

Levantine cultural characteristics were not only evident in family life, but in religious observances as well. While the Sephardim observed the Jewish holidays and Jewish traditions relating to the life cycle, they did so in their own distinctive fashion, with their own foods, songs, and customs. Sephardim loved to celebrate and looked for occasions to have parties and to get together with family and friends.

The newly arrived immigrants naturally tended to perpetuate the way of life they had known in the old country. But once they had settled here a while, the forces of assimilation began to interfere with the preservation of the old ways. Although a superficial glance at the Sephardic colony of New York before 1920 might reveal a fairly monolithic Hispano-Levantine Jewish community, a more careful analysis would reveal growing cultural tensions within the community.

Among the Sephardic immigrants, as among all other immigrants, there was an internal conflict between the forces of assimilation and those of maintaining a strong ethnic identity. There were factions in the community that urged radical Americanization, leaving all vestiges of Sephardic-Jewish life behind; on the other hand, there were those who argued vigorously for the preservation of the Judeo-Spanish language and culture and for the strict adherence to the old traditions. These two opposing forces fought for dominance within the general community and within the mind of each individual Sephardic immigrant. Most of the Sephardim were ambivalent and chose, by indecisiveness, a middle ground.

Since Sephardic identity was closely associated with the Judeo-Spanish language, the preservation of this language in America became an important cultural issue. On the one hand, Sephardim realized it was vital to learn English and to have their children attend the public schools. But some questioned the value of preserving an ancient Judeo-Spanish language in the United States. And there were some who maintained that as the national language of the Jewish people was Hebrew, the ultimate goal should be to drop both Yiddish and Judeo-Spanish and return to the use of Hebrew. An article in *La America* (December 9, 1910) exhorted, "Where there are many languages there is no nation; one nation must have one language only. And no Jew can deny that our maternal language is only Hebrew and none other." If, however, Sephardim should learn Hebrew for the sake of their Jewishness and English for the sake of getting along in America, what would then happen to Judeo-Spanish?

Gadol himself argued for preserving the Judeo-Spanish language among the children. Many parents who sent their children to the Sephardic Talmud Torah schools questioned the importance of teaching Judeo-Spanish to the children. Gadol contended that they would need to know the language in order to communicate with their relatives in Turkey. He thought Judeo-Spanish should be taught until the day arrived when Hebrew was the mother tongue of all Jews of the world. Gadol lamented that the young children were learning neither Judeo-Spanish nor Hebrew. He stressed that Judeo-Spanish was the link between the Sephardim in the United States and those in the Orient.

Other articles appeared in *La America* that dealt with the question of the Judeo-Spanish language. An article by Joseph Capouya (November 27, 1914) argued that Sephardim needed to preserve Judeo-Spanish, but not as separatists. Rather than the language limiting them to the confines of their own community, it should serve as a valuable supplement to their knowledge and increase productivity, strengthen community movements, and help the Sephardim to know themselves better. There was also a certain sentiment among assimilationists that the Sephardim should forget the Spanish language as soon as possible since it was associated with an unpleasant history, namely, the expulsion from Spain in 1492 and the isolation of the Jews in the Ottoman Empire for the past four centuries. The assimilationists felt that two languages, Hebrew and English, were more than adequate to meet all the needs the Sephardim could have. An article by Abraham Bazaravo (August 15, 1913) asserted that since Hebrew was the language of all Jews, it was the medium that could potentially bring Sephardim and Ashkenazim together. "Every people requires two things: a language and a country. Moreover, we need to work together to regain our ancient homeland in Israel."

The fact is that much of the theoretical discussion about the need for Judeo-Spanish was irrelevant to the reality of Sephardic life in the United States. It was only natural that the children of immigrants who were going to the public schools would adopt English as their mother tongue. Most of the immigrants, in spite of their best efforts, would never be able to use English as comfortably and as naturally as they used Judeo-Spanish. The isolation of Jews in Turkey and the Balkan countries that had maintained Judeo-Spanish over the centuries did not exist in the United States. On the contrary, the younger generation had no cultural pressures on them to maintain this language. Rather, the overwhelming pressure was to learn English and drop the "foreign" language.

The first American-born generation of Sephardim learned Judeo-Spanish as the language of their parents and their homes. Yet, they would seldom use the language outside the context of their family and close friends. The subsequent generation, for the most part, only knew enough Judeo-Spanish to communicate with their grandparents. The language of their homes had become English. By the third and fourth generations, Judeo-Spanish had completely ceased to be a language of communication. Now, where it is known or studied, it is usually for nostalgic or scholarly purposes.

The immigrant generation was torn by the conflict arising from the desire to maintain the old ways in the face of the powerful social forces of America. *La America* was an articulate voice urging that Sephardim manage to handle this conflict in an intelligent way. Gadol did not see Americanization as a necessary threat to the preservation of tradition and urged that Sephardim maintain their cultural and religious traditions, yet learn English, become American citizens, and adapt to American life.

The tensions created by the forces of assimilation versus the forces of preservation were evident among all immigrant groups. But complicating the crisis for the Sephardim was the fact that their ethnic identity was in itself a combination of elements. They were a Spanish-speaking people; but they were not part of any other existing Hispanic ethnic group. They came from Turkey and the Balkan countries; but they were separated by religion and social barriers from non-Jewish immigrants from the same regions. They were Jewish; but were clearly not of the same ethnic characteristics as the Yiddish-speaking Ashkenazic Jews. In short, the Sephardim were an entity unto themselves and diverse among themselves.

The Sephardic immigrants had a variety of opinions about themselves in relation to others. On the one hand, they had a strong self-image, thinking of themselves as the offspring of nobility, the heirs of a great past, and as a proud, self-respecting, and independent group. On the other hand, there were also deep feelings of inferiority. Overwhelmed by the numerous Ashkenazim, awed by the many successes of their Ashkenazic coreligionists, Sephardim came to see the Ashkenazim as models of success. In some cases, this led to admiration; in other cases, this feeling led to jealousy and antagonism. For some Sephardim, anything the Ashkenazic Jews did was ideal; while for other Sephardim, anything the Ashkenazim did was wrong or harmful.

Moise Gadol was a staunch believer in the need for Sephardim to maintain their own distinctive identity. Yet, he thought that the Sephardim could best fulfill their destiny by integrating themselves as much as possible into the Ashkenazic society. The main aspect of the Sephardic identity was, after all, Jewishness. Therefore, it was logical that the Sephardim should, in time, merge into one group with the Ashkenazim and be considered as one people with them. This process did not mean that Sephardim had to give up their own culture; it only meant that they could no longer hope to preserve their ways in the same fashion as they did in the old countries.

The Sephardic immigrants, to be sure, had much difficulty in their first encounters with Ashkenazic Jews. Gadol himself wrote (December 9, 1910): "Many of our Turkinos tell us with tears in their eyes that they are not believed by the Ashkenazim to be Jews." It was a regular complaint of Sephardim that the Ashkenazim did not receive them as Jews, thinking that they were Greeks, Italians, or Turks. Gadol believed that his newspaper had been influential in making the Ashkenazim realize that the Sephardim were in fact Jews. He noted that before the appearance of *La America*, the Ashkenazim did not think the Sephardim were Jews, even if they showed them their prayer shawls. But now that the Ashkenazim had seen that Sephardim had a newspaper printed in Hebrew letters and that the Judeo-Spanish language was a reflection of genuine Jewishness, Ashkenazim had begun to call Sephardim the "Jews of Jerusalem," as though the Sephardim were even more holy than they.

In an article reporting a new union of Sephardim and Ashkenazim in Turkey, Gadol rejoiced and hoped it would be a symbol of continuing cooperation between the two groups. Indeed, a goal of *La America* was to unite the Sephardim and Ashkenazim here in the United States. He condemned those who tried to keep Sephardim and Ashkenazim separated. "We are all children of one great nation, we must all unite, union is power."

But Gadol was not one to compromise the honor of the Sephardim or to swallow his pride if he felt offended by the Ashkenazic community. He did not believe in peace at any price; rather, he wished the Ashkenazim would accept the Sephardim as equals in every way and work together for the advancement of the Jewish people.

On February 8, 1912, the Progressive Oriental Society (composed mainly of Ashkenazim from Turkey) held a meeting with the intention of bringing Sephardim and Ashkenazim closer together. Speakers included Rabbi David de Sola Pool of the Spanish and Portuguese Synagogue, and Nessim Behar. There were also several speeches by Ashkenazic leaders. One of the speakers was A. Kretchmer, an Ashkenazi, who spoke at length. His talk disparaged the Sephardic Jews of Turkey, indicating that they were merely ignorant laborers and had played no role whatever in the Ottoman Empire. He asserted that the Ashkenazim were superior to Sephardim in various ways. Interestingly, Kretchmer spoke in Yiddish so that the Sephardim in the audience applauded along with everyone else when he was through, since they could not understand what he had said. But Gadol, who was present, understood Yiddish and he took copious notes of the speech in order to let the Sephardim in the United States and in Turkey know what Kretchmer had said. In the pages of *La America*, Gadol began a concerted campaign against Kretchmer and another Ashkenazic speaker of the day, Seff. He refuted their assertions and called on all Sephardim to protest vigorously against these charges.

In the March 15, 1912 issue of *La America*, Gadol printed a mock dialogue between himself, Joseph Gedelecia (president of the Progressive Oriental Society), Kretchmer, Seff, Nessim Behar, Alfred Mizrahi, and several others. The dialogue began with a statement by Gedelecia objecting to *La America*'s critique of his friend Kretchmer, implying that it was unfair of Gadol to attack these men since the Progressive Oriental Society had been supportive of *La America*. Gadol responded expressing his appreciation of the support that *La America* had received from Gedelecia's society. "I never attacked you or your society. I would not have attacked Kretchmer and Seff unless they had first attacked all Oriental Sephardim. If they had spoken kindly about our people, I would have praised them instead of criticizing them."

Kretchmer and Seff rebutted: "Oh, devil of an editor! Our intention was not to attack the Sephardim, but only to make the Ashkenazim aware of the Sephardim so that they can help them." Gadol replied: "If that was your intention, you did not need to invite our people, fooling them into thinking you'd speak in Spanish as was written in the advertisements. If I had not taken issue with you, my journal would be a timid thing which does not know how to defend the honor of our people. The Ashkenazim who found out what was written in *La America* thought that Kretchmer and Seff deserved even worse treatment from us. If our people would have understood you then, you would have been showered with abuse." Gadol went on to praise Nessim Behar as "the noblest Oriental Sephardi in New York."

Kretchmer and Seff then asked: "What can we do now to correct our error?" Gadol replied: "You have only one way, and that is to confess and repent in the presence of the same Yiddish-speaking people: we have sinned, we have erred, we have transgressed, and to promise not to speak any more like this, since now you recognize that the Sephardim are people who have a journal which knows how to defend their honor." However, Kretchmer and Seff retorted: "We will never do that. It is better for us to destroy *La America* so that we can begin again to speak what we like about the Sephardim." Gedelecia was then made to say that a new paper was needed to counteract the influence of *La America*, which would promote him personally as well as his organization. "Fool of an editor, haven't you learned yet that with the truth you cannot make money in America?" Alfred Mizrahi chimed in: "I do not know Yiddish, but if you pay the price, I will publish *La Aguila* in order to ruin *La America*." The newspaper *La Aguila* is then personified and made to say: "I am made up of lies and falsehoods. *La America*'s eagle stands above the word *emet* (truth) but I stand over the word *sheker* (lie)."

As could be expected, Kretchmer and his colleagues did not appreciate Gadol's criticisms and mockeries of them. Kretchmer wrote an article for the Yiddish newspaper *Taggeblatt* (March 15, 1912), in which he maligned Gadol. Gadol was outraged by the article and sent a letter to the editor of the *Taggeblatt*. He printed a Spanish translation of his letter in *La America*. Gadol's letter made the following points: "The article by A. Kretchmer which appeared in your journal was full of attacks and calumnies against me. I did not criticize any other speakers of that day, only Kretchmer and Seff who challenged the prestige of our people, especially those from Turkey. These two speakers ignore the intelligence and nobility of our race; ignore our great men and our Jewish press, our deputies in the Ottoman parliament, the national Jewish spirit of our people; they ignore our merchants, capitalists, our charitable men and our self-help institutions. What impression could all these attacks make on the Ashkenazic Jews? I felt it my obligation to publish in my journal the truth of the matter and to set the record straight.

"Kretchmer attacked me for trying to make a separation between Sephardim and Ashkenazim. If you check all the back issues of this newspaper you will see if this charge is true or not. The opposite is true. I have tried to bring the groups together in union. The motto of *La America* is: All Israelites are responsible one for the other. If Kretchmer knew Spanish and could read my paper he would not attack me as he has.

"I publish much about the Ashkenazic institutions here, and the papers in Turkey reprint them. I always praise the work of the Ashkenazic institutions. Isn't Kretchmer ashamed to say that I am against the Ashkenazim? Indeed I did not even attack Kretchmer himself but only the words he used against us. Moreover, I did not attack the Oriental Progressive Society. Cannot Kretchmer see that I work each day for my people, not for financial gain as he imagines? My journal is not subsidized by any society but only is able to survive due to my enormous moral and material sacrifices as well as through the aid of my readers who now appreciate the value of our newspaper."

Just as Gadol would not tolerate unsympathetic criticisms of the Sephardim by Ashkenazim, he was not reluctant himself to point out areas in which the Ashkenazim seemed to surpass the Sephardim. In *La America* (November 25, 1910) Gadol noted that there were numerous Jewish publications in New York City entirely due to the efforts of the Ashkenazim. "Before maintaining their bodies with bread, they maintain their spirit." He admired the intellectual and cultural life of the Ashkenazim, their many organizations, their schools, and their ambition. In urging his Sephardic readers to become American citizens, Gadol pointed to the Ashkenazic immigrants who all became citizens and were therefore able to progress. The Ashkenazim attended English classes and citizenship classes in large numbers. He asked the Sephardic Jews to follow this example. An article in *La America* (November 14, 1913), by an author who signed his name "Yehudi," contrasted the situation of Sephardim and Ashkenazim. "Yehudi" maintained that the Sephardic immigrant labored long and hard. Judaism's ideals became abstractions to him and he did not have the time or interest to give his children a good education in Judaism. On the other hand, Russian Jews learned English, sent their children to colleges, established schools and journals, synagogues, and study places. They learned the ways of America and were able to reach high positions. The Ashkenazim were becoming the leading industrialists, teachers, doctors, and lawyers. "And we Sephardic Jews?" The author's clear implication was that the Sephardim did not have the drive or vision to succeed in contrast to the Ashkenazim.

The feelings of inferiority expressed in the article by "Yehudi" were further elaborated in another of his articles in *La America*. He claimed that Sephardic Judaism in the United States was like a navy without capable captains or sailors, lacking proper leadership. "Spanish Judaism is nothing. We have no achievements or distinguished personages. We are only concerned with maintaining ourselves and not with fostering our spiritual development."

Gadol believed that if Sephardim would become involved in the major Ashkenazic organizations, they would be positively influenced by their Ashkenazic coreligionists. They would become part of organized Jewish life and make their contributions to the general Jewish community. Gadol saw the organizations as bridges that could bring the Ashkenazim and Sephardim together. Moreover, the Sephardim could learn much from their participation in the successful Ashkenazic organizations.

Gadol was involved, for example, with the New York Kehillah. This was a major effort of New York Jewry to bring together the diverse elements of the Jewish community into one umbrella group. The Kehillah included a broad spectrum of synagogues and organizations. Gadol reported in *La America* (February 3, 1911) that of the 784 organizations affiliated with the New York Kehillah, not one of them was a Turkish society. Yet, Gadol assured his readers, the Kehillah was very interested in the Sephardic community and wanted their involvement. Gadol called on the Sephardic societies to affiliate with the Kehillah and to send delegates to its conventions. Several Sephardic societies did follow his advice. Once the Federation of Oriental Jews was established in 1912, it too was involved in the work of the New York Kehillah.

Judah Magnes, the president of the Kehillah, made several valiant efforts to help the immigrant Sephardim. The New York Kehillah sponsored a conference on January 2, 1913, at which many leaders of the Sephardic and Ashkenazic community were present. The purpose of that meeting was to see how the Oriental Jews could be best assisted. The Kehillah agreed to establish an annual fund of $15,000 to assist the Sephardim and appointed a committee to implement the budget. David de Sola Pool was actively involved in this work. While this conference seemed to be an auspicious event for the Sephardim, the actual results of the conference were limited. With all the promises, good wishes, and allocation of theoretical funds, the Kehillah itself was too weak to see the plan through. Gadol grew irritated by the lack of action. He had a personal interest in the budget, since $750 was to be allocated to *La America*. Two months after the conference, Gadol still had not received one cent from the Kehillah for *La America*. "We cannot live on promises," he wrote with ire. The Kehillah held its fourth annual meeting on April 12, 1913, and the question of the Turkinos came up. A committee was established to look into ways of assisting them. In an editorial comment in *La America*, Gadol wondered how much more time would pass before anything was really done. "We have little faith in these promises; we have to help ourselves." At the conference of the Kehillah, almost all the Sephardic societies were represented, an indication of their growing involvement in general community affairs.

Gadol urged Sephardim to become involved in other Jewish organizations. In particular, he favored belonging to Bnei Zion, especially since that organization had a life-insurance plan that its members could join. Gadol also supported the Hebrew Immigrant Aid Society and continually prodded Sephardic involvement in its work. He believed that if Sephardim would contribute to the general Jewish funds, they would gain respect and come to have a voice in policymaking.

Aside from asking Sephardim to participate in Ashkenazic organizations, Gadol also encouraged them to take the initiative and invite Ashkenazic participation in Sephardic projects. The Federation of Oriental Jews successfully rallied support for the Jews in Turkey and the Balkans who were suffering due to the Balkan Wars. *La America* (December 20, 1912) reported that a meeting was held with Sephardic and Ashkenazic leaders (including Gadol) to call a mass meeting of all Jews to come to the aid of the suffering Jews in Oriental countries. It was clear that Gadol and others were bringing about a better understanding between the two groups of Jews. Yet, in spite of the steps of progress, the masses of Sephardim and Ashkenazim were still isolated from each other and, in many cases, antagonistic.

While Gadol was vigorously defending the Jewishness of the Sephardic immigrants and urging the Ashkenazim to accept them as fellow Jews in every way, there were elements within the Sephardic community itself that were moving further away from Jewish identity. In *La America* (November 25, 1910) Gadol reported that a number of young Sephardic men who had been in the United States for some time were no longer interested in Judaism nor were they proud of their Judeo-Spanish background. They wanted to become Americanized as fast as possible. Another article (January 5, 1912) stated that Ashkenazim were proud to be Jews because Jews were influential in American society, yet some Sephardim were ashamed to be Jews. The article urged Sephardim to be proud of themselves as Jews. The argument was that the Americans themselves loved the Jewish nation and there was no reason to hide one's Jewishness. "Brothers! Let us demonstrate clearly in every place that we are Jews! The name of the Jew in America gives honor! You will find work more quickly by demonstrating that you are Jews!"

The fact was that the Sephardic immigrants did not have time, money, nor the talent to establish proper Jewish schools for their children. Since the economic pressures were so great, the immigrants themselves—even if they wished to observe the Jewish laws and customs—often found themselves compromising their principles in order to make a living. Desecration of the Jewish Sabbath was not uncommon; the printery of *La America* itself was open on Saturdays for most of the years of its existence. The pages of *La America* reported various incidents of Sephardim violating basic laws of Sabbath, kashruth, and Passover.

A letter to *La America* from Jack Farhi informed readers of a missionary group located on Second Avenue. It sponsored moving pictures with free admission and gave away free gifts. The movie, of course, was on a Christian theme with the aim of gaining converts. Farhi noted that Sephardim—men, women, and children—attended the movies in order to obtain the free gifts. He lamented this situation. "It isn't enough that when we come to the United States we give up our religious observances; have we moved so far that we now allow ourselves to go to missionary places?" Farhi urged the Sephardim not to attend these movies and his suggestion was applauded by Gadol. Although it is unlikely that Sephardim did in fact fall prey to the missionaries, the fact that people could even think of attending such movies was itself a sign of a weakened Jewish identity.

The Sephardic immigrants found themselves in an oppressive and complicated setting. Newly arrived from the Levant, the chaos of the Lower East Side must have seemed overwhelming. They needed to keep their past, because their identities were rooted in it; but they needed to break away from their past in order to adapt to America.

The conflicts apparent in the Sephardic struggle for self-definition continued to trouble the Sephardim for the next several generations. Even today, when many of the old conflicts have been resolved, Sephardim still grapple with the problem of their specific Jewish and Sephardic identity. While Sephardim now, by and large, are fully Americanized and generally have become more understood and appreciated by the Ashkenazic community, sensitive Sephardic Jews still know that there is something quite distinctive and unique about their culture. In spite of the external vestiges of assimilation, a Sephardic soul still burns brightly and strongly within many thousands of the children and grandchildren of the readers of *La America*.

Moise Gadol, the editor of La America.

*Albert Amateau, c. 1913. Born in Rhodes,
Amateau was an officer of
the Federation of Oriental Jews.
He was one of the chief protagonists
in Gadol's dispute with La Vara.*

*Rev. Dr. David de Sola Pool,
minister of Shearith Israel
during the period 1907–70.*

Henry S. Hendricks,
long-time president of Shearith Israel.
He was active in the Berith Shalom
and the Sephardic Community.

Professor Maír José Benardete,
Sephardic philogist. He was the first
Turkish Jew to become a public school
teacher in the United States.

Albert Torres, publisher of La Vara.
He undertook the arrangements for
Gadol's funeral after hearing that Gadol
was to be buried in potter's field.

*Rev. Dr. Henry Pereira Mendes (l.),
minister of Shearith Israel
from 1877–1920, and
Rev. Joseph de Abraham Benyunes,
leader of the Sisterhood's
settlement house
on the Lower East Side.*

*The Angel family and neighbors, c. 1910, in Rhodes.
The author's family left soon after for the United States.*

The Progressive Jewish Boys Club, c. 1915.

The Alba Sephardic Club in the early 1920s.

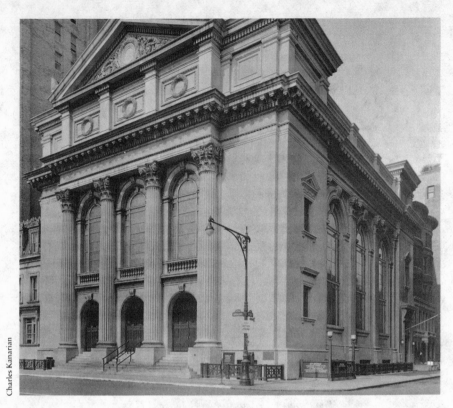

Congregation Shearith Israel,
the Spanish and Portuguese Synagogue in the city of New York.

The interior of Shearith Israel.

*The synagogue of the
Janina Jews, on Broome St.*

*133 Eldridge St.,
the site of the Shearith Israel
Sisterhood's settlement house.*

The building of the Sephardic Brotherhood,
at 20 West 114th Street.

5

Toward a
Unified Community

Before the emergence of *La America* in November 1910, the Sephardic community of New York had no central organization. It was basically a conglomeration of individuals from various cities of the Levant, each trying to make his or her own way through the quagmire of life on the Lower East Side. The few societies that had been organized prior to 1910 were small and were not concerned with the general situation of those outside their membership. The Sephardim had no voice in general Jewish or American affairs nor were the immigrants interested in having such a voice. Although they lived in difficult conditions, they always dreamed of becoming wealthy. There were enough examples of immigrants who had arrived with no money and who, through hard work and the willingness to take risks, had become successful owners of factories. Each new immigrant rationalized that he, too, had a chance. Discussions of idealism, unity, and community were of secondary importance to these newcomers.

Moise Gadol realized that the masses of Sephardim were not ready to develop great cultural institutions, schools, or even a central community organization. He saw how hard they worked and how little they earned. He knew that most of the immigrants had had a limited education before coming to the United States. He could see how fragmented the Sephardim were as a group—few individuals were concerned with others who were not from the same native city. Gadol knew all this; yet, this knowledge did not deter him from his goal.

The pages of *La America* were filled with Gadol's proddings: the Sephardim needed a voice; the Sephardim needed to unite; the Levantine immigrants should help themselves by cooperating with each other. For a while Gadol was a lone voice. There were few who paid much attention to his recommendations. But his was a persistent voice.

Realizing that the existing societies were too jealous of their independence to merge into one central Sephardic community organization, Gadol began to argue for a federation of the various societies. On March 22, 1912, *La America* announced on the front page the establishment of the Federation of Oriental Jews of America. A meeting had been held on March 18 at the home of Shelomo Emanuel, president of the Ahavath Shalom of Monastir Society. Representatives of six societies attended, along with Gadol. These men decided to establish a federation of the existing Oriental societies with each group maintaining its own organization. However, each group would also contribute a certain amount to the Federation and the Federation itself would serve the general needs of the Oriental community and would represent them in general Jewish and American organizations. The goal of the Federation was to help all Sephardim, not only in New York, but throughout the United States. It intended to provide moral, social, and economic help. It agreed to have nothing to do with religious rituals or services—those areas of concern that were best left to the individual societies. The Federation would try to resolve any disputes arising among the members of the Oriental community and would provide social work and counseling to families or individuals. It was also hoped that the Federation would establish a central Talmud Torah, a community center, and English classes. It was agreed that each society would contribute twenty-five cents per member each year to finance the projects of the Federation and that each contributing society would be represented on the Federation's board.

Following this initial announcement, Gadol and several others worked diligently to convince the leadership of all the societies to support and join the Federation of Oriental Jews. Gadol called on the presidents of the societies to hold membership meetings that would resolve to join the Federation and appoint a delegate to it. Gadol offered to serve as liaison between the individual societies and the new Federation.

On April 7, 1912, a meeting of the Federation of Oriental Jews of America was held. Of the thirteen societies that had been invited, nine sent representatives. Provisional officers were elected: Joseph Gedelecia as president and Albert Amateau as secretary.

At the April 21, 1912, meeting of the Federation, twelve societies were represented. A constitution committee was appointed. The representatives were informed that at the next meeting each society would have to give an accounting of its membership and would be billed accordingly. Each society was to be represented by its president and three delegates.

The next meeting was held on May 5. Aside from the representatives of the Sephardic societies, there were also representatives of Shearith Israel, including David de Sola Pool, and Rachel Toledano. Rabbi Pool expressed the good will of Shearith Israel and the willingness of this historic Sephardic congregation to help in all matters concerning the Federation. Toledano informed the group that the Sisterhood of the Spanish and Portuguese Synagogue was interested in establishing a center for Sephardic immigrants at 180 Chrystie Street. The presence of representatives of Shearith Israel was at this time considered a boon to the Federation of Oriental Jews. Shearith Israel had an impressive reputation throughout the Jewish community, being the oldest Jewish congregation in North America (founded in 1654). A number of its members had distinguished themselves in Jewish and civic affairs and it was considered desirable to have such a powerful and established force on the side of the new immigrants. Indeed, Pool was elected honorary president of the Federation of Oriental Jews at its meeting of May 19, 1912. Gadol said of Pool's appointment, "We can glory with such a person at the head of our organization."

Because the Federation came into being largely through the efforts of Moise Gadol, he exerted a considerable influence on the newly founded organization. Gadol would often remind the delegates to the Federation of the importance of *La America*. He indicated that running the paper was really too much for one man to handle and suggested that the newspaper should be supported by the Federation, as it was the only available mouthpiece of the Federation to the entire community. The Federation did appoint a committee that was responsible to come up with recommendations for *La America*. It was suggested that the presidents of the societies recommend that their members subscribe to *La America* and that these subscriptions be collected at their meetings. Another suggestion was to have a raffle, the proceeds of which would be turned over to *La America*. Gadol thanked the Federation and urged that these recommendations be implemented promptly, since the paper was in critical financial condition.

The Federation delegates took themselves quite seriously. They believed that they were the true representatives of the Levantine Jewish community in New York, and to a certain extent, in the entire United States. The meetings were characterized by a spirit of conciliation, as the delegates strove to keep peace among the various contending societies. Trying to be impartial, the governing board of the Federation offered its support, at least in theory, to any Sephardic organization that requested it. For example, the Federation agreed to take part in a fourth of July celebration sponsored by Congregation Shearith Israel. It also decided that the presidents of the societies should attempt to sell tickets to their memberships to a picnic sponsored by the Tikvah Tovah Society. At its meeting on July 28, 1912, the Federation agreed to assist the small Talmud Torah founded by the Ahavah Ve-Ahvah of Janina. It also suggested that this Talmud Torah be merged with the one operated by the Arabic-speaking Jews of the Rodefei Tsedek Society in order to form one large Talmud Torah for all Oriental Jews.

The Federation of Oriental Jews did in fact establish a Talmud Torah at 73 Allen Street. There were no tuition charges at all. The teacher at the school spoke Spanish, Arabic, and Greek so that all segments of the Sephardic community could feel that their children were receiving proper instruction. Pool donated $10 to the school while other members of the governing board made contributions of smaller amounts. This Talmud Torah had been started by the Ez Hahayyim Society but was now to be run under the aegis of the Federation.

At the meeting of the Federation held in October 1912, Gadol again brought up the question of *La America*. He indicated that the non-Spanish-speaking Jews from Janina and the Arab countries said that they did not wish to support the paper because they did not understand Spanish. Gadol believed that since most of the immigrants were Spanish-speaking, *La America* did serve the general needs of the community. Moreover, if the financial condition of the paper were to improve, he saw no reason why sections in other languages could not be added. Yet the reaction from the delegates was lukewarm at best and hostile at worst. David Carasso, the president of the Ez Hahayyim Society, spoke sharply against the paper and attacked Gadol personally. Gadol, who was himself vice-president of the Ez Hahayyim Society, was shocked and outraged by Carasso's criticisms. At the meeting in November, the question of *La America* again came up and was accompanied by debates and discussions, but no solutions were reached.

Gadol had suggested that the Federation call a mass meeting and invite both Sephardim and Ashkenazim. The Federation could offer a concert in Yiddish and Spanish and have various speakers addressing the crowd. Admission tickets would be sold to this event and a significant amount of money could be raised for *La America*. Yet the Federation delegates would not implement this suggestion. In December, Gadol was still arguing for his paper. "If the Federation does not help now with a little expense on its part, it will need to incur a great expense in the future to establish a new paper."

The Federation appointed another committee to help *La America*. Gadol believed that the Federation should send representatives to meet with Ashkenazic leaders who understood the value of a publication such as *La America*. The Federation, however, never actually helped *La America* materially. This was a source of disillusionment for Gadol, since he realized that his sacrifices and efforts on behalf of the newspaper were not really appreciated. The Federation, which was composed of the leaders of the Sephardic community, did not take *La America* seriously and never considered it the vital organ that Gadol believed it was. Disgust with the leadership's nonchalant attitude toward his newspaper led to Gadol's dissatisfaction with the entire operation of the Federation.

The meetings of the Federation concerned themselves with a

number of items of importance to the community. At the meeting of December 22, 1912, it was announced that an information center for young Turkinos had been set up at 186 Chrystie Street and was open from 7 to 9 P.M. on Wednesday evenings and 3 to 5 P.M. on Sunday afternoons. Young people were invited to come and talk about whatever was on their mind. This information center was established through the efforts of the Sisterhood of the Spanish and Portuguese Synagogue. One speaker attended this meeting to urge the Sephardim to watch their children and keep them away from Christian missionaries who were busy in the downtown area. At the same meeting, a letter was read that had been sent to the Federation by a number of young Sephardim announcing the establishment of a musical society for the young people of the community, asking the Federation to offer moral support. This offer of moral, not material, support was approved unanimously. At this meeting, there was also a discussion of efforts to inform the Ashkenazic leaders about the problems of the Sephardic community.

A seeming breakthrough in the affairs of the Federation was reported at the meeting held on January 12, 1913. Gedelecia reported that the New York Kehillah had agreed to a fifteen-thousand-dollar allocation for the Federation, a sum that would be distributed over a period of five years. With this money, the Federation believed it would be possible to obtain the services of a chief rabbi and be able to maintain a number of institutions within the Sephardic community. Yet this hope, too, led to disappointment. Many hours were spent discussing the allocation of this money, but none ever materialized.

Good intentions and promises do not build communities. At the first annual meeting of the Federation of Oriental Jews, held on April 27, 1913, Jack Farhi spoke eloquently. He told the delegates not to depend on the promises of the Ashkenazim or of any outside societies. Rather, each Sephardic society should give 40 to 50 percent of its total revenues to the Federation. In this way, the Federation could be independent and self-sufficient. The Hayyim Va-Hessed Gallipoli, of which Farhi was president, had agreed to contribute three to four hundred dollars per year to the Federation. He called upon all other societies to follow this example. A suggestion made in March was that each individual should pay one sum directly to the Federation, not paying any other dues to the separate societies. The Federation would then allocate funds to the societies. That suggestion was rejected.

The problem of finances was an overriding one for the Federation. It never could generate enough support, and its plans to win increased revenues were unsuccessful. At the meeting of May 11, 1913, the delegates dealt with the problem of the closure of the downtown Talmud Torah due to a lack of funds. Gadol suggested that each Sephardic Jew in America should be taxed one dollar annually in order to provide for the work of the Federation. Although this resolution was passed, it was never implemented nor was it even possible to implement it.

To be sure, there were several philanthropists among the members of Shearith Israel who were willing to offer financial assistance. Ephraim Benguiat made a sizable contribution to support the downtown Talmud Torah, saying that he would meet all costs if necessary but that he believed all the Sephardim were obliged to donate at least three dollars a year to support the school and the other projects of the Federation. Henry Pereira Mendes, the minister of Congregation Shearith Israel (the Spanish and Portuguese Synagogue), indicated that his congregation would undertake to pay all the expenses for the uptown Talmud Torah in Harlem. Gedelecia responded by saying that the uptown Talmud Torah was well supported by the Sephardim at present and that it was the downtown school that needed assistance. Apparently, Shearith Israel did not wish to take responsibility for the downtown school since its own Sisterhood was already active on the Lower East Side. The synagogue did not want to compete with the Sisterhood. These offers by Shearith Israel were not met with a warm response.

Albert Amateau claimed that the Spanish and Portuguese community had the *obligation* to bury without charge any Sephardic Jew who died. With the money the Sephardic societies would save by not having to provide burial space, the Federation would then be able to meet all its other obligations. Such an unreasonable request might have received a sharp answer. However, David de Sola Pool simply informed Amateau that Shearith Israel would indeed provide burial for any Sephardic Jew as long as he was a member of Shearith Israel. (In point of fact, Shearith Israel did provide cemetery space to bury indigent Sephardim—at little or no cost to the family.) Finally, the Federation unanimously voted that Shearith Israel would undertake to pay all the expenses for the uptown Talmud Torah while the Federation itself would stimulate the members of the community to pay for the downtown Talmud Torah.

While the meetings of the Federation dealt with matters of importance to the Oriental Jewish community, the organization itself was for the most part powerless. Fine resolutions would be passed without any means of implementation. Any suggestion entailing an expense was almost always defeated. Any request that the individual societies give up even a slight amount of their autonomy was brushed aside as nonsense. In short, the Federation had no power whatsoever except that of moral persuasion; and in this respect, it was hardly successful.

Stunned by the Federation's inability and unwillingness to help *La America*, Gadol angrily wrote on June 20, 1913, that the delegates of the Federation were upset at having to give up so much of their time for meetings of the Federation on days when they could rest or enjoy a few hours of leisure in the sun. "We have only discussions and more discussions but nothing definite is decided." *La America* began publicly to tilt against the Federation, an organization Gadol himself—through *La America*—had initiated. It had proven to be, in Gadol's view, an unsuccessful experiment.

But the leaders of the Federation were not quick to admit defeat. Albert Amateau wrote several articles, which Gadol published in *La America*, explaining the origin and purposes of the Federation of Oriental Jews. In an article that appeared on August 22, 1913, Amateau stated: "We Turkinos in America are of two categories: either very ignorant or little educated. . . . Among the ignorant, many societies were formed and each president sought honor for himself. When the Federation was first formed, these presidents feared that they would lose their honors. They joined the Federation against their will, thinking it could not last very long. When they saw that the Federation was advancing they did all they could to make it fail. The masses of our people support the Federation and therefore it can succeed." Amateau called on all Sephardim to support the Federation so it could continue to help the community. An example of how the Federation effectively served the people was cited: the Federation had energetically pursued the case of a Sephardic man who had raped a Sephardic woman and had had him prosecuted by the authorities.

To get an idea of its limitations, one need only examine the balance sheet of the Federation of Oriental Jews for 1912 and 1913. As of October 31, 1913, the total income of the Federation was only $1,438.42, while the total expenses were $1,536.34, leaving a deficit of $97.92. On such limited funds, one could hardly expect the organization to employ a chief rabbi, operate synagogues, finance religious schools, and otherwise serve the community. Albert Amateau, believing that the Federation could succeed, presented a proposed budget at the meeting of November 2, 1913, which amounted to $6,000 for the coming year, including $1,500 for a chief rabbi. In order to raise the necessary funds to meet this budget, it was proposed that each society pay one dollar per member to the Federation. This resolution passed by a seventeen-to-six vote. Gadol, supporting this idea, stated that if individual members did not wish to pay the one dollar for the Federation, each society should be responsible to pay for them from their treasuries.

But Gadol was already weaving a new plan to unite the Sephardim of New York. He envisioned the formation of an Oriental Jewish Community of the City of New York. In theory, this new organization was to be completely different in scope from the Federation of Oriental Jews. While the Federation was supposedly a national movement, the Community would be solely a New York operation. At a mass meeting held on December 9, 1913, Gadol spoke of the need to establish an Oriental Jewish Community in New York, which would include everyone without distinction as to city of origin. This Community would provide day-to-day help for the Sephardim and would assist in matters of immigration and employment. Furthermore, it would obtain a chief rabbi, sustain a religious school and synagogue, and secure the services of a lawyer and doctor to serve its members. The Community would also provide benefits in case of sickness. All these goals would be achieved if each member paid one dollar per month as well as a five-dollar entry fee. The Federation had proved incapable of handling these matters and Gadol was attempting to rally support for a new organization.

At this mass meeting, the leaders of the Federation also spoke. Gedelecia addressed the audience in English, not knowing Judeo-Spanish; he favored the new organization. Albert Amateau also spoke, stating that the immigrants came to America not to die but to live. They therefore needed a community that could help them with life, not merely with death. A provisional committee was set up to pursue the possibility of organizing the Community. Moise Gadol was elected to be one of the members of this committee.

The provisional committee of the Oriental Jewish Community met on November 16, 1913, and decided on the following provisions: 1) There would be no entrance fee to join the new organization. 2) Dues would be one dollar per month. 3) A member was required to pay three dollars in advance to cover the first three months of membership. 4) Members of both sexes aged sixteen through fifty would be accepted. 5) Each person must fill out an application form and be approved by two members of the organization who would testify that the applicant was honest. 6) Payment of the monthly dues must be in advance. 7) The executive committee would meet once a week and a general meeting of all the members would be held once every three months. 8) The activities of the Community would be published in *La America*.

Among the benefits for members would be free education for children in a Talmud Torah, and seats in a synagogue for the High Holy Days as well as throughout the year. The Community would have a paid secretary and an office. Each member would also have a five-hundred-dollar insurance policy in case of death. The Oriental Jewish Community appointed three delegates to the Federation. It planned to incorporate itself according to the laws of New York and to begin a registry of vital statistics of its members.

At its first regular meeting, held on November 23, 1913, eighteen of the twenty-three members attended. Joseph Gedelecia was elected president, Albert Amateau secretary, and Moise Gadol treasurer. Thus, the two main officers of the Federation succeeded in becoming the two main officers of the Community. This fact annoyed Gadol, since he believed that the Community should be a new and fresh organization. He feared that with Gedelecia and Amateau involved in the leadership, the Community might merely become an adjunct of the Federation.

Gadol addressed this meeting stating that the existing societies did not provide enough assistance to the Sephardim on a daily basis. "We should not and cannot rely on Ashkenazic institutions to solve our problems. We must support our own bureau to help immigrants. Moreover, the Community should make its own contribution to Mt. Sinai Hospital so that the Sephardic sick could be admitted there without charge. If we could make our Community work properly, our prestige will rise. We will be worthy successors of our great ancestors whom the Ashkenazim of the world respect so much. In union we will progress and gain in our self-respect." Gadol urged that the Community shouldn't help any Sephardic Jew who was not a member. "Our people are stubborn. If they receive something free during their difficult times, they do not later open their purse strings or pay anything in return when the crisis has passed. Sephardim must be taught that if they want the benefits, they must pay. In this way, we shall save our honor and guarantee the future for our membership."

At a mass meeting of the Community held on December 7 for Spanish-speaking Sephardim, more than five hundred people attended. Gadol addressed the audience, urging support for the Oriental Bureau of the Hebrew Immigrant Aid Society. "We must pay at least one dollar each to support it since this bureau deals only with Sephardic immigrants. We must support this bureau so that the Ashkenazim will not say that we expect to receive everything for free." Gadol stated that the Community would establish its own employment office, since the needs of the Sephardic immigrants were not being met by existing efforts. He stated, also, that Shearith Israel had promised many times to support the uptown Talmud Torah but, "we are impatient waiting for their aid."

In attendance were Alice Menken and Rachel Toledano of the Sisterhood of the Spanish and Portuguese Synagogue. Mrs. Toledano demanded the opportunity to speak. She publicly objected to *La America*'s statement that the Sisterhood's promises to help the Sephardim were empty. Gadol responded to her: "If the Sisterhood of the Spanish and Portuguese Synagogue wants to help us, it has to work in accord with our own community and not ignore our centers such as the Federation, the Community, and our journal. The Sisterhood had printed a number of circulars recently, shameful for the many errors, but did not use *La America*'s printing service, nor did they support *La America* though we have praised the Sisterhood's work many times in our pages without pay. We have gone three years with your empty promises and this has harmed us. The best thing is not to believe in promises, but to help ourselves." Gadol's speech was met with hearty applause by the large crowd. The battle cry of the Community, with its desire for independence and respect, was thus clearly proclaimed by Moise Gadol.

The Community held a mass meeting for Greek-speaking Jews on December 14, 1913, which drew only about fifty persons. Gedelecia, who chaired the meeting, would not allow Rachel Toledano and her associates to enter the meeting hall. This action led to disagreeable words between Gedelecia and Joseph Benyunes, the Sisterhood's downtown employee, but things soon settled down. In reporting this meeting in *La America*, Gadol professed not to know why Mrs. Toledano was so upset. He had only told her that the Sephardim were tired of her empty promises: "If the Sisterhood of the Spanish and Portuguese Synagogue intends to help, they have to discuss their plans with the Federation or Community. The Sisterhood has no right to collect funds for us; only our own organizations can do this. Our journal, which is the servant of our people, must speak always the truth and must criticize unjust things." Gadol wrote that if Mrs. Toledano thought *La America* had been unfair to her, she should bring her case to court or to the district attorney. "We are ready to show that our publication is just and does not intend to offend anybody."

The Federation, the Community, and the Sisterhood of the Spanish and Portuguese Synagogue were now embroiled in a series of charges and countercharges. By December 1913 Alice Menken of the Sisterhood had sent a letter to the Federation stating that the Sisterhood would take over the uptown Talmud Torah itself and henceforth wanted no more "cooperation" from the Federation. The Sisterhood, after this insult to the Federation, denigrated the Community as well. Gadol claimed shortly afterwards that Shearith Israel and its Sisterhood "opposed our Community without reason or justice. They are joined by various leaders of societies who fear that their societies will be weakened by the Community. But we want to work in harmony with everyone; those who work for disunion are trying to retard progress." Judah Magnes, president of the New York Kehillah, called a meeting of representatives of Shearith Israel and Sephardic organizations in order to bring about a reconciliation.

In spite of the dissension, the Community did make initial strides of progress. At a meeting held on December 28, 1913, it was agreed that new members need pay only one dollar in advance, not three dollars as had been proposed. The new organization had gained more than one hundred members in a short time. Although there was intense opposition from within the colony, Gadol felt that little by little it would succeed in winning over all the Sephardic Jews.

While the Community was trying to get itself on solid footing, the Federation of Oriental Jews continued its own activities. Of major concern to the Federation was the hiring of a chief rabbi. This matter was brought up repeatedly, resolutions were passed, monies were voted; yet, no Sephardic chief rabbi was ever actually employed by the Federation of Oriental Jews. The well-intentioned deliberations remained wishful thinking.

The Federation of Oriental Jews held a mass meeting on June 7, 1914, at the public school at 91 Forsyth Street. More than one thousand Sephardim of all backgrounds attended. The president, Joseph Gedelecia, listed the accomplishments of the Federation, referring to the three Talmud Torah schools that it sponsored, two in the downtown area and one uptown. Gadol considered this statement to be false. In reporting this speech in *La America,* Gadol stated that he did not know of these three Talmud Torah schools. The uptown school was sponsored by the Spanish and Portuguese Synagogue as well as by certain private individuals, not by the Federation. And, one of the downtown schools was supported by the Spanish and Portuguese Jews while the other was supported by the Jews from Janina. None was connected with the Federation. Gadol also took exception to Gedelecia's assertion that there were twenty-eight Sephardic societies with three thousand members.

An election of officers was held at the mass meeting, the results of which indicated the weak position of the Federation. M. Shinasi, a multimillionaire Sephardic Jew, was elected honorary president of the Federation. Yet, he did not even bother to attend this meeting. Edward Valensi was elected president. Gedelecia and two others were elected vice-presidents—but Gedelecia refused the office saying that his doctor and his wife forbade him from continuing as an officer of the Federation because of his deteriorating health. Albert Amateau was elected financial secretary and Moise Gadol comptroller. The speakers who had been listed to appear at the mass meeting did not show up nor did any representatives of the Spanish and Portuguese Synagogue attend. When the meeting adjourned at six P.M., there was a general dissatisfaction among those in attendance, especially concerning the elections.

In evaluating the position of the Federation and the Community, Gadol wrote in *La America* (June 12, 1914) that the Federation had done much good work since the time it was founded and that with its small income it could not have been expected to do more. It had succeeded in bringing the societies together, an accomplishment that had not been thought possible before. However, he felt that now that the Community had been established, the Federation no longer needed to deal with the problems of the immigrants and other day-to-day problems. It should only work to form organized communities in all the cities of the United States where Sephardim were residing and to centralize the societies in the various cities. The Federation should also obtain a chief rabbi for the Sephardim of the entire United States. In other words, the Community would now replace the Federation in all matters concerning the New York City Sephardim; while the Federation would henceforth be concerned on a national level.

But the Federation was not to follow this advice. The leaders continued to negotiate with the New York Kehillah and at the September 6, 1914, meeting of the Federation, a letter signed by Magnes on behalf of the Kehillah was read. The Kehillah agreed to pay $2,000 a year for a three-year period in order to employ a Sephardic chief rabbi. The pay for the rabbi was set at $2,500, and therefore the Federation only had to raise $500 a year. Each society represented agreed to pay $50 a year for this purpose.

Gadol himself was caught up in the enthusiasm of this offer and stressed the importance of obtaining a chief rabbi. He indicated that *La America* received numerous letters dealing with family problems and religious questions from rabbis in the various cities of

Turkey, Israel, and elsewhere. In spite of his good intentions, Gadol admitted that he himself could not understand the religious issues involved in many of these inquiries. It was necessary to have a chief rabbi to handle these problems.

But the Sephardic societies were slow to contribute. By January 1, 1915, the Kehillah had only received $350 from the Federation, and the Kehillah indicated that it would withdraw its offer of $2,000 a year unless it received the $500 within a short time. At a meeting of the Federation held on February 7, 1915, it was reported that the $500 had been raised but that the societies that had not yet contributed were also expected to participate. Abraham Galante, the noted scholar, was suggested as a possible candidate for this new position. Gadol opposed this choice, feeling that Galante had Reform tendencies and was not known as a Zionist—on the contrary, he said, Galante was a good friend of David Fresco, the editor of the Istanbul newspaper *El Tiempo* and a notorious anti-Zionist. Gadol stated that if Galante came as a leader he might be acceptable but he should not be appointed as a chief rabbi. The discussion about Abraham Galante in particular, and about obtaining a chief rabbi in general, occupied the members of the Federation during many meetings, yet no practical resolution ever resulted. For various reasons, the New York Kehillah did not follow up on its offer of the $2,000 per year, and ultimately the money raised by the Sephardim for the purpose of obtaining the chief rabbi was returned to the contributing societies.

The Federation's position continued to show weakness. At a meeting on December 13, 1914, Albert Amateau reported that the Federation simply could not continue its work due to a lack of funds. The societies had to pay what they owed or the Federation would be forced to dissolve. Aside from the financial problems, Gadol continued to point out other weaknesses of the Federation in the pages of *La America*.

The Federation of Oriental Jews held its annual meeting on June 11, 1915, at 186 Chrystie Street. At that time Edward Valensi was elected honorary president and Joseph Gedelecia was once again elected president. Gadol, who by now was exasperated with Gedelecia's leadership, was outraged by the election. In an editorial, he indicated that the meeting of the Federation represented backsliding for the Sephardic community. The Federation had become a small club of self-designated leaders not representative of the needs of the community. At the annual meeting, instead of inviting the entire community, the Federation just invited its executive members to attend. Only fifteen to twenty people were present. Gadol felt that the elected officials had been voted into office by too few people. Even those who attended had had no opportunity to voice their opinions. After Edward Valensi gave his presidential report, one of the delegates had wanted to comment, but Gedelecia had cut him off. According to Gadol, Gedelecia had become the "dictator of our colony." Gadol said that the Federation was no longer representing the Sephardim in any way and that support should be given to the Community instead.

However, the Community had not been able to gain widespread support and suffered from similar problems with leadership. A writer in La America complained that the Sephardim suffered from a grave illness—they did not know how to choose leaders. Gadol himself concurred by June 1915, writing that the very same people who had ruined the Federation were now badly serving the Community. Gadol proposed establishing yet another new organization, to be known as the Comunidad Israelite Sefardit de New York (the Israelite Sephardic Community of New York). This group would be strictly for the Sephardim, run by Sephardim and staffed by Sephardim. Gadol strongly favored not using "Oriental" in the new organization's title because the term Oriental was associated in the American mind with the Japanese. As American attitudes were not favorable to these Orientals, the Sephardim should not share the poor connotations of the term. Sephardim was the logical substitute, as it was a term that was enhanced by its people's illustrious history.

Gadol was harsh in his criticism of Gedelecia, citing an article that had appeared in a Yiddish-language newspaper in mid-1915, which had given an unfavorable account of the Oriental Jews of New York. The editor of the newspaper cited Gedelecia as the source of the information. Gadol responded by trying to discredit Gedelecia's facts and figures. He said that the Yiddish article had implied that the eighteen thousand Sephardim of New York were a welfare group, who lacked the means to support themselves honestly. In refutation Gadol listed a number of Sephardic individuals who had become wealthy and also stated, "Our people prefer working at any occupation, however humble, rather than to depend on charity. We are fed up with Gedelecia's false promises, his insults of our people. It is time for us to silence him so that he can no longer speak on our behalf." In a later article Gadol criticized Gedelecia as an ineffective leader: "Yet, he keeps the title of president [of the Federation], leading the Ashkenazic community to think that he is in fact our leader. We must not permit him to be at the head of 20,000 Sephardim, especially without having been elected by our people in a fair general election. He is not fit to represent us, but rather disparages us on every occasion."

Gadol continued to attack the Federation and to encourage the formation of a new Sephardic Community. A meeting was held on December 12, 1915, and approximately thirty people attended. Gadol opened the meeting with a speech explaining his goals in organizing this conference. After recounting the previous difficulties, he concluded that the Federation of Oriental Jews must be disbanded and the term *Oriental* must be abandoned in the name of any future organization; that a new Sephardic Community must be formed and that each member pay one dollar in its support; that a Sephardic Jew was needed to head the Community, one who knew the languages of the people it served; that this Community not assist any Sephardic Jew not affiliated with it; and that the Community must have as a goal the establishment of two large synagogues, one uptown and one downtown.

Following Gadol's remarks, the venerable Nessim Behar spoke emphatically about the need to establish a communal Talmud Torah. He also stressed the importance of helping the newly arriving Sephardic immigrants.

Albert Amateau, who was deeply involved in the work of the Federation, then took the floor. While agreeing that the term *Oriental* should be changed to *Sephardic,* he did not believe the Federation should be dissolved or abandoned. On the contrary, he believed it would be possible to fulfill all the objectives outlined by Gadol through the already existing Federation. Amateau suggested that a resolution should be sent asking the Federation to change its name to the Community of Sephardic Jews and to make reforms in its procedures. He thought the present organization could be preserved and the goals noted by Gadol be realized. Amateau's ideas were turned into a resolution that called on the Federation to change its name and to make the necessary reforms. The resolution passed and Gadol's more radical suggestion was brushed aside.

Although disappointed, Gadol continued to argue for a new Community in the pages of his journal. He also printed articles by other writers sympathetic to his point of view. On January 7, 1916, an article by Joseph Shaltiel entitled "We Are Sleeping" appeared in *La America*. Shaltiel stated that the Sephardim needed to be able to work cooperatively for the general welfare of all the Sephardim of New York and needed a Community organization. The following week's issue of *La America* also included a long article comparing the effectiveness of the Federation to the proposed Community. As could be expected from Gadol's bias, the article strongly favored a Community over a Federation.

But the idea of a Community was being undermined in various ways. Three existing societies, the Bikur Holim, which cared for the sick; the Hevra Kadisha, which cared for the dead; and the Ozer Dalim, which helped the needy, decided to unite and form a new organization. Their leadership asserted that if these groups were to unite and function properly, they would be able to perform many of the duties outlined for the new Community, rendering the Community unnecessary. Gadol was quick to point out that the effort to unite these societies would not be successful and he insisted that under the aegis of a central Sephardic Community they would be able to function more efficiently. He added that of the six dollars members paid in dues, three dollars could go to the Hevra Kadisha, one to the Ozer Dalim, one to the Bikur Holim, and one to sustain the communal office.

That Gadol was right in foreseeing the failure of the attempt to unite the three groups was quickly proven. The Ozer Dalim and Bikur Holim called a mass meeting for January 30, 1916. They distributed circulars with thirty signatures and tried to gain support for the proposed union. Only twenty-eight people showed up for the meeting, and not even half of the signatories appeared. Gadol pointed out that one signatory was Joseph Gedelecia and he blamed the failure of this meeting on Gedelecia. Since Gedelecia's name was associated with the project and he was discredited, people had no faith in this new merger.

The Ozer Dalim and Bikur Holim were not daunted by the failure of the meeting. On the contrary, they called another mass meeting in the downtown area in late February 1916. The meeting had been called for 1P.M. but by 3P.M. very few people had shown up. A number of the leaders of these two groups went to the Sephardic coffeehouses and dragged people to the meeting. By 4P.M., about eighty-five Sephardim were present. The meeting was chaired by Gedelecia. Contributions were requested, but the amount raised on that occasion barely covered the amount spent on advertising the meeting and only two dollars was left for the general fund. This effort ended in failure just as Gadol had predicted.

La America continued to print articles week after week urging the dissolution of the Federation and the establishment of a Sephardic Community. In March 1916 the leaders of the Federation invited Gadol to attend a meeting, apparently wanting to win him back to the movement. The steady barrage of criticism in *La America* could not help but annoy and frustrate the Federation leaders. Gadol wrote of his participation in the Federation meeting in the *La America* issue of March 17, 1916. Twenty people were present, only four or five of whom were actually representatives of Sephardic societies. Gadol addressed the group quite bluntly, stating that the Federation of Oriental Jews must be replaced by the Sephardic Community or must transform itself into a Community. He asserted that the Federation was finished—it had been unsuccessful in most of its projects and had consistently misled the people with false hopes and expectations.

Gadol noted that he had originally argued against the establishment of a Sephardic Community, thinking it would be seen as a separatist movement in opposition to the Ashkenazim. "But time has shown that there is no other way to advance the Sephardic people. It is only natural that the Ashkenazim look after other Ashkenazim both here and abroad. But who is looking after the needs of the Sephardim?" Following this speech, there was a heated reaction by those in attendance. Gadol would not retreat from his position and again emphasized that *Sephardic* must be used in place of *Oriental*. Gadol was particularly critical of the fact that the

Federation's officers had been elected not by the community in general but only by a few select delegates.

In an attempt to defuse these criticisms, the Federation leaders agreed at a meeting on April 8, 1916, to circulate copies of its constitution to all the Sephardic societies and clubs. However, Gedelecia said that the Federation did not have the money to print copies of the constitution and distribute them. Gadol immediately interjected that he would gladly print it for free in Spanish; but Gedelecia declined the offer, saying that English was also required. Gadol felt that Gedelecia did not want a fair election and did not want the community at large to be aware of the requirements of the constitution of the Federation. Gadol called for a legal election whereby all the people could vote and not just a few leaders. He asked that the elections be held at a mass meeting where people could decide once and for all if they wished to preserve the Federation or to establish a Sephardic Community. "This time we must put an end to despotism, autocracy; and we must shout: long live the people! Long live democracy! Long live equality! The will of the people must be done!"

The Federation's leaders still thought it possible to ignore Gadol. Instead of issuing copies of the constitution and having an open election, they again decided to limit voting to delegates in the coming election. Angered, Gadol sent a letter to Judah Magnes, who had been dealing with the Federation as the legitimate spokesman of the Sephardic community. Gadol condemned the autocracy of the Federation and stressed the need for a Sephardic Community. Gadol's letter attacked Gedelecia sharply. Magnes responded to Gadol's letter saying that it was impossible for him "to keep up with the difficulties and controversies that seem to disturb the Oriental or Sephardic Jewish community. I do sincerely hope that some way may be found of bringing about greater harmony and more united activity on behalf of the Jewish cause."

The Federation went ahead with its elections in June 1916. A few of the Sephardic societies sent delegates to participate. Someone read off the names of the nominees and called for any other nominations—there were no nominations from the floor. The list was read again and the officers were assumed to have been elected. The president was Joseph Gedelecia. The Federation did not call any meetings until November 26, at which time the delegates discussed how they might help the victims of the war in Turkey and the Balkan countries.

Gadol intensified his efforts to get a Sephardic Community started. He appealed not only to the Sephardic sense of pride, but to practical considerations that directly affected the Sephardim and their families. In March 1916 he reported in *La America* that the Jewish Relief Committee had spent $500,000 for the suffering Jews of Galicia and Poland, but for the Jews in Turkey, this committee had only allocated $3,000. And for those of Bulgaria and Serbia, not even one cent had been set aside. The fact was, argued Gadol, that the Ashkenazic Jewish organizations were not looking out for the Sephardim.

Gadol found a sympathetic audience among the members of the Gallipoli Progressive Club. He attended a meeting of this society on Saturday night, March 24, 1917, to which nearly two hundred people came. Gadol called for a Sephardic Community with its own independent office. He asked that the Gallipoli Progressive Club take the initiative and call a meeting of all clubs and societies to form this Community. The Gallipoli Progressive Club accepted the challenge and a meeting of more than one hundred people was held on Saturday night, June 30, 1917. A provisional committee was elected to establish a democratic Sephardic Community. Two weeks later *La America* indicated that the Judeo-Oriental Community, which had been established as the original successor of the Federation, was calling a meeting to decide how to dissolve its assets in favor of the new Sephardic Community. This issue also reported that the first meeting of the provisional committee to establish a Community was held and that progress was being made. Finally, on October 14, 1917, a conference was held in order to establish the Community formally. Nessim Behar was supposed to serve as chairman but he arrived late. In his absence, Moise Gadol chaired the meeting. Although there was much discussion, no fixed results emerged. Again the movement toward a Community was stalled.

The provisional committee held meetings from time to time, but by May 1918 the Community had still not become a reality. Another group of people, dissatisfied with the sluggish progress of the provisional committee, decided to found the Community themselves. This committee placed a large advertisement announcing the formation of a Sephardic Community in the July 5, 1918, issue of *La America*. The notice said that six hundred members had already signed up but three thousand members were needed. This attempt also fizzled out.

On January 4, 1920, representatives of thirteen Sephardic organizations met with the goal of forming a Community. Again, a provisional committee was appointed. A meeting was held on January 25 at 105–7 Eldridge Street. One hundred people attended and organized the Sephardic Community. The participating societies agreed to pay one dollar per member in order to set up an office. This new effort seemed to have the possibility of real success. But Moise Gadol was not entirely happy with what was happening. After years of struggle and failure, the Sephardic Jews had been unable to unite themselves into a cohesive Community. The present effort, although it appeared to be a sign of progress, was not really initiated or organized by the Levantine Sephardim themselves. Rather, the Sephardic Community of New York was organized and led by individuals from Shearith Israel. Meetings were held at the downtown Berith Shalom Synagogue, a branch of Shearith Israel. Joseph Benyunes, the leader of Berith Shalom, was chairman of the meeting that formally founded the Community, on March 14, 1920.

Delegates of fourteen societies and clubs attended the founding meeting and agreed to support the Sephardic Community of New York. A committee was appointed to find a suitable place for an office and to hire a secretary. Benyunes was elected president and Behar and Gadol were elected to the executive committee. While at this early stage Gadol was willing to participate energetically in the work of the new Community, he soon came to feel that the people of Shearith Israel, and in particular its Sisterhood, were playing what he felt to be too great a role.

The Sisterhood of the Spanish and Portuguese Synagogue formally joined the Community. Henry S. Hendricks, a prominent leader of Shearith Israel, took an active role of leadership in the Community. The Sisterhood put a room in the Berith Shalom building at the disposition of the secretary of the Community, charging no rent for the space.

An article that appeared in *La America* in October 1920 reported that the Sephardic Community was making progress. Henry S. Hendricks had been elected chairman at a meeting where seven societies were represented. It was decided to send delegates from the committee to address each Sephardic society that was not affiliated. Five societies had already paid their dues while others had promised to do so soon. The Community was becoming a viable organization.

But there was no shortage of problems and internal dissension. At a meeting held on April 3, 1921, at the Berith Shalom building, 133 Eldridge Street, over fifty delegates attended. Representatives of all the Spanish-speaking societies were present, with the exception of the Mekor Hayyim Dardanelles. Hendricks, as chairman, introduced a guest, Rabbi Hayyim Nahoum, the former chief rabbi of Turkey. Rabbi Nahoum encouraged the formation of a central Sephardic Community and spoke of the need for union among Sephardim.

Some of the delegates expressed dissatisfaction that Hendricks did not speak Spanish, and so someone served as translator. Hendricks stated that the Community now had seven Sephardic groups paying one dollar per member. The Sisterhood of the Spanish and Portuguese Synagogue, instead of paying this fee, was giving free space in its building. On hearing this, Gadol objected strenuously, arguing that all societies should pay on the same basis. Apparently, though, his objection was overridden.

By the conclusion of the meeting, all the delegates present agreed to encourage their societies to affiliate with the Community. This was a tremendous boost, since, if the delegates could succeed, the Community would come to include nearly all of the Sephardic societies.

A committee was appointed to draw up a constitution for the Community. It was suggested that all Sephardim throughout the United States should contribute to the New York Community since it was to deal with immigration and other national matters. It was reported in *La America* that the Community had hired a secretary temporarily—for a five-week period—to care for the needs of incoming immigrants as well as to look after other responsibilities.

As the Community seemed to be making real progress, Gadol

became increasingly disillusioned with it. Of course, his dissatisfaction may have been a matter of pride, as he was not personally responsible for the formation of the Community, but the fact is that the Community would probably never have come into existence without the years of agitation by Gadol. Gadol was involved in the leadership of the new Community and did have an influential voice in its workings. The root of his dissastisfaction probably lay in his belief that the Community was not an authentic creation of or representation of the Levantine Sephardim themselves. Being extraordinarily proud and stubborn, Gadol violently resented the assistance of "outsiders." He could not understand why the Levantine Sephardim were unable to arrange their own affairs. He had turned against Gedelecia because he was an Ashkenazic Jew who did not speak the languages of the Sephardim. Now he turned against Hendricks, the grandee of Shearith Israel, who could only speak English. A Sephardic Community, according to Gadol, could not exist unless all Spanish-speaking groups affiliated and formed a new executive board—with a president who understood the aspirations and needs of the Sephardim and spoke both Spanish and English.

Other individuals and groups seemed to share Gadol's concern. In its issue of December 2, 1921, *La America* reported that the Salonika Brotherhood pulled out of the Community because Hendricks could not speak Spanish and wouldn't allow an election to take place for a new executive board. The Salonika Brotherhood formed its own central organization and changed the name of its society to the Sephardic Brotherhood. This group intended to establish a Sephardic center and to unite the other Sephardic societies with them. This move annoyed Gadol, as he felt their aims conflicted with the Community. He wished them to unite with the other groups, oust Hendricks, and take over the already existing Community.

Gadol believed that a Community needed $20,000–$25,000 to prove its stability to the public. With such a fund it would have to be recognized as a viable and permanent institution. Lack of adequate funds undermined confidence in the project and Gadol believed that there could not be any real progress until all of the societies supported the effort wholeheartedly.

The withdrawal of the Salonika Jews and their establishment of the Sephardic Brotherhood basically destroyed confidence in the Community. It soon ceased to function. Again, the Sephardim found themselves at the starting point.

In the meanwhile, there were still voices calling for the reestablishment of the Federation of Oriental Jews. Albert Amateau believed the Federation was the correct solution to the problems of the Sephardim. He blamed Gadol and *La America* for ruining "the powerful Federation." In reacting to Amateau's charge, Gadol stated that the claim that *La America* ruined the Federation was absurd: Amateau was blaming *La America* instead of facing the reality that the Federation itself was the source of its own demise.

La America continued to print articles favorable to the establishment of another Sephardic Community. In the issue of February 23, 1923, an article by Bohor Hanna, a colleague of Gadol, stated that a communal movement was being led by the best individuals in the colony and should succeed. "It will be difficult at first, but we must not be discouraged." On February 27, 1923, a meeting was held at the Filo Center Club, 43 West 113 Street, in order to establish a Sephardic Community in New York. Raphael Amado was chairman, and representatives of eleven societies attended. A committee of seven was appointed to plan and organize the Community. At a meeting on March 20, also at the Filo Club, over thirty delegates representing seven societies attended. The Sephardic Brotherhood did not send an official delegate although the secretary of the Brotherhood did attend and said he was personally in favor of the new venture. The Brotherhood had declared itself in opposition to the Community and indicated that it would not take part. Gadol stated that the committee should ignore both the Sephardic Brotherhood and the Berith Shalom and work with all the other groups in the community. Jack Levy said that the Berith Shalom should not be excluded from the new Community since it was interested in this project. It was decided to send all Sephardic societies a copy of the plan of the Community as well as the proposed constitution.

This community movement aroused substantial controversy. A public debate about the need for a Community was held on April 22, 1923, at Laurel Garden in Harlem, pitting Simon Nessim against Raphael Hasson of the Sephardic Brotherhood. Both men agreed on the need for a Sephardic Community; however, they differed in the manner of creating it. Nessim eloquently argued that no individual society should found the Community and that the Sephardic Brotherhood could not represent the forty thousand Sephardim in New York. Hasson disagreed with this approach and believed that the Sephardic Brotherhood was the proper vehicle for the Community. There was a brief disturbance among several of the people who attended, but this incident passed quickly and the large crowd left the hall in relative harmony.

On April 23, over sixty delegates and prominent Sephardic figures attended a meeting at the Filo Center Club. Eighteen societies were represented, but not the Sephardic Brotherhood. All the societies approved the constitution in principle. Benyunes, of Berith Shalom, stated that he would do all in his power to help the Community. Gadol used the occasion to remind the audience how long *La America* had been propagandizing for the establishment of a Community. Gadol regretted that one group, the Sephardic Brotherhood, still was not participating and asserted that it was trying to ruin the communal movement, as well as to destroy his newspaper. Gadol tried to interest the delegates in purchasing shares in *La America* at ten dollars per share. Benyunes himself bought three shares, while five others bought two shares each.

The Community received a letter from the Sephardic Brotherhood, which was read at its May 28 meeting at the Filo Center Club. The Brotherhood stated that it would support the Community if all the Sephardic societies gave 75 percent of their funds and income to the Community. This offer was rejected. It had already been agreed that the societies would pay two dollars per member to the Community and would keep the remaining funds to care for their own internal matters.

A meeting of delegates to the Community met on April 29 at the Filo Center Club. John H. Levy was chairman. Levy, himself a Turkish Sephardic Jew, was a lawyer and a member of Shearith Israel. He reported that seven societies had paid their dues and the total amount received was approximately $2,000. He and Henry Hendricks had filed the appropriate documents for the incorporation of the Community.

La America announced (March 6, 1925) that the Sephardic Community of New York was making gigantic progress. At its meeting of March 4, over thirty delegates had attended, with Edward Valensi presiding. The Talmud Torah committee allocated $2,500 to the Community and promised an additional $2,500 toward the purchase of a communal building, which would contain rooms for a large Talmud Torah. The Community decided to use the $2,000 in its treasury for the purpose of obtaining a community building. It was decided to buy two buildings in Harlem, which had a total value of $35,000, and to remodel them into one large building. The renovation and the initial cost would come to a total investment of about $75,000.

The Community ultimately did buy a house on 115th Street. David de Sola Pool referred to the Community as a "stable and responsible organization." However, it had limited success. Like the Federation, it was based on the local societies, not on the community as a whole. In time, the petty grievances among the groups emerged and led to its disintegration. Moreover, as the Sephardic population moved away from Harlem, the community house became less and less relevant to the needs of the people.

The ideals for which Gadol had fought during the course of his publication of *La America* were never realized in fact. Certainly, numerous individuals were helped by the Federation and the various Sephardic community efforts. Yet, Gadol was unable to make the Sephardic Jews function as a community. The spiritual and material losses to the Sephardic people due to the absence of a central Community cannot be measured. However, it is certain that the Sephardim of that generation as well as of subsequent generations would have been a stronger people culturally and religiously if people would have listened to the proddings of Moise Gadol.

6

Old and New Sephardim Meet

Congregation Shearith Israel, the Spanish and Portuguese Synagogue in the City of New York, was founded in 1654. The oldest Jewish congregation in North America, since 1897 it has occupied a magnificent synagogue building on the corner of Seventieth Street and Central Park West. Prior to the arrival of Sephardic immigrants from the Levant, Shearith Israel was the only Sephardic synagogue in New York City. Its religious services and *minhag* (ritual) followed the practices of the western Sephardim, particularly those of Amsterdam.

Shearith Israel was without doubt one of the most distinguished congregations in New York City, and among the most outstanding Orthodox Jewish congregations. Under the religious leadership of Henry Pereira Mendes and later of David de Sola Pool, Shearith Israel played a prominent role in all areas of Jewish life.

By the beginning of the twentieth century, most of the members of Shearith Israel were not of Spanish or Portuguese origin. Although a number of families could trace their ancestry to the Spanish and Portuguese Jews who arrived in the New World during colonial times, much of the membership was composed of Ashkenazic Jews who happened to find in Shearith Israel a meaningful spiritual home. Many of the members could claim some Sephardic ancestry, but very few were "pure" Sephardim—having Sephardic parents and grandparents going back through the generations. However, since the congregation was known as the Spanish and Portuguese Synagogue, it was considered by many to be the spokesman and representative of the Sephardic people in New York as well as throughout the country.

The members of Shearith Israel prided themselves on the decorous and dignified service of their synagogue. The congregation boasted a professional choir, an elaborate religious ritual, and a beautiful synagogue building. Most members were well integrated into American society. Indeed, members of the synagogue held leading positions in government, commerce, and intellectual life.

How does a congregation of established and refined members, calling itself "Sephardic," react to an influx of poverty-stricken, poorly educated immigrants who call themselves "Sephardim?" How does a congregation following a highly structured Western-style service relate to a noisy and energetic group of coreligionists whose service is Orientalized?

The venerable Sephardic congregation in New York and the newly arrived Sephardic immigrants from the Levant—separated by centuries of history—were now coming together as estranged relatives. Although each group recognized its deep relationship with the other and the essential unity between them, they would need time to grow accustomed to one another. There were simply too many differences that came between them.

As an institution, Shearith Israel was delighted with the arrival of Sephardim in New York. There had been so little Sephardic immigration during the previous century that Shearith Israel had become somewhat of an island within the overwhelmingly Ashkenazic Jewish community. There was a genuine fear among leaders of Shearith Israel that the Sephardic *minhag* of their congregation was in jeopardy since there were so few natural bearers of this tradition in New York. The *Shearith Israel Bulletin* of February 1912 noted: "The great increase in the number of Sephardic Jews in America is a happy guarantee of the survival and spread in the United States of the ancient *minhag* of our congregation." The synagogue really believed that its members and the Sephardic immigrants would become partners in a unified Sephardic commu-

·

nity. Shearith Israel hoped to attract at least some of the Sephardic immigrants as members.

Yet, while Shearith Israel was happy in principle with the arrival of the new Sephardim and while it was glad to receive individual Sephardim as members, it did not know exactly how to deal with the masses of new Sephardic immigrants. Shearith Israel and its Sisterhood made many attempts to work with the Sephardim, but to a large extent these efforts resulted in disappointment.

From the point of view of the Sephardic immigrants, Shearith Israel was an object both of reverence and of resentment. They could not help but be impressed with the grandness of the synagogue and its apparent wealth and dignity. They took great pride in knowing that the very first Jews to arrive in North America were Sephardim, the founders of Shearith Israel. Moise Gadol, visiting the synagogue in November 1910, had elaborate praise for Shearith Israel. He said that its beauty surpassed the finest synagogues in Europe. The "perfect services" were accompanied by a magnificent choir, and the participants in the synagogue service dressed with the greatest elegance. "In the faces of all can be seen our chosen people: 'You have chosen us from all the nations.'"

On the other hand, there were those among the immigrants who resented the services at Shearith Israel since they were not conducted in the manner of services in Oriental countries. There were also those who felt that Shearith Israel members looked down on the newcomers. Many expected Shearith Israel to be their salvation and raise them from their misery; when Shearith Israel was unable to perform to their expectations, they became disillusioned and hostile to the synagogue. Yet, in spite of these factors, Shearith Israel and the new Sephardic immigrants did succeed in doing much positive work together.

The Sisterhood of the Spanish and Portuguese Synagogue was particularly interested in assisting the Sephardic immigrants. It established an Oriental employment bureau to help Sephardim find jobs. The *Shearith Israel Bulletin* in March and April 1912 appealed to members of the synagogue to help find jobs for the Sephardic immigrants, especially jobs that would not involve the violation of the Sabbath. The Sisterhood understood that the "Oriental brethren, proud though poor, ask of us only an opportunity for honest employment." The Sisterhood established an Oriental committee whose sole task was to stay abreast of problems within the Sephardic immigrant community and to provide whatever services were required. It had operated a settlement house on the Lower East Side in order to assist the Jews of that area, and by 1912, the settlement house dedicated itself exclusively to the needs of the Sephardic immigrants. A synagogue, Berith Shalom, was established in this building. The Sisterhood's settlement house sponsored a variety of activities for adults and children and provided many needed social services. As the programs expanded, the neighborhood house became inadequate and facilities were twice moved to larger quarters: to 86 Orchard Street in 1913, and then to 133 Eldridge Street in 1918.

The pages of *La America* reflected both the obvious and the more subtle aspects of the relationship between Shearith Israel and the new immigrants. On the front page of the issue of February 9, 1912, there was a letter written by David de Sola Pool inviting all Sephardim to attend a meeting at the Sisterhood settlement house in order to discuss the establishment of classes for Oriental Jews. The meeting, held on February 13, was attended by fifty or sixty people including Moise Gadol. Pool addressed the group, indicating that the Sephardic immigrants shared the same Sephardic customs observed by Congregation Shearith Israel. The two groups, he insisted, had a great deal in common and had every reason to consider each other as members of one group, as they had been brothers in Spain centuries ago.

This was an auspicious beginning to the meeting. However, things then turned for the worse when a woman who was originally from Morocco and now a member of the Sisterhood of the Spanish and Portuguese Synagogue rose to speak. She was well intentioned, certainly; yet her talk hopelessly lacked an understanding of the essential needs of the newcomers. Among other things, she told the Sephardic immigrants that she would see to it that the Sephardic girls learned to play the piano and to speak pure Castilian Spanish instead of their Judeo-Spanish. These skills, far removed from the daily needs of the people, were hardly vital interests to those gathered at the meeting. This lady's speech reflected a cultural haughtiness and gentility and implied that she, and the Sisterhood, knew more about what was important in life than the immigrants themselves. Following this speech, N. Taylor Phillips, a leader of Congregation Shearith Israel, spoke, urging the Sephardic immigrants to become not only good Americans but to remain good Jews.

Moise Gadol believed that all the speech-givers meant well, but their addresses did not bode well for any real promise of progress. In reporting the events of this meeting in *La America,* Gadol wrote that if Shearith Israel did in fact wish to provide a service for the Sephardim, it should establish a first-rate Talmud Torah. He said there was no reason to teach Castilian Spanish when there were many more pressing needs. Pool, in response to Gadol, announced that Shearith Israel would establish a Talmud Torah for the Oriental Jews.

On page one of *La America*'s edition of March 1, 1912, Gadol published an open letter to Shearith Israel. He called on the venerable Sephardic congregation to establish a large Sephardic club on Chrystie or Rivington Street, where the Sephardic immigrant population was concentrated. He thought a building should be provided and an honest and capable person should be hired as the club's director. The building would serve as a center and include a library, rooms for public meetings, lectures, and entertainment programs, and classrooms for a Talmud Torah. The Sephardic immigrants would contribute to this project and be partners in the venture.

Instead of establishing this center, though, Shearith Israel thought it best to let the Sisterhood continue to operate its own settlement house and provide services to assist the Oriental Jews. But because the Sisterhood's settlement house was the private possession of one group, it could not fulfill Gadol's wish for a community-based cultural center. For all the good that it did, the Sisterhood's house was not an outgrowth of the Sephardic community but was an institution that was established and operated by "outsiders."

While Gadol was struggling to rally the Sephardim behind a community-based organization, and while the idea of a Federation of Oriental Jews had been brought to the public's attention, Shearith Israel was trying its best to attract Oriental Jews to its congregation and to increase its influence among the people. The Sisterhood invited the Oriental Sephardim to attend Shearith Israel on the eve of Purim, Sunday night, March 3, 1912. Over five hundred people came and were treated to a magnificent party with abundant food and drink. At this celebration, one Sephardic speaker praised the "noble Congregation Shearith Israel" for caring for the needs of the immigrant Sephardim just as Mordecai and Esther cared for the Jews of old. The president of Shearith Israel closed the evening, thanking everyone for coming and inviting them to use the synagogue for all their religious needs. In reporting on this gathering in *La America*, Gadol added a postscript: Rabbi Pool had agreed to present Gadol's open letter to a special meeting of the leaders of Shearith Israel. Gadol was confident that Shearith Israel would act favorably and establish a Sephardic cultural center to aid their brethren. Gadol thanked Shearith Israel for the Purim party and all the good it was planning to do on behalf of the Sephardim.

With the successful Purim celebration behind them, the Sisterhood of the Spanish and Portuguese Synagogue continued its work with even more energy and enthusiasm. In April 1912, the Sisterhood announced English classes, which were to be held both downtown and at 2 West Seventieth Street. It also announced that it operated an employment bureau, which received applications for jobs on Sundays from 11 A.M. to 1 P.M. at 2 West Seventieth Street.

On July 4, 1912, the Sisterhood held a special celebration for the Oriental Jews at the synagogue on Central Park West. Copies of the Declaration of Independence were printed in English and Judeo-Spanish. The gathering was attended by prominent members of Shearith Israel as well as by a city official. Free refreshments and musical entertainment were provided.

Shearith Israel had conducted free religious services for the High Holy Days since 1909. These services were held in the synagogue's auditorium and were attended primarily by Oriental Jews. During the 1912 holidays, Shearith Israel succeeded in attracting a substantial number of Oriental Jews to this service. Gadol reported that a large percentage of the "best and most intelligent of our people" preferred to pray on the High Holy Days at Congregation Shearith Israel. "On the one hand, we are glad to see the association of our Sephardim with Shearith Israel. But on the other hand, we regret that they prefer to sit downstairs in the auditorium at the free service rather than to pay their way and sit in the main synagogue.

This is against the dignity of our people, especially since most of those who attended the free service could well afford to pay for seats in the main synagogue."

Gadol was not only angry with the Turkinos who were content to take things for free; he was also upset with Shearith Israel for offering the free services. Gadol himself attended these services at Shearith Israel in 1913 and discovered that 90 percent of the worshipers were "middle-class" Turkish Jews. Gadol believed that these individuals should have been permitted to occupy empty seats in the main synagogue rather than sit downstairs in an auditorium. He felt that Shearith Israel was degrading the immigrants by having them attend services downstairs, and he strongly urged the Sephardic Jews to stay away from the so-called overflow services and attend their own synagogues.

While the leaders of Shearith Israel could not comprehend Gadol's criticisms, thinking that he should have been grateful to the synagogue for providing free services, Gadol was defending Sephardic pride. He did not want the immigrant Sephardim to become accustomed to taking charity. He felt that if they were to rely on the overflow services offered by Shearith Israel, they would never make an attempt to build their own synagogues, to stand on their own feet. While Shearith Israel was offering temporary help, it was not teaching the Sephardim to become independent and plan for stable synagogues of their own. Where were these Sephardim who attended the overflow services at Shearith Israel during the rest of the year? Were they members of Shearith Israel or any other synagogue? Did they contribute in any way to the development of Sephardic Jewish life in the city? The fact was that Shearith Israel offered these people a way out of Jewish involvement, although it appeared that the synagogue was trying to attract them to Jewish life.

The Sisterhood of the Synagogue held a Sukkot party for Oriental Jews on Sunday night, September 29, 1912. Again, this event was a great success and attracted a large crowd. Again, the celebration included lavish refreshments and a program of speakers, and again, it was free.

For all their good intentions and the expenditure of much time and money, the leaders of Shearith Israel and the Sisterhood were unable to win over the warm support of the masses of Sephardim. Certainly, a number of the Sephardic immigrants were delighted with Shearith Israel's gestures and benefited from the many services provided by the synagogue and its Sisterhood. Some became members of Shearith Israel on Seventieth Street or of the Berith Shalom Synagogue of Shearith Israel on the Lower East Side. Sincere effort and dedication always can win some success. Yet, to a large degree, the old Spanish and Portuguese establishment failed to gain the confidence of the masses of Sephardim because they could not entirely empathize with the latter's situation.

When the Sisterhood established its synagogue and center at 86 Orchard Street, it sponsored a dedication celebration on Sunday night, November 30, 1913. This event symbolized the gap that separated the old and the new Sephardim. Quite a few of the immigrants did attend this celebration. One of the ladies of the Sisterhood addressed the audience, telling them that the center was being established by the Sisterhood in order to help the Oriental Sephardim. Services would be held each day and on the Sabbath, and the building would house a Talmud Torah, English classes, a literary club, and a variety of societies where individuals could learn to sing, dance, and participate in other activities. Those in the audience who were newly arrived immigrants believed these words and applauded frequently. Henry Pereira Mendes, minister of the Spanish and Portuguese Synagogue, recited a psalm and then delivered a speech in Hebrew. He introduced Joseph Benyunes who was to serve as the *hazan* of the synagogue on the Lower East Side. Benyunes spoke humbly, stating that "he was neither a sage nor a rabbi but only a simple person who read his prayers with pleasure for the benefit of our Sephardim." Another speaker of Shearith Israel, N. Taylor Phillips, remarked that the Sisterhood moved its downtown headquarters from 216 East Fifth Street to 86 Orchard Street to be nearer to its Sephardic brethren. David de Sola Pool then spoke. He said that Shearith Israel would help support the existing Talmud Torah schools of the Sephardic community and would cooperate with the Federation of Oriental Jews and other Sephardic organizations. Shearith Israel would accept members in the new synagogue only if they were not already affiliated with any other synagogue. Moreover, members would have to pay

regular dues. Following Pool, a woman member of Shearith Israel spoke in Arabic, although there were practically no Arabic-
speaking Jews present. This was done, it seems, merely for show.
When some Sephardim wished to hand out circulars about a mass
meeting for the proposed new Sephardic Community, one of the
ladies of the Sisterhood objected. This objection led to bad feelings among the audience.

In reporting this celebration, Moise Gadol wrote that he had
had enough of the Portuguese Jews. "They always show themselves
as though they want to help us. . . . Many times they have promised
to sustain our uptown Talmud Torah. . . . We are convinced that
they want to help us as equal Sephardim which we are, since they
are the rich ones and have been in America for centuries and we are
today their subordinates. But in reality, they have done nothing
palpable to help us. For three years all we have gotten are empty
promises. By relying on their empty promises we lose the possibility
of obtaining true aid elsewhere. We will not let them offend our
dignity. We have a Federation and a new Community and only
through these organizations will their help be accepted. If they
really want to help us, we are ready to be helped and to give them
thousands of thanks."

The fact is that Shearith Israel did want to do its best for the
Sephardim pouring into the United States; but it wanted to help on
its own terms. Instead of operating within the Sephardic communal
organizations (as poor and inadequate as they were), the Sisterhood
felt it knew better what was good for the Sephardim. Consequently,
in spite of the much good that the Sisterhood did, there was a
certain degree of resentment and hostility among some Sephardic
immigrants. Trying to smooth over the growing friction, Mendes
wrote a letter to La America in which he stated that he considered
all the Sephardim in New York as members of his congregation,
united in brotherhood and history; he also wrote that he was always
glad to help Sephardim whenever the occasion arose. Realizing that
Oriental Sephardim preferred their own customs, Mendes welcomed
them to join Shearith Israel if they were so inclined. He called on the
Sephardim downtown to support the work of the Sisterhood.
Reacting to this letter, Gadol asked Mendes how one could become
a member of Shearith Israel, not as a charity case but as a real

member with all the privileges and rights. He also asked for a copy of the synagogue's constitution. (Mendes never provided this information to *La America*.) Gadol wrote that the Sisterhood could win support only if it behaved sincerely and assumed limited goals that could be achieved.

The tensions between Shearith Israel and the Oriental Jewish organizations intensified. Judah Magnes, head of the New York Kehillah, felt it necessary to call a meeting of representatives of Shearith Israel and the Oriental community in order to discuss areas of conflict and to bring the two groups together. A meeting was held on February 2, 1914. At that time, David de Sola Pool complained about *La America*, saying that the Sisterhood and Shearith Israel had not intended to pose as the heads of the Oriental Jewish community as *La America* had claimed. The small committee that met on that day was presented with the idea of establishing a *kolel*, a general Sephardic community organization, which would have representatives of the Spanish and Portuguese Synagogue as well as representatives of the Oriental Jewish community.

But on March 6, 1914, Gadol printed an article entitled "What's with the Kolel?" He noted that although some of the influential people at Shearith Israel had enthusiastically spoken about establishing a *kolel*, no action had been taken. Gadol was angry that this joint effort appeared to have been quietly abandoned. Apparently, the individuals in Shearith Israel who were involved in this project came to the conclusion that it was best for the Spanish and Portuguese Synagogue and the Sisterhood to do things their own way rather than to attempt to be involved in a perpetual debate with contending Oriental Jewish groups.

In the same month, *La America* reported that the uptown Talmud Torah had been taken over entirely by the Spanish and Portuguese Synagogue. Gadol was infuriated by this move since the school had in fact been established by Oriental Jews and had appeared to be doing well. The Spanish and Portuguese Synagogue undertook to finance the school but had gradually asserted more and more influence over its operation. The man who had founded the school, Yaacov Nehama, was dismissed as a teacher. Nehama took his students and continued under the auspices of the Ez Hahayyim Society. "Now the Portuguese do not even pay the remaining teacher at the uptown Talmud Torah and it appears that the school is dormant. This is all the aid of the Portuguese who pretend to sustain Judaism. They prefer to spend money for Purim celebrations instead of sustaining the Talmud Torah. They are praised in the Yiddish papers for helping the Turkish Sephardim and they collect money under this pretext."

Gadol's hostility toward the Sisterhood and Shearith Israel soon found more nourishment. In March 1914 the Sisterhood sponsored a Purim party for Oriental Sephardim. It was, as usual, a generous party and there were a number of speakers promising to do many good things for the Oriental Jews. Gadol, who attended the event, obtained a copy of the Sisterhood's annual financial report and found that the Sisterhood allocated the money it spent on Purim celebrations from its charity fund. "Therefore everyone must know that to eat at such parties of the Sisterhood is to eat from money taken from charity." Gadol went on: "Brothers, we must maintain our dignity and not permit this society of Portuguese ladies to play with the honor of our people." He was particularly disturbed by the fact that the Purim celebration entailed great expense and that the money could have been better spent. "We ask the honored public if it is called an act of charity to spend four or five hundred dollars to put on a celebration for Purim with public money." He thought the money should have been used for a Talmud Torah or other worthwhile projects, not for one-time parties.

Henry Pereira Mendes replied to Gadol in *La America*, refuting the charges that the Sisterhood had considered the money spent on the Purim celebration as charity. He also rejected the charge that the Sisterhood had raised funds among the Ashkenazic community in order to help the Oriental Jews. He stated that the Purim party had cost only $35, and that the funds for the party had not been obtained from the public. Mendes regretted the hostility of *La America* toward the Sisterhood. Gadol responded that his statements referred to the Purim party of 1912 and were based on the Sisterhood's own financial statement. "There was a sum of $792.90, which was listed as money dedicated for the education of Oriental Jews; but in the list of activities all we found was that the Sisterhood distributed copies of the Declaration of Independence on Purim to three hundred Turkish Jews. The funds were listed by donors, most of whom were Ashkenazim. Which is incorrect, our publication or Dr. Mendes's letter? . . . Our Sephardic Oriental Jews have this newspaper to defend their honor and dignity. . . ."

In spite of Gadol's antagonism, the Sisterhood's settlement house and synagogue thrived. The Sisterhood of the Spanish and Portuguese Synagogue established a Jewish Friendship Circle for young Sephardim on the Lower East Side, the first youth organization of its kind for Sephardic children. The settlement house also provided a camp fund, which enabled poor Sephardic children to attend summer camp; an employment office; classes and clubs for adults; and counseling by a social worker. The synagogue was directed by Joseph Benyunes and, for a short time in 1914, it was served by Reverend Aharon Benezra. Members paid fifty cents a month, which entitled them to burial privileges. They were expected to attend synagogue services regularly and enroll their children in the Talmud Torah. Gadol claimed that it appeared that members of this synagogue who died, though they paid their dues regularly, were buried in the Shearith Israel cemetery as charity cases. He told the Sephardim not to be fooled on this matter. Other Sephardic societies, he thought, provided more services for less money. He insisted that the Oriental Sephardim should unite to form their own Community to save money: it would cost each person only three dollars a year and each would be entitled to all the services needed for life and death.

Benyunes called a meeting of Oriental Jews in order to criticize *La America*'s attack on the Sisterhood's settlement house and the synagogue at 86 Orchard Street. Gadol responded by saying, "Those who know our work know that we do not criticize anything or anyone without good reason. We had to point out that the Spanish version of the constitution of the Berith Shalom synagogue does not include the point in the English version which says that members would be buried by the Hebrah Hesed Ve-emet [i.e., charity]." As it happens, Gadol was quite mistaken in his charge. The burial society of Shearith Israel is known as the Hebrah Hesed Ve-emet. This society arranges for the burial of all members of Shearith Israel and is in no way considered to be a charitable service for the poor. The fact is that Shearith Israel did designate a section of its cemetery in Cypress Hills for the use of Oriental Jews. Among those buried in this section were some whose families could not afford the costs of interment. In other words, there were charity cases buried in this section of the cemetery, although by no means were burials of members of the downtown synagogue considered to be charity cases.

With Gadol constantly sniping at the Sisterhood of the Spanish and Portuguese Synagogue and at the synagogue itself, it is not surprising that he was not held in high regard by the leaders of the settlement house and synagogue at 86 Orchard Street. Illustrating the bad feelings between the settlement house and Gadol was an incident that occurred in September 1914. Gadol, as president of the Sephardic Zionist Organization, wanted to use the facilities of 86 Orchard Street for the group's meeting place in order "to do honor" to the Portuguese Jews who always proclaimed their wish to embrace the Oriental Sephardim. Since leaders of Shearith Israel had spoken out in favor of Zionism there was no ideological reason why the group should have been turned away. Yet, Gadol's request was rejected with the reason that since Gadol had criticized the actions of the Sisterhood and Shearith Israel, there was no place for his Zionist society at 86 Orchard Street. Typically, Gadol used this as a further example of the selfishness of the Sisterhood. "Why should the Zionist society suffer because of its president, who may be replaced in the future in any case? Our Sephardic Zionists in fact have no need of the Portuguese. We can find better locations. This action on their part is simply another demonstration of their antagonism to us." Yet, complained Gadol, "our people still support 86 Orchard Street. On the contrary, we should place this locale in excommunication (*herem*) since it is anti-Sephardi and anti-Jewish nationalism." Gadol noted that if the Sephardim themselves had their own Community and chief rabbi, "it would be possible to separate ourselves entirely from these Portuguese Jews who pretend to help us." He indicated that his criticisms were directed only at the synagogue on 86 Orchard Street, not to the main synagogue on Seventieth Street and Central Park West.

One of the major problems that plagued the Sephardic immigrants was their inability to unite to form large synagogues or Talmud Torah schools. There were a number of attempts, but none was successful. In October 1915 several Oriental Sephardim called a meeting to establish a Talmud Torah and synagogue in Harlem. Very few attended this meeting, and among the first people to arrive were Pinhas and Rachel Toledano. Mrs. Toledano, because of her involvement with the Oriental Jewish community, had become to some the symbol of the Sisterhood of the Spanish and Portuguese Synagogue, with all the good and bad that went with that association. Gadol had a special antipathy for her and criticized her in the pages of *La America*. At the meeting, the Toledanos asked what was wrong with the existing Talmud Torah in Harlem, which was under the auspices of the Spanish and Portuguese Synagogue. Shelomo Emanuel, the chairman of the meeting, replied that the school was inadequate, the children were not learning enough, and there were too few teachers. Mrs. Toledano then stated that the Sisterhood would be glad to assist the Oriental Jews in founding their own Talmud Torah. She also complained about articles against her that had appeared in *La America*. Gadol, who was present at this meeting, stated that he always respected and sympathized with his Portuguese brothers and if he criticized the great and impossible promises that they made it was in the name of truth and in the interest of the colony. He appreciated good work whose goal was to make the community independent. He said that Mrs. Toledano had said that Shearith Israel wanted the Oriental Jews to become members of the synagogue; yet, Henry Pereira Mendes had never sent a copy of the synagogue's constitution as was requested nor did he provide any schedule of membership fees. Emanuel chimed in, saying, "If Shearith Israel does not treat us as equals and bring us into their synagogue with respect, then that historic synagogue is destined to disappear in a few years." Mr. Toledano, who was himself a leader in Shearith Israel, was told, "Many of our Turkinos could pay for seats during the High Holy Days and did not need to be treated as charity cases by Shearith Israel."

Despite these hostilities and public outbursts against representatives of Shearith Israel, the work of the synagogue on behalf of Oriental Jews continued. The building on 86 Orchard Street was a beehive of activity and its synagogue attracted many members. In March 1916 *La America* reported that the Spanish and Portuguese Synagogue at 86 Orchard Street had 160 Sephardic families as members. It sponsored celebrations attracting hundreds of people.

The plays presented by the children of the Talmud Torah were excellent and well received by large audiences. The success was so notable as to evoke a complaint from the president of the Ezrat Ahim Society on the Lower East Side, who lamented that the Portuguese at 86 Orchard Street had won over many members of his society. Since they attended that synagogue they wanted to use the Ezrat Ahim treasury for their own purposes. Even Gadol himself had to admit that only the Spanish and Portuguese Jews—of all the Sephardim in New York—had synagogues that were distinguished and had an atmosphere of sanctity in the true sense of the word. Only the synagogue at Seventieth Street and the branch at 86 Orchard Street operated in dignified manners, while all other Sephardic services were plagued by a lack of decorum and religious inspiration.

In 1918 Joseph Benyunes, leader of the synagogue at 86 Orchard Street, announced in *La America* that due to the great success of the Sisterhood project, a building located at 133 Eldridge Street was being purchased to house the synagogue Berith Shalom as well as a Talmud Torah. The move to larger quarters was necessitated by the expansion of the settlement houses's services and by the large number of people taking advantage of them. The new building would house a Bikur Holim society to care for the sick, a kindergarten, library, employment office, and clubs. Benyunes welcomed all Sephardim to take part in this great effort: "We are ready to make it the community center so much needed by the Sephardim of New York."

On May 12, 1918, the building at 133 Eldridge Street was dedicated, with over one thousand people attending the dedication ceremony. Gadol went through the five floors above the synagogue to inspect the classrooms of the Talmud Torah, which at that time had an enrollment of 162 children. There were meeting rooms, a library, and a large hall under the synagogue sanctuary for celebrations. Gadol was forced to admit that the Sisterhood of the Spanish and Portuguese Synagogue deserved credit for this marvelous achievement and hoped the Sephardim would frequent the new building.

It is difficult to argue against success. In *La America,* July 9, 1920, Gadol reported on page one that the Berith Shalom synagogue had over five hundred members and was still growing. Gadol himself became a member. He was elected to serve on the financial committee as well as on the synagogue committee. It appeared that the Sisterhood's hard work had finally achieved its goal.

But this tranquillity was short-lived. On September 11, 1921, Berith Shalom held a general meeting at the request of fifty members who wished to bring complaints against some of the officers of Berith Shalom. Henry S. Hendricks, of Shearith Israel, was then serving as president of the Berith Shalom and chaired this meeting. Gadol signaled that he wished to speak but Hendricks would not recognize him, saying that Gadol was no longer a member of Berith Shalom, as he had failed to renew his membership in May. Gadol insisted on the right to speak. The matter came to a vote and it was the decision of those present to let Gadol have the floor. The editor of *La America* then proceeded to address the congregation. He wanted to know if Berith Shalom was under the control of the five hundred members who maintained it, or if it was merely a puppet organization of Shearith Israel? Moreover, Gadol demanded a constitution for the Berith Shalom. He stated that he had written to Hendricks a number of times urging the president to see to the writing of a constitution but had never received a clear reply. Gadol did not renew his membership, he claimed, because it was a crime to belong to a society that had no charter or constitution; it was contrary to the laws of this country. But he considered himself to be a member of Berith Shalom until such time as he received a letter informing him that he had been dropped. Somehow, Gadol's criticisms were temporarily put aside, but the problems did not go away.

On January 29, 1922, Berith Shalom held an open meeting for its members, and one hundred people attended. Gadol later referred to this event as "the revolting meeting of Berith Shalom." Annual reports were given at length in English and Spanish. When at last the time had arrived for election of officers, many of the members said that they wanted a Spanish-speaking president and that they opposed the reelection of Henry Hendricks. Raphael Hasson, a Spanish-speaking Sephardi, received the majority of votes. Hendricks objected, though, saying that Hasson was a socialist and did not believe in the religious traditions. Hendricks then presented a list of officers as suggested by the nominating committee and, in spite of the objections of the members present, declared the list to be elected. The people were indignant. Hendricks stated that his words must be accepted and that his acts were done in the interest of Berith Shalom. Following this episode, it seems that a group of dissidents hired a lawyer in order to contest the election. Gadol wrote in *La America* that he did not believe that the Berith Shalom had its own charter but that it was actually under the charter of the Sisterhood of the Spanish and Portuguese Synagogue. In effect, the members of Berith Shalom paid dues but had no right to vote or make demands or direct the programs. They simply paid to support the autocratic method and rule of the Sisterhood. The credibility of the Berith Shalom was severely challenged and this led to the disenchantment of many members.

The situation continued to deteriorate. Gadol publicly urged members of Berith Shalom to reject Shearith Israel as their guardian. He wrote that the Spanish and Portuguese Synagogue had consistently shown disrespect for the Oriental Sephardim. On Sukkot of 1924 "the great scandal in the great Portuguese synagogue" occurred. The sukkah of Shearith Israel on Seventieth Street was not very large and it was impossible for everyone to find seats in it. The president of Shearith Israel, Mortimer Menken, stated that members of the synagogue had priority and that nonmembers should enter the sukkah through another door. According to Gadol, fifty or sixty Jews were actually turned out from the sukkah. He used these facts as examples of the disrespect Shearith Israel had for the immigrant Sephardim and urged them to break away from Shearith Israel and the Berith Shalom. Mortimer Menken and Joseph Benyunes wrote a letter to repudiate Gadol's statements. They claimed that his charges were all false and concluded that ". . . the relationship between our two congregations [Shearith Israel and Berith Shalom] remains one of full understanding, complete cooperation, and of earnest religious work with the Sephardic community of the city." During this period, David de Sola Pool wrote a letter to pacify Mortimer Menken, who was close to losing all patience with the immigrants. Pool wrote: "We should be prepared to forgo much for the sake of harmony and peace, for the sake of the broader interests of our own congregation, for the sake of the welfare of the Oriental Sephardic community, and more especially for the sake of their American-born children who can so easily be lost without our friendship and solicitude."

In spite of these fine sounding words, the relationship between Shearith Israel and Berith Shalom continued to deteriorate. During the spring of 1925, Berith Shalom formally dropped its association with Shearith Israel.

By that time, though, the downtown synagogue and settlement house were already in the midst of a decline. In a perceptive report in 1926, Louis Hacker wrote of the changing character of the Sephardic community on the Lower East Side. He indicated that the Sisterhood's settlement house had steadily been losing influence as Sephardim were moving away from the area. No new immigrants needing their services were arriving.

Following the break with Berith Shalom, Shearith Israel continued to try to attract the Sephardim to its synagogue on Central Park West and Seventieth Street. These efforts were crowned with some success.

As the American-born generation of Sephardim on the Lower East Side was growing into adulthood, they developed a deeper appreciation of Shearith Israel than their parents had demonstrated. They could understand the language better, and could appreciate the history and tradition of the ancient Spanish and Portuguese Synagogue. Because they were already Americanized, the American-born Sephardim were able to identify more closely with Shearith Israel and not feel alienated by the members of that distinguished synagogue. In efforts made to unify the Sephardic community from 1925 and on, Shearith Israel's influence was noticeable. The old hostility, epitomized by Moise Gadol's attacks, had softened. A grandson of one of the Turkish immigrants to the United States, a subscriber of *La America,* is now the rabbi of Shearith Israel!

7

The Struggles of *La America*

The Sephardic immigrants in New York and throughout the United States formed self-contained colonies that were isolated to a large extent from general Jewish and American life. The Sephardim had to establish their own newspapers and cultural activities to communicate their ideas and values to their fellow Spanish-speaking coreligionists. Multilingual Sephardic leaders were often bridges between the Sephardim and the outside world.

The most impressive cultural endeavor in the early part of the century was the publication *La America*. In retrospect, one must be awed by the incredible intellect and energy of Moise Gadol. *La America* represented a cultural accomplishment of American Sephardim that stands as a monumental tribute to its editor and the immigrant Sephardic generation of which he was part.

Gadol founded *La America* as a weekly paper so that the Sephardim would be recognized as legitimate Jews and be represented in Jewish and American affairs. At his own expense, he obtained the services of H. Rosenberg of 131 Henry Street, a publisher of Jewish-Russian materials, and arranged for the production of the first seven issues. The newspaper was far from successful in the beginning, with very few people purchasing copies. Ironically, the Yiddish newspapers in New York expressed sympathy for the new Judeo-Spanish publication and even printed several articles about the Sephardic immigrants; yet the Spanish-speaking Sephardim themselves showed little interest in the journal.

When Gadol's money ran out, he sought other ways to keep the paper going, believing that *La America* was essential to the Sephardic community. He was prepared to make any necessary sacrifice on behalf of his project. Gadol persuaded a few young Sephardic men to invest their money in *La America* and they formed the Oriental Printing and Publishing Company, at 190 Chrystie Street. Publication of the newspaper, which had stopped on February 17, 1911, was now resumed on April 14, under the aegis of the new company. Yet, even with a group of partners, *La America* was only able to appear for fourteen more weeks before being forced to close. Refusing to lose hope, Gadol once again began publication of the newspaper on December 22, 1911, after which time it appeared regularly, once a week on Friday, for a number of years.

Gadol saw his journal as a "national, literary, political, and commercial weekly" and as the authentic voice of the Oriental Spanish Jewish community. Its intent was to help the Sephardim in every way, to foster the ideals of the community, and to defend the honor of Sephardic Jewry. An article in the April 21, 1911 issue claimed that *La America* played "a most sacred role" in enlightening our brothers, ridding them of obscure thinking, uniting them in a community, representing them and keeping them informed. Gadol believed his journal was indispensable, that it could serve as a powerful instrument of education and major molder of public opinion. He also believed that he, as its editor, could be extremely influential in the community, more than an orator or legislator.

In the August 16, 1912, issue of *La America*, Gadol ran an article on the front page proudly announcing that the United States government had granted authorization for *La America* to be mailed in the category of second-class mail. Gadol viewed this authorization as an official acknowledgment of the United States government—his newspaper was the legitimate spokesman for the interests of the Oriental Jews in this country. He hoped that because of this recognition, all large companies, commercial institutions, political parties, and individuals would place advertisements in the newspaper. In a burst of optimism, he foresaw the opportunity of increasing the number of ads dramatically, of expanding the number of pages of the journal—which heretofore had been only four or six pages— and even of publishing the newspaper on a daily basis. Although the newspaper did improve its condition somewhat, the lofty expectations of the editor were not to be realized.

Gadol was a fiery and impassioned journalist, courageous and self-sacrificing. He knew that in order to succeed he had to produce a newspaper that could be read and enjoyed by the masses of Sephardic immigrants. He included information about conditions in Turkey and the Balkan countries, reporting as much as possible about the hometowns of the Sephardic immigrants in the United States. He described in detail the various organizations of the Jewish community in New York that could be helpful to the Sephardim. He constantly encouraged the Spanish-speaking immigrants to attend English classes and to become American citizens.

In order to be of service to the immigrants, Gadol printed the American immigration laws in Judeo-Spanish both for the benefit of the Sephardim here as well as for those still in the old countries who may have been planning to migrate. He explained the political system of the United States, describing the positions of the Democratic and Republican parties on various issues.

Gadol offered English lessons in the pages of *La America*. In one column he printed Judeo-Spanish words; in the next column he offered the English equivalents but in Rashi script (a type of Hebrew print); and then, in a third column, he would list the English word in English letters. Sometimes he even provided Yiddish equivalents for Judeo-Spanish words since many Sephardim worked in factories with Yiddish-speaking managers, owners, and employees.

Aside from the news items and materials about American life, the pages of *La America* included Judeo-Spanish poems written by Sephardim in the United States and abroad. There were also essays on many topics: on child-rearing, willpower, the role of women in American society, the need for labor unions. There were historical articles about the Jews of the United States, about American history in general, and about the histories of the Jewish communities in Turkey and the Balkan countries.

The scope of *La America* reflected Gadol's belief that this newspaper was not merely the voice of the Sephardim of the Lower

East Side or even of New York City, but was the real voice of a national movement. *La America* had correspondents and agents throughout the United States, in all cities where Sephardic communities existed. It also had agents and correspondents in foreign countries to keep the American audience informed of events throughout the Sephardic world.

Although Gadol was himself a very serious man, he recognized the need to make his newspaper appeal to the masses. In the September 12, 1913, issue of *La America,* Gadol welcomed to New York the editor of the humorous newspaper in Salonika, *El Satan,* Moise Solam. Solam had written a number of pieces for *La America* under the pen name of "Un Salonikli." Gadol contracted with Solam to reprint some of the humorous material from Solam's newspaper. These pieces were entertaining and included jokes, satires, and light verse.

In January 1916 Gadol announced a change in the format of the newspaper, with the aim of gaining more popular support. Three new features were added: a section of Judeo-Spanish proverbs and sayings, correspondence from readers, and a series of articles on the history of the Jews in America. In order to provide his readers with religious and spiritual guidance, Gadol would include articles about all the major Jewish holidays as they approached. On January 28, 1916, he printed a number of poems by the famous Spanish Jewish poet Yehudah Halevi, also providing a historical sketch about this outstanding Sephardic figure in order to give his readers pride in their heritage. He ran a number of articles about heroes of the Jewish past such as the Prophet Isaiah. During 1922, the newspaper included a serialized version in Judeo-Spanish of Victor Hugo's *Les Misérables.*

Although Gadol carried almost all of the burden of the newspaper on his own shoulders, he did at times obtain the services of collaborators and writers. For short periods of time, he succeeded in hiring managing editors, but in no case did their tenure last very long. Among those who collaborated in the writing and editing of *La America* at one time or another were Aharon Elias (Ben Eliyahu), Joseph B. Levy, Albert Cohen, Barukh Pardo, and Joseph Varsano.

The cultural significance of *La America* was not limited to its literary function. The newspaper's office became a clearinghouse for the Sephardic community on many questions. People turned to Gadol for advice on business, American citizenship, immigration procedures, and on how to locate missing friends or relatives. Gadol was ready to answer all questions and to give as much time as necessary to help an individual solve his or her problem. His office became so busy that he soon realized the impossibility of his dealing with everyone's problems and still finding time to manage his newspaper and personal life. On the front page of the July 5, 1912, issue of *La America,* he indicated that he would provide free-of-charge services only to those individuals who were subscribers of the newspaper.

Even when *La America* began to enjoy a modicum of acceptance from the Sephardic community, the newspaper was far from being a financial success. On the contrary, Gadol's recurring complaint was that the paper received inadequate support from the community. In the first issue of *La America,* the subscription price was announced at $3.00 per year; this was soon reduced to $1.50 since very few people had subscribed. The price of ads was also kept extremely low in order to encourage advertisers. Gadol's critics—and they were many—claimed that *La America* was too small and too expensive. They felt that the editor was exploiting the Sephardim by charging exorbitant rates. Since he had the only Judeo-Spanish newspaper in the country, his critics were fast to point out that this monopoly tended to Gadol's financial advantage. The critics did not realize that Gadol had spent $200 of his own money to produce the first four issues of *La America* and had been only able to draw one hundred subscribers, from whom he collected only $70. The rest of the money was lost, not to mention his time and trouble. Gadol knew very well that if the newspaper didn't gain readers, businesses would not place ads. Without the revenues from subscriptions and ads, the newspaper could not survive.

The general lack of support given *La America,* especially in the early years, is a reflection of the cultural life of the Sephardic immigrants. Money was scarce. There was little time for reading newspapers, even though the articles were geared specifically to the needs of the readers. Because of the difficult economic conditions, and because many of the immigrants arrived in New York with little education, a cultural organ such as a newspaper had difficulty in succeeding.

One of *La America*'s perennial problems was the failure of numerous subscribers to pay their subscription fees. Moreover, it was common for one person to buy the newspaper and then share it with many others. In the third issue of *La America*, November 25, 1910, Gadol expressed his frustration: "We proceed without any encouragement on the part of thousands of Turkish Jews who live here and who do not understand the value of such a journal, with the exception of a few intelligent ones without whose aid the journal will not be able to continue to appear."

In the May 17, 1912, issue, Gadol announced that the financial condition of the newspaper had improved but requested that his subscribers should pay in advance and assist the newspaper by soliciting advertising and announcements. "The editor has not tired of working in the interest of our nation, has not spared his time, energy, and ideas from every point of view." Gadol often indicated that he received many letters of praise and encouragement from Sephardim throughout the United States and, indeed, from leaders throughout the world. Yet in spite of these sympathetic letters, he received very little material aid to sustain his journal. In spite of persistent notices in the newspaper, the majority of readers were content to promise to pay their subscription fee, but not actually to pay it.

Gadol placed the facts about *La America*'s finances before the public on various occasions so that people would realize that he was not becoming rich at their expense. He repeated the fact that he had been financially hurt by the publication of the newspaper and had suffered economic losses during the first four months of the journal's existence. When he established the Oriental Printing and Publishing Company, with the help of Asher Benveniste, Isaac Farhi, Joseph Abolafia, and Eli Hananiah, he succeeded in raising $600 in capital. He purchased the necessary printing machines and types for $1,000, putting $200 down and agreeing to monthly payments. The expenses of publishing a four-page weekly in 1912 came to $60 per week, or $3,000 per year, not including the payments on the machinery, and not including the salary of the editor. In October 1912, *La America* only had five hundred subscribers. If all of them paid on time, this would bring only $750 of revenue to the paper. In reality, though, he only received $500 per year from subscriptions since not everyone paid. An additional

$500 per year was raised through ads, a rather small amount, since according to Gadol, the readers of La America did not adequately patronize advertisers. The company did about $1,000 of business on other printing jobs and on the sale of books. The result was a deficit of about $1,000 per year. Gadol believed that it was necessary to have two thousand subscribers in order to cover the cost of publication, let alone expand the format of La America. He suggested that the various Sephardic societies give the paper a subvention or at least help in signing up subscribers. In the November 22, 1912, issue, Gadol indicated that the journal and printing company were about to close due to lack of financial support. "Our editor is very tired of this very difficult work carried out by him alone. . . ."

Gadol reminded his readers of the many accomplishments made possible by the publication of La America. In asking his readers to send their subscription fees, Gadol said that he did not think his readers were so cruel as to let the journal die. After all the unlimited sacrifices the editor had made to keep the newspaper appearing regularly, he felt the least the readers could do was to send in the money they owed.

Conditions seem to have improved somewhat, so that beginning with the issue of July 12, 1912, La America was expanded to six pages from four. In order to encourage subscribers to pay, Gadol planned to publish each week the names of those who contributed to the support of the journal that, in his opinion, was the "center of our people." Unable to achieve the success he wished from his readership, Gadol approached various Sephardic societies and the Federation of Oriental Jews for support.

By 1913, the position of the newspaper began to stabilize. La America was being sold at newspaper stands at 178 Chrystie Street, 105 Allen Street, and 70 Rivington Street. It had also begun to take more ads and gain subscriptions. Gadol believed that with further support, La America could be issued in both Spanish and English and expanded to eight or twelve pages. He hoped it could appear several times a week, perhaps every day. By the end of 1915, the newspaper had about one thousand subscribers.

During the first five years of La America, Gadol faced difficult challenges. Since La America was unable to maintain itself financially, Gadol had to earn a living in other ways. Not only did he need to earn enough money to support himself and his wife, but he had to make up the deficit of the newspaper. He was involved in the import and export of clothing, with dealings in the United States, Europe, Argentina, and especially the countries of the Levant. His business was known as the World Trading Company, which he advertised in *La America*. In 1914 Gadol, with Shabatai Graciani, Morris Behar, and Aaron Zadok, established the New York Shoe Polish Manufacturing Company, Inc., at 149 Park Row, the first Judeo-Oriental business to sell shares of stock. Each of the four men committed $1,500 and they planned to sell shares of stock to raise capital so they could expand the business. Their product was known as Sport Shoe Polish, and on the trademark was a Star of David and a statement that this was the best shoe polish available, money to be refunded to anyone who was not satisfied with its quality. However, this venture was not successful, since few people bought shares of stock.

The printery of *La America* always did some small printing jobs for the Sephardim, such as invitations and circulars. The newspaper also offered Judeo-Spanish books for sale to the public. In 1916 the journal began a new project it called "La Biblioteca del Pueblo" (The People's Library), for which the printing company would publish booklets of twenty-five pages and sell them for ten cents a piece. Each pamphlet would deal with some facet of Jewish history, so that Sephardic youth could have a better understanding of the glorious past of the Jewish people. The project was administered by Aharon Benezra of New York and the plan was to issue one pamphlet per month. The first was about the Prophet Isaiah; the second about Ezra the Scribe. However, this project was short-lived and produced little revenue.

In fact, none of the commercial ventures of Moise Gadol was very lucrative. Gadol's former partner, Joseph Varsano, has stated: "Gadol was a good man and a dedicated man; but he was not a good businessman." Gadol was never able to eke out more than an adequate living from all his commercial ventures. Varsano himself broke his partnership with Gadol (as had others before him) because *La America* simply was a losing proposition from a business point of view. It took the incredible dedication of Moise Gadol to keep the paper alive.

Gadol viewed himself as being engaged in a battle greater than any physical war. He wrote in 1912, "We will not be afraid of anything, we will go to this war with open arms until death, as faithful soldiers, for the honor of our nation. Our weapons are not cannons, knives or guns, but rather the smallest and most powerful weapon in the world. Our weapon is one small pen, the point of which wrote and will always write only the truth, which will break the hearts of the charlatans and intriguers . . . we will not lose hope before seeing that day which certainly will come, when it will be known that truth always triumphs."

Gadol was deeply hurt by the many people who criticized him. He called on his "intelligent readers" to silence the critics of *La America* and to encourage others to subscribe and support the journal. Why were the Sephardic masses so apathetic to this endeavor, he asked time and again. Could they not see how much good *La America* was doing for the community? Gadol's plaint, "Our people do not understand the value of my work," was especially directed at the Sephardim of New York City. Since most of the Sephardim of the country lived in New York, he had expected a significant number of subscribers and supporters from the community there. But his expectations had not materialized. Gadol blamed ambitious or ignorantly jealous Sephardic leaders of societies for the backwardness of the Sephardic colony in New York. Whenever the journal made progress, these incipient enemies reacted against him, feeling that *La America* threatened their own positions. Gadol told these leaders that he would never be discouraged, that he would remain independent, and that he would never sell his conscience, not even for millions of dollars. In the December 13, 1912, issue, *La America* reported receiving donations from Montgomery, Alabama, and a check from Atlanta, Georgia, for $16.25. Yet from New York City, where most of the Sephardim lived, *La America* only received two donations of three dollars each. Many of the New York subscribers had not even paid their subscriptions.

The financial problems of the newspaper led to certain unpleasant episodes. Some individuals felt they could have *La America* print whatever they wished if they provided a large enough contribution. One man from Seattle had sent in money so that his letter would be published in *La America*. Gadol responded to him:

"Unjust matters, we will not print even for a million dollars, and truth we will publish for free."

When the pages of *La America* described some unfortunate incidents that had occurred in Sephardic coffeehouses and restaurants, the proprietors of those establishments were upset and attacked Gadol and the newspaper. Gadol answered that he had printed these items in good faith, in the hope that things would improve. "And we are not afraid of anything, not even death." He announced that he would consecrate his life "for the good of the Jewish nation, although in place of thanks [I] will be paid by some ignorant people in the worst way."

In January 1913 Gadol received complaints from the Monastir Jews claiming that the paper's coverage of their theatrical performance was not as elaborate as for a similar event presented by the Jews of Kastoría. The Monastir Jews complained that the names of all the Kastorían actors had been noted but the Monastir actors had been cheated of seeing their names in print. Gadol responded that the Kastoríalis supported *La America* with many subscriptions, whereas there were only five Monastir subscribers, three in New York and two in Rochester, even though they were a larger community. Gadol was angry that the Monastirlis expected him to publish publicity for them at no cost. He also indicated that the play of the Kastoríalis was on a Jewish topic and was put on in order to raise funds for a Talmud Torah, whereas the Monastirlis put on a play of a French translation, having nothing to do with Judaism. In the next issue of *La America* Gadol published an article entitled "To Speak the Truth Is To Lose Friendship." The Monastir Jews were incensed by Gadol's response to their complaint. In order to pacify them, Gadol listed the names of all the actors in their play and also the names of the committee members. He then gave a public declaration that he would not make any more sacrifices on behalf of societies that did not financially assist the journal. This response further aggrieved the Monastir Jews. In fact, a circular was posted in a Sephardic café that slandered Gadol. Gadol felt that the circular was so vile that he would not dignify it with a response. He was subject to similar abuse periodically.

Some of his most bitter experiences related to competitive Judeo-Spanish newspapers. On February 18, 1912, some circulars appeared in the Turkino coffeehouses of the Lower East Side announcing the appearance of a new Judeo-Spanish daily newspaper, *La Aguila*, scheduled to appear that week. The founder of this project was Alfred Mizrahi, who in 1911 had started the Hispano-Jewish Publishing Company in order to raise funds to support his efforts. In reacting to the emergence of a competitive newspaper, Gadol first stated that he welcomed any new journal. But he went on to say that Mizrahi was filled with pseudointellectual pretensions, that he would print anything in his newspaper if he were paid the right price, and that the new paper could only be inferior to *La America*. Gadol was so convinced of his own greatness that he had no patience for anyone who competed with him. His opposition to competitors stemmed not from mere jealousy, but from his overwhelming arrogance in thinking so highly of himself and his own work.

The first issue of *La Aguila* appeared on February 23, 1912. Startlingly, it referred to itself as "the only Spanish-Jewish paper." Gadol reacted strongly. "All of our readers are revolted by the great falsehood of *La Aguila*, beginning with its statement that it is the only Spanish-Jewish newspaper. In its February 25 issue it stated that it is the only daily Jewish paper, a fact which remains to be proven." *La Aguila* used almost the same masthead as *La America*. Gadol complained that *La Aguila* had nothing Jewish in it since its editor had not studied Jewish history or Hebrew and Gadol believed that *La Aguila* was in fact the organ of the Oriental Progressive Society, which was composed mainly of Ashkenazic Jews from Turkey. He was confident that although Mizrahi tried to discredit *La America* in every possible way, *La Aguila* would not be successful.

A period of attack and counterattack followed. In *La America* of March 8, 1912, Gadol charged that *La Aguila* fraudulently claimed to be a daily journal but in fact came out only sporadically. The editor of *La Aguila* included a report on several Yiddish lectures dealing with the Sephardim. Gadol wanted to know how this was possible as Mizrahi did not understand a word of Yiddish. The editor of *La Aguila* defended Ashkenazic speakers who had spoken disparagingly about the Sephardim. Gadol said that Mizrahi must have been bought off and accused him of defending the maligners rather than the supporters of the Sephardic community.

La Aguila was far from a successful venture. Although it called itself a daily, it missed thirteen days of publication between numbers five and eighteen. Mizrahi found it difficult to pay his workers on time and the paper failed fairly soon. In the April 5, 1912, issue of *La America,* Gadol included a boxed notice: "Necrology. The only Spanish-Jewish daily, *La Aguila,* has died. May its soul rest in hell."

On October 3, 1915, another Judeo-Spanish weekly began publication under the name *El Progresso,* with Morris Nissim as editor. Nissim, originally from Salonika, was known as a progressive young man of socialist ideals. Before undertaking his newspaper, he had come to Gadol asking for advice. Gadol indicated that he admired Nissim's courage and did not consider that the fledgling newspaper would endanger the existence of *La America.* Gadol offered to help *El Progresso* in the area of references for advertisements.

But in spite of this original goodwill, Nissim—perhaps misdirected by others—published articles that called into question the honor and dignity of Gadol and *La America.* Although he was outraged, Gadol stated that he would not enter into polemics with Nissim. In evaluating his competitor's newspaper, Gadol found that each week it reflected a different point of view and printed whatever people would pay to have printed.

In December 1915 *El Progresso* began to appear under a new name, *La Boz del Pueblo* (The Voice of the People). The first issue contained an article ridiculing Jewish religion and praising socialism. Gadol protested, telling his readers not to bring the newspaper into their homes since it contained articles that could harm the spirit of young people. Gadol satirically renamed the paper "La Boz del Guerko" (The Voice of the Devil).

Gadol consistently maintained that he welcomed good competition since he felt the Sephardic community was large enough for more than one Judeo-Spanish weekly and that competition would stimulate general interest in the Sephardic press. But he was quite upset by what he called "dirty competition." *La Boz del Pueblo,* according to Gadol, was a bad paper, full of falsehoods, spelling mistakes, vulgarities, and sacrilege. He felt the new paper was a discredit to the Sephardic people. *La Boz del Pueblo* tried to provoke Gadol with numerous hostile articles, but Gadol refused to answer any of the charges. He believed the public would realize that he was right and his competitors wrong.

La America was able to withstand the competition, although it continued to struggle for survival. In February 1920 Gadol reported that *La America* had a good outlook for the future and was succeeding in winning widespread support. He indicated his wish to turn his printing and publishing establishment into a public corporation, and announced plans to sell $20,000 of stock, at the rate of $5 per share. Once he raised at least $5,000 of this amount, he planned to relocate the *La America* offices in larger quarters. He assured his readers that his proposition was a good business offer and that no one would lose a cent by investing in it. He thus prepared to establish the Spanish Jewish Printing and Publishing Company, Inc. As with all his previous business ventures, this one also was doomed to failure. Although a number of people did buy shares of stock, the total amount raised was far less than the $5,000 needed.

In 1922, *La Vara*, another Judeo-Spanish weekly began publication. It was founded through the efforts of former employees of *La America* and one of its initial goals was to destroy *La America*. It was clear to Gadol that *La Vara* offered competition far more serious than any of the other competitors he had faced in prior years. *La Vara* was a popular, entertaining newspaper, and it appealed to the masses, unlike the high-minded *La America*.

The struggle between *La America* and *La Vara* was one of the ugliest episodes of Sephardic life in the 1920s. The main personalities in *La Vara* were Albert Levy, the editor, and Moise Soulam, the assistant editor. Both of these men were active in the Sephardic Brotherhood, and Gadol believed that they were not serving the Sephardim honestly, but were only acting as spokesmen for the Brotherhood.

The feud that was to erupt between Gadol and *La Vara* was a particularly bitter one, and the details of the dispute, as well as personal attacks on one another, appeared regularly in both *La America* and *La Vara*. (The following reconstruction of the feud is based on reports in *La America,* which—as could be expected— were totally sympathetic to Gadol. However, the relevant minutes of the Sephardic Brotherhood were also consulted. These minutes provide a different point of view, as did Albert Amateau, who was directly involved in the dispute against Gadol.)

The dispute began to unfold in the pages of *La America* in the issue of August 29, 1922. Gadol reported that former employees of his newspaper had founded *La Vara* through immoral and improper means. They had copied the list of *La America*'s subscribers and clients from Gadol's office and sent issues of *La Vara* to all of *La America*'s subscribers in order to win them over. Unsuspecting readers may have thought that *La Vara* was itself issued by Gadol. Enraged, Gadol indicated that it had taken him many years to develop his list of subscribers and clients and that his ungrateful employees had robbed him with the intention of destroying his newspaper. Subsequent issues of the newspaper continued to harp on the immorality of the founders of *La Vara* and Gadol did not hesitate to attack his competitors by name. *La Vara* responded to these attacks by publishing criticisms of Gadol.

As this dispute gained momentum, the Sephardic Brotherhood became directly involved by issuing a criticism of Gadol's attacks on *La Vara*. In replying to the Brotherhood (*La America*, October 13, 1922), Gadol stated that he had no intention of offending the prestige of the Sephardic Brotherhood; in fact he was still a member of the Brotherhood. He was attacking the editors of *La Vara* as individuals, and he believed that they were unfit to serve as officers of the Sephardic Brotherhood. In a later issue, Gadol specifically stated that it was not in the interest of the Sephardic Brotherhood to give offices to Moise Soulam, Albert Levy, and Morris Gattegnu. The issue of November 10, 1922, included a satirical poem ribbing *La Vara;* the issue of November 24, 1922, included an open letter to Albert Levy, criticizing the editor of *La Vara*, who had poked fun at the satirical poem.

As *La Vara* made progress and the condition of *La America* began to deteriorate, Gadol's attacks became more strident. In the issue of February 9, 1923, Gadol wrote that he had patiently withstood all the insults of his competitors, the former workers who had betrayed him. He believed that he was showing restraint, trying to demonstrate that he was not afraid of competition. He hoped that by giving his readers the opportunity to judge the inferiority of *La Vara* for themselves, the sincere and loyal subscribers of *La America* would ultimately rise to the support of Gadol's newspaper.

Not leaving the matter entirely to public opinion, Gadol consulted a lawyer who assured him that he could have *La Vara* closed and the editors put in prison for their criminal acts of theft, slander, and illegal competition. But before proceeding with the case, Gadol publicly asked his competitors to stop issuing insults against him and his journal. He put them on notice that if their unfair and illegal competition continued, he would do what was necessary to defend his dignity, and they would have to suffer the consequences. *La Vara* continued its attacks, and Gadol reported (May 4, 1923) that he was going to hire a lawyer. In the same issue, he printed an open letter from a Hebrew teacher in New Lots (Brooklyn) condemning Albert Levy for his unethical articles in *La Vara*.

In the meanwhile, Gadol had published an article critical of the Sephardic Brotherhood, charging that the Brotherhood had paid *La Vara* to control the news and had even offered a payment to *La America* in order to silence Gadol from encouraging the formation of a central Sephardic Community, which the Brotherhood felt would provide competition. As could be expected, the Sephardic Brotherhood did not appreciate Gadol's article and they initiated a lawsuit against him for slandering their organization and officers, and they actually had him arrested. The minutes of the Sephardic Brotherhood for January 31, 1925, indicate that bail of $500 was set for Gadol and his partner Albert Covo. The case was referred to a grand jury as a case of misdemeanor. The Brotherhood also summoned Covo and Varsano, both members of their organization, to appear at a meeting to explain why *La America* published this article against the Sephardic Brotherhood. The men appeared at a meeting on February 8, 1925, and claimed that they were not responsible for the article themselves.

While the Sephardic Brotherhood was attempting to establish its case, Gadol was working to find support for his own case. On the first Wednesday night of February 1925, Gadol attended the meeting of the Sephardic Community held at the Filo Center Club in Harlem. He addressed the group, indicating that *La America* had always worked for the sake of a united Sephardic community and that it had always had a constructive relationship with the Sephardic Brotherhood. He told how he had been subjected to great calumnies and insults and was now involved in a court case.

Edward Valensi, the chairman, asked the twenty-five or thirty delegates of the societies for their opinion: was *La America* constructive or destructive? Gadol was asked to leave the room during the discussion. The upshot was that all agreed to appear in court in order to testify that *La America* was a good, honest, and constructive newspaper, dedicated to the welfare of the Sephardim. Gadol thanked the delegates for their support.

La America of February 6, 1925, included several articles highly critical of the Sephardic Brotherhood. Gadol indicated that his lawyer had said that there was nothing criminal about the articles that he had published in *La America* and that he was able to verify all the facts in them. The Sephardic Brotherhood's meeting of February 8, 1925, attempted to come up with a solution whereby the entire matter between Gadol and the Brotherhood could be settled out of court. The Brotherhood made the following demands: *La America* must provide the names of the authors of articles critical of the Sephardic Brotherhood (a number of articles had been unsigned, or signed with fictitious names); *La America* must retract the charges against the Sephardic Brotherhood mentioned in these articles; and *La America* must pay the Sephardic Brotherhood $150 to cover its court costs.

Albert Amateau told the members of the board of the Sephardic Brotherhood that the case could still be dropped while it was in the hands of the district attorney; however, if the case were referred to a jury, the Sephardic Brotherhood could no longer withdraw its charges. Some discussion followed, and one individual indicated that *La America* would not pay the $150. After further discussion, it was agreed that the Brotherhood would send a letter to Joseph Varsano absolving him of any responsibility for the publication of articles hostile to the Brotherhood and a letter to Albert Covo, indicating that the Brotherhood would not press charges against him.

La America reported this meeting in a somewhat different way. According to the newspaper, it had been Albert Covo who had indicated to the Sephardic Brotherhood that *La America* would not pay even one cent to cover the legal costs of this case. The

Brotherhood members then agreed that they would raise the $150 themselves but asked for a guarantee that Gadol would no longer attack the Brotherhood in the pages of *La America*. Covo responded that he could not control Gadol in any way and would not attempt to do so. One of the members of the board of the Brotherhood volunteered to speak to Gadol personally, with the principal intention of settling the matter. But the attempt to solve the matter peacefully failed.

La Vara of June 15, 1923, attacked Gadol's character, calling him a liar and troublemaker. The president of the Sephardic Brotherhood, Albert Amateau, signed the article, which had been approved by the executive committee of the Brotherhood. This article was accompanied by a caricature of Gadol. The minutes of the Sephardic Brotherhood for March 3, 1925, indicate that the Brotherhood believed that all charges against Gadol could be verified and adequately supported by evidence.

Gadol brought a case against Albert Amateau, Albert Levy, and Moise Soulam, representatives of *La Vara* and the Sephardic Brotherhood. He began his testimony stating that Amateau had come to the editorial office of *La America* in August 1924, accompanied by three friends, to make peace. He said that he had performed many good acts on behalf of Amateau and was annoyed that Amateau had published a full page of terrible insults against him. Amateau admitted signing the article and invited Gadol to attend a meeting of the Sephardic Brotherhood to straighten things out. Gadol told Amateau that he had resigned as a member of the Sephardic Brotherhood and did not wish to bring his case to it; rather, he would bring the charges to an American court.

The lawyer for the Sephardic Brotherhood attempted to verify the charges made against Gadol, claiming that the editor of *La America* was a "falsifier and an intriguer." In the subsequent court sessions, Gadol defended himself and proved the charges to be false. The lawyer of the Sephardic Brotherhood tried to have the matter settled out of court following the first session, but Gadol was insistent that the case be carried through to its end. He felt that his honor was at stake and he wanted a complete vindication of his character. Following the second court session, another attempt was made to have the matter settled out of court and at that time Gadol agreed to discuss the matter privately. However, this effort failed and the third court session, on Friday, April 3, took place in the magistrate's court. Gadol read from the pages of *La Vara* that claimed that he was "a wicked man, a falsifier, an intriguer and a coward." The *La Vara* articles also claimed that Gadol had actually committed certain crimes. The articles ended calling on Gadol to confess the "unpardonable crimes which he has committed." After reading these charges, Gadol asked Amateau and the editors of *La Vara* to prove any of them.

The fourth session took place on Friday, April 24, in the magistrate's court in Harlem. There were approximately eighty to one hundred Sephardic spectators. The lawyer of the defendants asked Gadol: "Isn't it true that you attacked the journal *La Vara* saying that it is dirty and its editors were thieves?" Gadol responded: "I always published the truth. All which is written in the poem is true. The editors are thieves. They have never denied this nor do they have the courage to lie. Why didn't they proceed with their case against me? Why are they afraid? They themselves know that they are thieves. They founded their business by robbing the addresses of my subscribers and clients. Their journal is dirty, this is true . . . everyone knows that *La Vara* is a journal written in the most profane language and does not serve anything more than as a demoralization of our people."

During the course of the cross-questioning Gadol made the following eloquent defense of *La America:* "The ideals of my journal were to defend the interests and the dignity of the Sephardic people. I have always worked for the centralization of all the societies into one strong Sephardic community for the good of the public in general. I have always worked to help immigrants with all their troubles through the Jewish immigration society without having the immigrants required to pay anything, so that no one would be exploited by imposters. I argued much for this goal [of helping Sephardic immigrants] and in 1912 founded a bureau for the protection of Sephardic immigrants in the same Jewish immigration society. I have always propagandized for education, advising our people to frequent the public schools in order to Americanize; I have always propagandized for the national Jewish ideal—Zionism—and to sustain the Hebrew religion; I have always published everything which is helpful from the point of view of humanitarianism."

The following dialogue took place between Moise Gadol and his own lawyer, Mr. Schneider, as recorded in the pages of *La America* by Gadol.

SCHNEIDER: Were you always editor of *La America*?

GADOL: Always.

SCHNEIDER: Have you earned money through this journal?

GADOL: I have always lost much money with this journal.

SCHNEIDER: And how are you able to sustain your publication?

GADOL: The sustenance of the journal was always derived in part through subscriptions and through announcements, and in great part from the profits realized from our printing business, from the sale of books, from notarial work, and whatever other source of revenue. All these sacrifices were made in order to sustain one journal for the good of the public. For me there is nothing more than to wish for a life which is very simple, the result of labor which is very difficult.

SCHNEIDER: And what made you give your life to such a difficult labor and one of such responsibility without profit?

GADOL: I had done business in my native land. From my youth I was interested in public matters and when I came to America I saw that the Sephardim here suffered due to the lack of a journal to bring them together. I used all my energies in order to realize this idea [of a journal] and when I succeeded, then came the danger.

SCHNEIDER: What do you have to say about this journal *La Vara*, number 42.

GADOL: This journal *La Vara* was born with the unique intention of ruining my journal, my business, and my reputation. This number 42 is not the only one they published against me. They had begun for forty consecutive weeks before this number and they continued [to attack me] following this number until today, when they still continue the same insulting writings. Amateau and the Sephardic Brotherhood were not content merely to publish page 8 of this journal [*La Vara*] against me, but they reprinted the same page in two thousand sheets separately and distributed them freely through the efforts of David Nahmias. Their idea was to spread their denigrating insults and defamations of my character. I always did all the good I could for them, and for this they paid me back with such an evil action. I cannot explain it. Their malice against me is without measure; it is for this reason that I felt myself obligated to address my case to the court.

JUDGE (addressing Amateau): Is it true that you published two thousand separate circulars of the contents of the same page of the journal [*La Vara*]?

AMATEAU (turning a thousand different colors, from the source of his heart giving a false answer): No!

GADOL: In the next number of *La Vara*, number 43, one can read a letter of thanks to Mr. David Nahmias for his having circulated these two thousand circulars.

Following this day in court, the lawyers of both sides again attempted to reach a settlement privately. In *La America*, May 8, 1925, Gadol stated that he pressed his case in court not for the sake of vengeance but only to prove his own integrity. He felt totally vindicated by the results.

In 1941 Gadol wrote a description of the outcome of the case. "At the end, their lawyer was told by the magistrate that he must hold his three clients on heavy bail for the grand jury, because they could not prove a letter of the six months' continuous criminal writings. When they realized they would be in jail many years, then they understood the American justice in courts, through such honest, fair and able magistrates, as his honor magistrate March proved to be. Then they put various prominent Sephardim to induce me to drop my complaint against them from court. Finally I consented, telling them that I do not wish to see my worst enemy in jail, especially Sephardim who ate bread from my hands for many years in my newspaper and printing establishment. I explained that I leave it to God, the greatest judge of the universe, to pay them as they deserve and they shall not receive any punishment from human hands. I ordered both lawyers to drop this shameful case from court. They cried from joy, hearing my verdict in their behalf. They kissed my hands, promising to be good toward me in the future. They published a denial, that all their writings against me were false with the only idea to destroy my business. I continued to publish *La America* for a few months. Seeing their unbearable competition, I became disgusted and sold my plant of ten thousand dollars for only five hundred. I called and paid all my small creditors."

Gadol still could not see any virtue in *La Vara:* "I was revolted reading their filthy paper full of immoral writings instead of educational, as I did it for fifteen years. Their paper became the protector of swindlers and crooks instead of persecuting such as I always did without fear. Only people of crooked characters became their supporters."

Gadol had won the battle, but lost the war. His own business had been damaged severely by the competition of *La Vara*. The "humoristic" journal was gaining popularity while *La America*—especially as Gadol wanted it to be—was steadily losing ground. By the summer of 1925 the era of *La America* had come to an end and the era of the dominance of *La Vara* in the Sephardic community had begun.

Albert Amateau, in retrospect, feels Gadol never achieved full success for several reasons. Certainly a prime explanation is that a majority of Gadol's prospective readers could not read Judeo-Spanish although they could speak it. And of those who could read the language, many disliked the peculiar Bulgarian expressions, accentuations, and spellings that Gadol used. Sephardim from Greece and the Arab lands did not understand the language at all. Gadol never received the financial help he envisioned; he failed at obtaining support from the New York Kehillah, Congregation Shearith Israel, and the Federation of Oriental Jews. Gadol alienated various segments of his audience; for example, the Turkish immigrants misinterpreted his advocacy of Zionism as a threat to the Jews still in Turkey.

Amateau has stated: "The frustrations and the privations he underwent soured him to the point of paranoia, which brought him ostracism and animosity." Certainly, much of what Amateau has said is correct. However, Gadol's failure can be seen in a different light. Gadol was a brilliant man, far ahead of his time, his ideas so progressive that the semiliterate immigrants could not appreciate him. Moreover, since the Sephardic community was splintered according to cities of origin, Gadol was really an outsider, since relatively few Jews had come from Bulgaria. His visionary messages could not be appreciated, especially as they came from a "stranger."

Furthermore, the petty jealousies of various Sephardic leaders militated against giving too much prominence to Gadol and his journal, which they viewed as threats to their individual leadership. Obviously, Gadol had personality flaws and Amateau's criticisms must be given full weight. But the fact is that Gadol was a man out of tune with his generation and this was the source of his frustration and failure. He spoke of ideas and principles far too advanced for his audience. Prophets are seldom popular; but they leave a message that has eternal meaning.

With the closing of *La America,* Gadol had difficulty reorganizing his life. To tide him over, several friends offered him temporary work, but he was soon compelled to seek a more stable livelihood. Gadol described this period of his life in a letter written in 1937 to the editors of *La Vara.* "My dear deceased wife who always helped me with my work on the newspaper was also forced to start work in a beauty parlor, as I began a career selling clothes through shoe-repair shops, and doing well in a short period of time. Our offices were at 703 Brighton Beach. I worked under the name Brighton Leather and Finishings Company and my wife's famous beauty parlor was called René's Beauty Shop. We did well, were independent and satisfied, able to buy an automobile. But five years later all this came to an end, on July 6, 1933, the day of the death of my dear wife." Gadol was financially assisted by friends during his wife's fatal illness.

His letter continued: "And so I was left alone, without my companion, without a home, and the two viable businesses were sold for a pittance. I remained [in my small place] thinking what I ought to begin to do. . . . A friend from Bulgaria, Aaron Shabati, born in my city, came to see me with his wife, Sarah, who was born in Russia. They insisted on taking me into their house to recuperate, to see what I would do in the future. So I lived in their house at 158 Herzl Street, Brooklyn, for four years, from August 1933 until July 1937, constantly thinking what I ought to do next."

Gadol's letter went on to discuss how an acquaintance had cheated him out of several hundred dollars and exploited his business talent. Gadol took legal action against this one-time friend. "Then I had to move. I went to live at [my current address] 144 Beach 91 Street, Rockaway Beach. Many of my interested friends have offered me several important positions from which I hope I can arrive at a better future, even better than when I had the printing plant and the newspaper." Gadol visited the offices of *La Vara* and was received cordially. "The publishers of the current newspaper have stated that they would accept my good advice and ideas in order that everyone may progress." Gadol hoped once again to enter the world of journalism. Indeed, he wrote several articles for *La Vara* and published a pamphlet that attempted to prove that Christopher Columbus was a Sephardic Jew.

Gadol entertained hopes of establishing another newspaper and applied for financial backing from the Federation of Jewish Philanthropies and from Rabbi David de Sola Pool of Shearith Israel. But by the late 1930s, he had become bitter, melancholy, and even mentally unstable, and could gain no support from the community. He died on June 11, 1941, a poor, alienated, and generally forgotten man.

8

Zionism among the Sephardim

Following centuries of exile and persecution, the national aspirations of the Jewish people emerged with strength in the nineteenth century. An early proponent of the reestablishment of a Jewish nation in the Holy Land was Rabbi Yehudah Alkalai (1798–1878), who was born in Sarajevo. Alkalai, a prolific writer and controversial speaker, was an early major voice in the development of modern Zionism. He wrote in both Judeo-Spanish and Hebrew and did much of his preaching among the Sephardic masses of the Ottoman Empire.

The idea of Jewish national unity was not primary to the Jewish people at this time. Accustomed to living in the Diaspora under the rule of other peoples, Jews could hardly imagine controlling their own destiny in their own country. And there were two major groups who opposed the idea. Religious zealots had long felt that the Jews would only return to the land of Israel with the arrival of the Messiah, and assimilationist Jews were opposed to the revival of Jewish nationhood, believing it was more important to work for freedoms in the countries in which they lived. Reform Jewish leaders rallied behind the motto: "Berlin is our Jerusalem." The Reform movement purged the Jewish prayer book of references to the return to the Holy Land and to the coming of the Messiah.

The masses of Jews were concerned with the daily problems of earning a living and supporting their families. Great ideals about the establishment of a Jewish homeland were distant dreams to most people, who could hardly imagine themselves moving to the desolate, remote land of Israel.

The Zionist movement grew because of the dedicated effort of a few brilliant and passionate Zionists who agitated forcefully and tirelessly for the emergence of a Jewish state and who were able to withstand verbal and physical abuse, from Jews and non-Jews alike, in their struggle to forge a new destiny for the Jewish people. By the 1880s idealistic Jews from throughout the world began to move to the Holy Land to establish new Jewish settlements. They cleared the land, built schools and synagogues, developed industry, and prepared themselves for self-rule. Yet, the masses of the Jewish people were apathetic or antagonistic to the new movement.

Within most Jewish communities, small circles developed to foster the goals of Zionism. They worked to convince their people that the Jews were entitled to a land of their own where they would be free of persecution, where they could flourish in an authentic Jewish civilization, and where they could have pride and security. The idea of Zionism occupied the Sephardic communities, as well as the far more numerous Ashkenazic communities.

Henry Pereira Mendes, minister of the Spanish and Portuguese Synagogue in New York, was a noted spokesman on behalf of Zionism. His younger colleague, David de Sola Pool, was also enthusiastic in his advocacy of Zionism, and actually spent several years with his family in the Holy Land. Through the influence of these Sephardic rabbis, the yearning for the establishment of an independent Jewish state spread among the Jews of New York and, indeed, throughout the United States.

Zionist groups in New York planned mass rallies to gain support from the Jews. The second issue of *La America* (November 18, 1910) announced that a meeting had been held on November 14 at Cooper Union Hall, where orators had spoken about their visits to the Holy Land and the resurgence of the Hebrew language there. In spite of the rain, more than five thousand enthusiastic people attended.

Moise Gadol was deeply committed to Zionism from his earliest youth. As a young man in Ruschuk (now Ruse), Bulgaria, he had founded a Zionist society and served as its first president. Upon coming to New York, he continued to preach in favor of Zionism. At that time Palestine was under the control of Turkey. Jewish newspapers in Turkey expressed the fear that Zionism might endanger their position. They saw Zionism as a direct threat to Turkish sovereignty, since the proposed Jewish state would be in Palestine, a possession of Turkey.

Gadol's Zionism was different from the Zionism of the Ashkenazic Jews. While the Ashkenazim argued for an independent Jewish state in Palestine, Gadol advocated a Jewish state in Palestine under the government of Turkey. He felt that the Turkish government could be persuaded to allow Palestine to become a Jewish state while yet remaining part of the Turkish empire. Gadol argued in *La America* that those Jews who went to Palestine should become Turkish citizens and learn both Hebrew and Turkish. As good Zionists, the Jews had to show Turkey that they did not wish to steal Palestine, but intended to improve the land.

Gadol's point of view was opposed by the Ashkenazic Zionist leaders. Gadol lamented that the Ashkenazim did not understand the Sephardic approach to this question and were not aware that the Ottoman Empire had been better to the Jews than many Christian countries.

In a practical vein, Gadol used the pages of *La America* to encourage Sephardim to settle in Palestine. In 1912 an article reported that Spain was trying to attract Moroccan Sephardim to Spain, but had not been very successful in this effort. Spain had started a Spanish-Hebrew association in Tangier. Gadol met the editor of the Spanish Catholic journal *Las Novedades* who asked Gadol if he thought Jews would return to Spain. The editor of *La America* answered that "any Jew who went to live in Spain deserved the hatred of all Jews in the world." Gadol asserted that the only place for Jews to migrate to was their own ancient homeland, Palestine, certainly not to the country that had expelled its Jews in 1492.

In attempting to convey Zionist ideals to the Sephardic immigrants, Gadol used several approaches. One was to encourage Sephardim to participate in general Zionist rallies. He advertised a Zionist celebration that was to be held on Sunday February 2,

1913, and urged the Sephardim to come in great numbers, to show the Ashkenazim how numerous and enthusiastic they were. However, only one hundred Sephardim came to this meeting of about two thousand. Gadol was invited to address the audience in Spanish but refused, saying too few Sephardim were present.

Although he continued to encourage Sephardim to participate in general Zionist rallies and organizations, Gadol was active in fostering Zionist organizations among the Sephardim themselves. In February 1914 the Oriental Jewish Maccabee Organization of America held its founding meeting with Gadol as one of the main speakers. The group's goals were to develop the gymnastic skills and physical strength of its members, to foster the Hebrew language, to defend the national honor of the Jews, and to join the Zionist Federation of America. Gadol stated that he hoped that other Sephardic communities in the United States would follow the example of this group. The Maccabee group got off to a good start. Morris Benveniste was its first president and Joseph Lasry its first vice-president. Raphael Levy and Selim Sitton also served as officers. In order to encourage this new venture, the Educational Alliance offered a room in its building as well as a teacher to lead the members in gymnastics, for which, each Maccabee member would pay the Educational Alliance $2.50 per year.

On July 25, 1914, the Zionist Sepharadim Society of New York was established, largely through the efforts of Nissim Habib. The organization was also called the Sephardic Zionist Union. Gadol was elected the first president of this group. *La America* reported that the Turkish Sephardic Jews were ardent believers in Zionism and sang the "Ha-tikvah" enthusiastically. Subsequent issues of the newspaper reported the brilliant successes of the Zionist Sephardic society, praising its meetings, lectures, and rapid growth within the community. The organization held its first mass meeting in August 1914 with more than four hundred people attending. Gadol served as chairman. The day chosen coincided with the Hebrew date the ninth of Av, a day of Jewish mourning and fasting, commemorating the destruction of the First and Second Temples. In opening his talk, Gadol stated: "Today is the ninth day of Av. Must our people always suffer? No. The Jews of the twentieth century are going to put an end to the Exile. . . . The ninth of Av was the day when our fathers were content only with the laments of *Eikhah* [Book of Lamentations] and the dirges over the great destruction of our glorious past. But we their children, in this century of civilization, are no longer content merely to remember the past. Crying and singing dirges do not help us. Just reading our books with black covers will not bring the redemption to us. It is, rather, by thinking better how we can win our lost kingdom that the redemption will come. Many say that the messiah is Zionism. . . . Zionism only wants to make Palestine a Jewish center under the protection of the constitutional government of Turkey." Gadol then quoted from the prophets who taught that the Jewish people would succeed not by force or might, but rather by the justice of their cause.

A number of other speakers also addressed the audience. It was announced that dues would be 10¢ a month; $18.40 was collected at that meeting. In the August 21, 1914, issue of *La America*, it was announced that the Sephardic Zionist society had approximately 150 members and was in need of a meeting place for a literary club. It was also suggested that it would be desirable if a number of Sephardim could cooperate to open a restaurant named "Zion"—which would have a meeting space in a room upstairs, while the main floor would be used for a profitable restaurant. In the following week's issue of *La America*, it was announced that the group ordered Zionist buttons for its members. It also proposed to find a suitable club room, to translate Jewish theatrical pieces, and to call a mass meeting.

During World War I, the Sephardic group of New York took the initiative to sponsor a memorial for Jews who fell in the war. It also issued a strong protest, addressing a resolution to Washington, D.C., that the war should be put to an end. The organization held a day of prayers for peace, at which Moise Gadol presided.

The Sephardic Zionist Union in New York held a major program in honor of Hanukkah in 1914. Over a thousand people attended, including more than one hundred Ashkenazim. The evening featured numerous speakers, including Gadol, the president of the group.

At a meeting on January 6, 1915, the Sephardic Zionist Union agreed to put on a play, *Bar Kokhba;* to make a constitution; to

affiliate with the Zionist Federation of America; and to subsidize
La America.

The initial success of the group was followed by a period of
rapid decline. A meeting held on May 2, 1915, drew only thirty
members of the three hundred. This had been billed as an important
meeting and letters were sent to the membership urging them to
attend. The meeting had to be postponed due to the poor attendance.

La America (March 10, 1916) printed an article about the
Zionist movement among the Sephardic colony in New York. It
noted that the Maccabee society had faded out after only a short
while and no attempt was being made to reorganize it. Moreover,
the Sephardic Zionist Union had become ineffective. The leaders
and members were too busy with their own private businesses.
Taking the cue from this prodding, the Maccabee group reorganized
and called a picnic and concert to be held in Juniper Park, Long
Island, in May 1916. The Maccabee society held its first conference
in September 1916 at 134 Eldridge Street. The president was Albert
Halfon. Nessim Behar addressed the group of approximately eighty
about the goals of Zionism and the need for Sephardim to become
American citizens.

Another meeting was held in October 1916, drawing a good
crowd and featuring intelligent discussion. A gymnastic and literary
night was held on December 25, 1916 at the Lyceum Hall. Nearly
three hundred Sephardim attended. However, as with so many
other endeavors within the Sephardic community, internal dissension soon erupted. The Maccabee society had not placed any ads in
La America and had ignored Gadol. Gadol wrote an article in *La
America* (December 29, 1916) complaining that the Maccabees did
not appreciate the value of the press and therefore would be unable
to achieve full success. "Because they ignore us, they cannot gain
the interest of our people." Gadol also pointed out that the Maccabee Zionist society did not have a charter and was not legally
recognized, whereas the Sephardic Zionist Union was a legally
chartered organization.

Matters worsened when the Maccabee society published a
journal that included an article about Zionism in the Sephardic
colony of New York. The article said: "Until now there had been
no continual movement to organize the Sephardim in the national

movement [Zionism]." Gadol refuted this statement, stating that the Sephardic Zionist Union had been founded three years earlier and had been working continually on behalf of Zionism. Furthermore, he asserted that since the inception of *La America*, it had devoted much space to Zionist teachings and ideals.

As the Sephardim worked to improve their own organizations, the general Zionist movement took almost no cognizance of them. The nineteenth Zionist Congress was held in Philadelphia in 1916. Gadol noted that the Zionist Federation ignored the thousands of Sephardim in the United States. He pointed out that it was the Sephardim who were the first to call for the resettlement of the land of Israel and that Zionist ideals could only be achieved with the cooperation of the Sephardim in Turkey, America, and elsewhere.

Perhaps to rectify this problem, a Zionist Sephardic propaganda committee was founded in January 1917, its goal being to involve all the Sephardic societies in general Zionist activities. Among the initial leaders were Sephardic and Ashkenazic representatives of various factions within the Jewish community. The main Sephardic voices were those of David de Sola Pool and Nessim Behar, who urged that Sephardic societies take a greater interest in Zionist affairs and directly involve themselves in the movement for a world Jewish congress. Gadol wrote that any representatives of the Sephardic societies should be pure-blooded Sephardim. This statement was intended to counteract the influence of Joseph Gedelecia who presented himself as a leader of the Sephardim, but was himself an Ashkenazic Jew.

In the meanwhile, a clear split emerged within the Sephardic community concerning the strategy of Zionism. The Maccabee Sephardic movement had adopted the general Zionist platform calling for the establishment of an autonomous Jewish state in Palestine. Gadol maintained that this program endangered the Sephardim in Palestine as well as those in Turkey. Gadol continued to argue for a Jewish center in Palestine under Turkish rule. The Zionist leadership responded that if it followed Gadol's advice, it would lose the support of the masses of Russian Jews.

Gadol noted in *La America* that many Sephardim shared his views on Zionism. He urged Sephardim not to show any disloyalty to Turkey during the course of the war. "Our people must remain silent and not take part in any Zionist work that endangers the Jews of Palestine and Turkey."

The situation of Jews in Palestine had indeed worsened. Gadol sent a telegram to a Jewish leader in Spain, Abraham S. Yahuda, asking him to inquire whether Spain would intervene to help the Jews of the Holy Land. Yahuda did so and Spain responded favorably. Gadol printed a form letter in *La America* that was to be sent by the presidents of the Sephardic societies to the U.S. Department of State, indicating that Spain was ready to help the Jews of Palestine by intervening with the Turkish government. The letter urged the Department of State to attempt to stop the massacre of Jews in Palestine. In June 1917 *La America* reported that King Alphonso XIII of Spain had intervened to help the Jews in Palestine. Gadol asked all societies to write to the king of Spain expressing their appreciation for his efforts.

Zionist activities continued to expand among the Sephardim. A Zionist rally sponsored by the Greek-speaking Jews in November 1918 drew three hundred people. Joseph Beja wrote an article for *La America* (May 7, 1920) that stated that public opinion had been won to the Zionist cause. Beja called on the Sephardim to do their share in aiding in the restoration of Israel.

While more individual Sephardim became supporters of the Zionist ideals and became involved in general Zionist organizations, the Sephardic Zionist groups still had difficulty maintaining themselves. The Maccabee society became dormant by 1920. The Sephardic Zionist Union was also relatively quiet. Gadol believed that only by having strong Zionist groups could the Sephardim have a voice in general Zionist affairs. Individual Sephardim who belonged to general Zionist groups were overwhelmed by the vast Ashkenazic majority. Gadol noted that in Turkey and elsewhere Sephardim maintained their own Zionist organizations rather than remain part of the Ashkenazic groups. He felt that the Ashkenazim would listen to a strong Sephardic organization.

In February 1922 the Maccabee group, which had been located on the Lower East Side, dissolved itself, giving up its place at 263 Grand Street. However, a new Sephardic Maccabee society began in Harlem, at 226 Lincoln Avenue. At that time many Sephardim were living in Harlem and the new group won the support of the Sephardim of that neighborhood.

Once Turkey lost control of Palestine, Gadol's position was no longer tenable. The general Zionist platform was universally adopted. All Sephardic organizations and societies actively supported the Zionist cause, not merely by enthusiastic rallies and singing of "Ha-tikvah" at all public gatherings, but by providing financial support to the growing Jewish community in Palestine. The struggle to win the support of the Sephardic masses to Zionism, waged by Moise Gadol and others, was crowned with complete success.

Years later, the Union of Sephardic Congregations held a convention on May 21–22, 1949, and reacted joyfully to the creation of the State of Israel and its acceptance into the United Nations. The representatives to the convention adopted the following resolutions: "This convention of the Union of Sephardic Congregations hails the progressive achievements of the United Nations in working for world peace and international cooperation, and it rejoices in the United Nations' sponsorship of the creation of the State of Israel and its acceptance of the State of Israel into the family of the United Nations of the world."

An additional resolution was also adopted: "This convention of the Union of Sephardic Congregations thrills with pride at the establishment of the State of Israel and its acceptance in the United Nations. It calls on the Sephardic congregations of the United States for continuing and increased support of Israel in this critical moment of destiny, and of the Sephardic Talmudei Torah [religious schools], Yeshivoth, and other Sephardic communal institutions in Israel."

The convention discussed at length ways in which the American Sephardic community could be of assistance to the Sephardim in Israel. It urged that the communities in Israel organize themselves into representative and comprehensive committees that could properly advise the American Sephardic community about the needs in Israel.

Since a very large percentage of Jewish immigrants to Israel derived from Sephardic communities in Africa and Asia, it was only natural to expect that American Sephardim would be vitally concerned not only with Israel in general, but with the welfare of their fellow Sephardim in the newborn state. Israel occupied and continues to occupy a central role in Sephardic community life.

9

Economic Life

Albert Matarasso, one of the leading intellectuals in the Sephardic community of New York, delivered a lecture in 1941 in which he described Sephardic life in New York between 1910 and 1920. Speaking in Judeo-Spanish, he addressed an audience composed primarily of those who, like himself, had actually arrived in New York during that period. "This Sephardi upon immigrating into this country was obligated to lift himself up on the day following his arrival and go out to find work in order to fill his stomach. He found himself disillusioned of the belief which he had prior to immigrating, that in this country dollars grow."

Indeed, the immigrants came to the United States with great expectations. The wealth supposedly available in New York had become a matter of folk mythology in the countries of the Levant. The first responsibility of the Sephardic newcomer was finding shelter and food and some form of employment. Many intended to stay in the United States only long enough to attain prosperity, at which time they planned to return to the cities of their birth and become benefactors there. Many others wished to remain in America, but they too recognized the responsibility of earning enough money not only to support themselves but to send back to their relatives on a regular basis. It was a matter of family pride that those who came to the United States should send money to their families. An immigrant who failed to earn enough to be able to send funds to relatives abroad was considered a disappointment to the family.

In 1910 *La America* noted that most Sephardim in America lived in misery and poverty. Yet in spite of their horrible economic condition, they still tried to send back as much money as possible to their families. They spent very little on themselves in order to accumulate a sizable nest egg quickly.

The Sephardic immigrants, for the most part, did not have adequate formal education and most came with no capital. Very few knew English. Emigrating from a premodern land to an industrialized western country was no simple matter. The masses of Sephardim came as individuals or in small groups, not as part of a communal migration. They arrived young and inexperienced and their adjustment to American life was mixed with pain, loneliness, and ambitious hopes of success.

In 1910 *La America* reported that there were then about five thousand Spanish Jews from Turkey in New York, with other communities in Seattle, Cincinnati, Chicago, Philadelphia, and other cities. Because of their eagerness to succeed, Sephardim would work at almost any job rather than remain without income and rely on charity. They accepted low wages and menial jobs. In 1912 *La America* reported that the weekly salary of many of the workers was only five or six dollars.

Sephardim in New York found jobs in various factories on the Lower East Side. Some sold candy in movie houses, although the workers had to pay the theater owners for the right to do business in the theaters. Sephardim could be found working as waiters, dishwashers, shoeshiners, fruit vendors, and peddlers. Sephardim who had been in the United States for a few years and already knew a bit of English sold postcards in stores or from street stands.

The most important Sephardic commercial enterprise at that time was the cigar factory of the Shinasi (Ashkenazi) brothers, Turkish Jews who had made a fortune in the tobacco industry. Their cigar factory employed nearly two hundred Sephardim. Aside from giving the workers an income, the Shinasi brothers also provided a dramatic model of the financial success possible in the United States.

In spite of their willingness to work at almost any job, there was still a very high rate of unemployment among Sephardim. The coffeehouses were filled with people who felt helpless and crushed. Even those who had succeeded in finding jobs were usually not satisfied with them and were looking for better positions.

Through the pages of *La America*, Moise Gadol offered guidance to the Sephardic immigrants concerning the development of proper attitudes and work habits. He encouraged them to learn English—even Yiddish—so that they would have an easier time finding employment. He saw himself as a self-appointed spokesman for the good character of Sephardic Jews and he used every opportunity to convince the public that the Sephardim were excellent and responsible workers. In a report on the Oriental Bureau (January 19, 1912), Gadol wrote: "In general, the Oriental Jew is active, energetic and intelligent." Gadol spent time trying to find jobs for his coreligionists. People would come to the office of *La America* and ask his advice, which he freely gave. He became involved in the lives of many unemployed Sephardim.

Moreover, as director of the Oriental Bureau of HIAS, Gadol devoted numerous hours to helping Sephardic immigrants adjust to New York life and find employment. He believed that unless the Sephardim were economically independent and self-sufficient, they would be unhappy and unable to develop properly in this country. Gadol's goal was to find jobs for the unemployed and to find better and cleaner jobs for those who were already employed in low-paying occupations.

Of course, the ultimate responsibility for success belonged to the immigrants themselves. It was necessary for them to take the initiative to attend English classes and to improve their working skills. Gadol attempted to interest the local Yiddish press in the problems of the Sephardim. He tried to encourage Ashkenazic Jews involved in commerce and industry to hire Sephardim in their factories and offices.

In 1912 an interesting article appeared in *La America,* signed by a Miss A. The author quotes Gladstone to the effect that initiative and orderliness lead to success. "We must convince ourselves that we Oriental Jews have the same aptitudes as our Yiddish brothers, and in consequence, like them, we also are able to achieve things. We need to show initiative and to be systematic." The article went on to say that Sephardim must swallow their pride, control their tempers, and work as hard as they can. "Some of our Sephardic factory workers quit their jobs and are presently unemployed. Why did they quit? Because they prefer being unemployed rather than suffering the affront to their dignity by phrases from their employers such as 'hurry up,' 'go ahead,' 'come on.' These phrases should not discourage us, but rather we must continue to do our work calmly and in this way we will succeed."

This message was not lost on the Sephardim. David N. Barocas, who came to New York from Turkey as a young boy, remembers how even the children of Sephardic families would find paying jobs for themselves. "The younger children attending school were mindful of their severely restricted economic conditions at home. To help their parents some of them shined shoes on street corners; some sold candy at the corners of the Bowery and Delancey Street; others were employed by concessionaires in motion-picture houses and still others went to work part-time, in factories. Somehow they knew that only through hard work they could achieve a measure of success, independence, and peace of mind."

Gadol provided advice and assistance to the Sephardic immigrants in matters of their employment. In order to ameliorate conditions of Sephardic employees, he was not afraid to criticize the powerful Schinasi brothers in a front-page article of *La America* (May 16, 1913). Gadol called on them—"in the interest of the health of our coreligionists who work in your factories"—to allow the employees to work only five days a week rather than the six days they presently worked. Gadol asked that the employees be off work on Saturday as well as Sunday. To make up for the lost day, he suggested that employees might work longer hours on the other five days. This plan, argued Gadol, would prove beneficial to the health of the employees and would also be good for those Sephardim "who love the repose of our Sabbath."

The Sephardic immigrants did not at first recognize the value of unionizing. Gadol printed articles dealing with the importance of unions and the progress that could be made by a united work force. A specific incident occurred within the Sephardic community that gave Gadol the opportunity to express his opinions on unions. A group of Sephardic young women who were factory workers went on strike in January 1913. They had been working under terrible conditions for practically no pay. The owner of the factory would not give in to the strikers' demands and a number of the women violated the strike and returned to work. The remaining strikers were beginning to lose patience and the strike was threatened with failure. Gadol addressed a rally of these workers and told them: "For the past two or three years, the Ashkenazim have not considered you to be Jewish but rather thought you were Italians or Greeks since you did not know how to speak Yiddish or English. However, since the journal *La America* has appeared and the Oriental Bureau has been founded, all the Ashkenazic Jews understand that you are Jewish of one blood and faith with them. The Ashkenazic union reaches out its hand to help you! You must appreciate this!" He told them that Ashkenazic women succeeded because they belonged to unions and as a result worked in cleaner jobs and received more pay. "It is vital that the Sephardic workers belong to unions and continue to strike for better working conditions and pay. Have patience. Good does not come without suffering!" These words apparently gave the Sephardic women the courage to continue with their strike and win their demands.

In 1916 a labor problem erupted in the electric-battery industry, where many Sephardim worked. In the Interstate Electric Battery Company, four hundred of the seven hundred workers were Turkish Sephardim. They worked fifty-four hours per week with little pay. The three hundred other workers demanded less hours and more pay and threatened to strike unless their demands were met. The management gave in to them. Seeing this, the four hundred Sephardic workers organized themselves and sent a delegation to the management making the same demands. However, the management refused and even insulted them. The Sephardic workers decided to strike, and the other workers joined the strike in sympathy. Faced with this walkout, the management gave in to the demands of the Sephardic workers who won the same terms as those who were members of the Brotherhood Metal Workers Union. Sephardim came to realize that they, too, should join the union.

Seeing the success of the workers at the Interstate Electric Battery Company, Sephardim in other electric-battery companies also made demands of their employers and struck. The workers joined the Brotherhood Metal Workers Union and had union speeches translated into Spanish. The various strikes of the Sephardim in all the battery factories ended with victory for the workers. The united effort was rewarded.

While Gadol saw the value of Sephardim joining existing labor unions, he also suggested that there be a union of Sephardic workers. If this union were to collect dues of one dollar a month, the Sephardic workers would have excellent benefits and greater influence. But Sephardic workers were content to join the unions of their trades and saw no pressing need to establish a specifically Sephardic union.

In spite of the generally bleak economic conditions that engulfed the Sephardic immigrants, there were a number of bright spots in the economic picture. Unquestionably "the most remarkable Turkish Jews here" were the Shinasi brothers. They were born in Manissa (now in Turkey) and came to the United States in 1892. They established a small cigar factory selling their merchandise on the streets. The business prospered and they were able to expand their operation. Although they had arrived in New York without any money, by 1911 they had become the proprietors of two sizable cigar factories that did millions of dollars of business each year. Their cigars and cigarettes were marketed under the name Shinasi Brothers. They sold their factory to the Tobacco Produce Company in 1916 for 3.5 million dollars.

After one of the brothers, Shelomo Shinasi, died on Yom Kippur, 1919, an article appeared in *La America* about his death and funeral. He had died at his fashionable home on Eighty-ninth Street and Riverside Drive. His funeral was performed according to the practices of the Reform Jews, although Shinasi was a Sephardic Jew and it was expected that it would have followed Orthodox Sephardic practices. It appears that Shinasi's wife and sister had wanted an Orthodox funeral but that his only son, Leon, had refused. Contrary to Orthodox Jewish law, the deceased tobacco millionaire was embalmed and laid to rest in a metal casket. The funeral was performed by Rabbi Stephen Wise, an important Reform rabbi. *La America* reported that Shelomo Shinasi left an enormous estate, bequeathing ten million dollars to worthy public causes, including a substantial amount to establish a Shelomo Shinasi Memorial Hospital in his native city. Gadol indicated that

Leon Shinasi needed to be informed that his father's money should be used to help the suffering Sephardim better their lives and establish a meaningful community. But Gadol's words were not heeded by this Americanized son. Shortly afterwards, *La America* noted that Leon Shinasi was reported to have donated one thousand dollars to a Christmas fund. Gadol praised his humanitarian sentiments, but asked, "Is it possible that he will not do the same for his own coreligionist Sephardim? We who know the noble character of Leon Schinasi are sure he will do much for the Sephardim." However, with all their millions of dollars, the Shinasi family preferred to contribute their money to general humanitarian causes rather than to their own needy coreligionists in New York.

The Shinasis did hire many Sephardic workers, and publicly stated that they hired Sephardim in order to help them. Yet, those who wished to detract from the reputation of these wealthy businessmen stated that the workers were exploited with low wages in the tobacco factories. While the Sephardic immigrants took pride in the fact that they had millionaires among their people, they could not help but note that these millionaires had little identification with their Sephardic brothers and sisters.

The pages of *La America* reported other economic ventures organized by Sephardim during the second decade of the twentieth century. The issue of February 21, 1913, announced the establishment of an Oriental mercantile cooperative association. This company was founded by a group of young Sephardim with the aim of establishing a chain of stores that sold diverse items of clothing as well as groceries. They hoped to set up shops both uptown and downtown. Almost all of the founders were Turkish Jews and they indicated that they would hire other Jews of Turkish origin.

La America of January 21, 1916, published an article entitled "The Progress of Our Sephardim in New York" that stated that the Sephardim were making significant economic progress. Most had money in the bank and many new manufacturing companies were being established. Hundreds of Sephardim were involved in manufacturing clothing. Some of the new immigrants who did not know English found work in various factories making electric batteries. The Sunshine Battery Company at 92 Prince Street was founded by Eliah and Jack Crespi, who were originally from Ankara. The

Universal Electric Novelty Company at 278 Division Street was begun by Gabriel Caspi and Moise Mizrahi, who were originally from Dardanelles.

Many businesses caught the attention of Moise Gadol. Among them was a garment factory owned by Jacob Cohen, born in Kastoría, which was located at 110 Grand Street. The factory employed many young Sephardim. The Grand Handkerchief Manufacturing Company was owned by Jack Cohen and Benny Mayo of Kastoría. Nessim Behar visited the Sunshine Table Manufacturing Company at 120 Columbia Street whose owners were Sephardim, graduates of an Alliance Israélite Universelle school in Turkey. Their company was prospering and Behar rejoiced that the owners maintained their profitable business while still observing the Sabbath. Samuel Yahya, born in Constantinople, owned the Adams Paper Company, which sold great quantities of paper. Jack David Hananiah, originally of Smyrna, was the first Sephardic Jew in New York to become a dentist. Unfortunately, he was murdered in his office by a former patient. His brother Ely also became a dentist.

At this time Sephardim began entering the professions. Maír José Benardete was the first Sephardic Jew from Turkey to be licensed to teach in American public schools. John Hezekiah Levy was a successful lawyer. Sephardim also became involved in the insurance business.

In the summer of 1920, Gadol took a trip to the Catskill Mountains to see how the Sephardim were doing in that region. He went to the Carmel Hotel, owned by the Russo brothers and an Ashkenazic partner, and found it to be a beautiful, well-run place. He met a number of Sephardic guests there, and was happy to note that Sephardim in New York were prospering to the extent that they could spend some of the summer in these luxurious environs. The owners of the hotel went out of their way to make Gadol feel welcome and comfortable. While in the Catskills, Gadol visited the Caleb brothers, who owned magnificent villas for the tourist trade and who had become quite wealthy. Gadol wrote that although he seldom gave any importance to wealthy people, because he usually found them to be arrogant, the Calebs seemed democratic, well-liked, and not inflated with their own self-importance. The Calebs were born in Albania, but their family was originally from Janina.

Gadol, along with other Sephardic spokesmen, pointed with pride to the progress being made by the Sephardim. In 1916 he wrote that the Sephardic community was often characterized in the press as being of insignificant economic means. He felt this gave the wrong impression: the fact was that Sephardim were ambitious and hardworking. Their success was more notable than many other immigrant groups.

Yet, some Sephardim suffered from feelings of inferiority in relation to the Ashkenazic Jews. They wondered why Ashkenazim were more prosperous and successful. If several Sephardim had big factories, the Sephardic immigrant could point to many Ashkenazim who had larger factories. If the Sephardim could boast of a number of wealthy people, the Ashkenazim could boast of many more wealthy individuals. Looking for solutions, Gadol suggested that the Sephardim establish their own bank so they would be able to borrow more readily. He felt that the Ashkenazic and American banks did not treat Sephardim fairly.

The fact is that the Sephardim did do quite well for themselves. The more affluent were moving to Harlem, New Lots in Brooklyn, and the Bronx. The overwhelming poverty and feelings of desperation that had overcome them upon their arrival in New York gave way to success and mobility. They worked long hard hours but almost all of them succeeded in working their way out of poverty. One striking example of the Sephardic success story is embodied in the life of Louis Rousso. He came to New York as a young man from the city of Monastir, a tiny, poverty-stricken town in what is now Yugoslavia. Rousso began his life struggling at job after job making only several dollars per week. In 1979, he retired as chairman of the board of Russ Togs, a leading clothing manufacturing company, which is listed on the New York Stock Exchange and has a volume of several hundred million dollars per year. When Rousso was asked to account for his success he answered directly: "It was simply hard work and determination. I knew I wanted a better life for myself and my family. I worked and made sure that I would succeed."

But financial success, in many cases, came with a heavy personal price. Fathers worked long hours and could spend little time with their wives and children, even on weekends. Compromises in religious observances were common. At first the worker might feel guilty for desecrating the Sabbath or eating forbidden foods. In time, he would stop thinking about these transgressions. His children and grandchildren would be even further removed from the traditional Jewish way of life. A poem by Preciado Levi, which appeared in *La America* (April 14, 1911), has a verse that says:

> We call out to God with all our hearts
> In order to demand pardon
> For all of our sins:
> May they be forgiven.

Material success has its price. The Sephardim in America paid dearly for theirs.

10

The Sephardic Diaspora in the U.S.

In 1913 David de Sola Pool estimated that between 80 and 90 percent of the Sephardim in the United States were living in New York City. Most of them spoke Judeo-Spanish but there was also a considerable population of Arabic-speaking Sephardim as well as Greek-speaking Sephardim. The pages of *La America*, as could be expected, primarily reflected the situation of the Judeo-Spanish Sephardim of New York. And yet, Gadol had agents in all the cities of the Sephardic diaspora in the United States to send in news items about their local communities. Therefore, *La America* does provide some interesting insights into Sephardic life throughout the country from this period.

The New York Jewish community had made a number of attempts to divert Jewish immigration from New York City. The theory was that conditions in New York were so congested and the financial and social burden on the local community so great that it was to the advantage of the immigrants to settle elsewhere. In 1907 the Industrial Removal Office, a Jewish organization begun as part of the Jewish Agricultural and Industrial Aid Society, sent a number of Levantine Sephardic immigrants to Seattle, Gary, Cincinnati, Toledo, Columbus, and Cleveland. The New York Kehillah attempted to establish Sephardic colonies in Glenham, New York, and Raritan, New Jersey.

Although these attempts only affected a very few of the immigrants, the result was the establishment of various communities throughout the country. Once a nucleus of Sephardim had settled in a city, they would send for family members and friends from their native cities to join them. In 1914 Sephardic communities existed in Seattle (about 600 people), San Francisco (about 100 people), Atlanta (about 100 people), Rochester (about 90 people), and Portland, Oregon (about 80 people). There were also small communities in Chicago, Los Angeles, Indianapolis, and Montgomery. All of these communities shared common cultural characteristics and common problems. The difficulties plaguing the New York Sephardim were evident on a smaller scale in the other Sephardic colonies: the Sephardim felt alienated from the general society and isolated from the Ashkenazim. Divisions based on geographic origin were common and their economic situation was difficult. The problems involved in educating the young to be both good Americans and good Sephardic Jews were evident everywhere.

The formation of the Oriental Brotherhood Society of Raritan, New Jersey, on May 22, 1912, was announced by Alfred Benjamin in the pages of *La America*. This community was quite small and did not last long. In 1915 *La America* noted that there were more than three hundred Sephardim living in New Brunswick, New Jersey. A society known as Ahavah Ve-Ahvah was organized by Jews from Salonika there. A second group, composed of members of diverse origins, belonged to the National Spanish Hebrew Society. The Salonika Society had a treasury of about $250 while the second group had only $120. Neither had a synagogue, religious school, nor a cemetery. There was an effort being made at that time to unite the two groups into one community.

But shortly afterwards a problem occurred in New Brunswick. The Ahavah Ve-Ahvah Society had allowed a young people's group to meet in its hall. Things were going well until the leaders of the society realized that many of the children in the group were from families who were not members of the Ahavah Ve-Ahvah Society. The society decided that it would not allow the youth group to meet in its hall. This decision aroused much antagonism.

Responding to this conflict, Gadol indicated that although the society had cause, its action had not been prudent. He suggested that instead of stopping the group from meeting, the society's committee should have tried to explain to all the Sephardim the need for supporting Ahavah Ve-Ahvah. While it was not fair for parents to have sent their children to the facility while not sharing in the financial obligations, in the long run the young people who participated would grow up recognizing their debt to the society and become members. He felt there was a clear moral obligation to the youth in spite of the negligence of the parents.

Philadelphia, Pennsylvania, had a small colony of Levantine Sephardim. In 1915 the Levantine Jews Society of Philadelphia was established. On December 27, 1917 it sponsored a celebration in the auditorium of Gratz College with over three hundred people in attendance. This celebration aimed at bringing the new Sephardim together with the members of the historic Mikveh Israel Congregation of Philadelphia. Moise Gadol and his wife attended this affair. The Levantine Jews Society in Philadelphia was led by Gadol's uncle, Samuel Gadol, but wasn't active long: some members left it to attend Mikveh Israel, while others joined Ashkenazic organizations.

In its issue of June 21, 1912, La America included an article from its new correspondent in Rochester, New York, Jack Elias. He reported about the sad cultural situation of the Sephardic colony there. There were about forty or fifty Jews of Monastir origin in Rochester who were of good character but had not received much formal education. Some were illiterate, and therefore had no reason to subscribe to La America.

In a subsequent article, Elias indicated that many of the Monastir Jews of Rochester were offended by his previous article because it had brought up the issue of illiteracy. Gadol stated that he had not meant to offend anyone by printing that article, but that it could be useful in prodding the Sephardim to make sure their children were receiving good educations. The problem of illiteracy was not confined to Rochester, but existed throughout the United States.

The Or Israel Monastir of Rochester was founded in 1909 through the initiative of David Albahari and Jacob Besso. When it received its charter in September 1912, it had a capital of about $300. The community in Rochester was active in various ways. La America in 1913 reported that a literary club among the Sephardim of Rochester, founded on November 10, 1912, was growing and already had thirty-eight members. Its president was Bohor Mayo. The club had purchased books from Jerusalem and was attempting to foster literary values. In 1914 *La America* noted that the Oriental Jewish Club in Rochester had opened at 108 Kelly Street as an offshoot of the literary club. It was praised as being the first such literary club among the American Sephardim. In the words of Gadol: "Literary clubs are the light and progress of a people." The Oriental Jewish Club sponsored theatrical evenings as well as other programs of cultural value. In general, their efforts were crowned with success.

The tiny Sephardic colony in Rochester had been divided into several groups. *La America* reported (July 17, 1914) that the two major groups, Or Israel Monastir and Agudat Ahim had united under the name Or Israel, with all members being equal. The Sephardic women of Rochester also organized themselves and were involved in charity work. *La America* praised the growing unity of the Rochester community.

In 1915 *La America* reported that the Sephardic community in Rochester opened a Talmud Torah with a volunteer teacher. The religious fervor of the community was described in a subsequent article, which noted a great celebration in honor of obtaining a new Torah scroll for the synagogue. There had been a procession through the streets of the city to the synagogue, which many Ashkenazic Jews had joined. The Ashkenazim had been impressed to see that the Sephardim "were really Jews." The Sephardic community purchased its own synagogue building and had a gala ceremony in September 1916.

Aside from the religious and cultural programs sponsored within the community, there were also social events, such as summer picnics so that members and friends could get together informally. A new society known as the Young Men's Sephardic Association of Rochester held occasional evenings of music and dance. The first such event took place in the fall of 1916 and was quite successful. All in all, the news from Rochester in *La America* described a community that was making considerable progress.

SEPHARDIC COLONIES IN THE MIDWEST

In 1910 *La America* reported about the Sephardic colony in Chicago, Illinois. A few groups of Sephardim lived there: about fifty to seventy Sephardim from Turkey, all of whom were employed; about forty to fifty Moroccan Jews, almost all of whom were engaged in selling tobacco; a small group of Romanian Sephardim, good-hearted and religious "but they were assimilated with the Ashkenazim"; and a tiny group of Portuguese Jews, some of whom were quite well off financially. The Portuguese did not speak Spanish, and were in effect separated culturally from the other Sephardim.

The Turkish Sephardim of Chicago only held religious services on the High Holy Days. Some of them did not even attend these services because of their shame of being Jewish. The Moroccan Jews attempted to pass themselves off as Catholics and spent their leisure time playing cards. Obviously, the forces of assimilation into American society were powerful and the small colony of Sephardic Jews in Chicago had difficulty maintaining its identity.

There was a Sephardic society in Chicago that by the end of 1910 had forty members and about $400 in the bank. The society became known as the Union Israelite Portuguese. By 1916 it had approximately $1,000 in its treasury, although its membership had remained stable. The society provided sick benefits for its members and held services for the High Holy Days. It also sponsored an annual ball. In 1916 another Sephardic group was established, Ozer Dalim. The two societies competed with each other and tensions within the community increased.

Of the fifty Sephardic families in Chicago in 1916, over two-thirds were members of the Union Israelite Portuguese. A leader of the Ozer Dalim Society claimed that his group had wanted to unite with the Union Israelite Portuguese but the larger group had rejected the application. In order to justify the existence of Ozer Dalim, Leon Legier wrote a letter to *La America* (August 11, 1916) in which he stated that the Sephardim of Chicago lived in two separate neighborhoods: the well-off and educated Sephardim on the South Side while the poor and ignorant ones lived on the West Side. Legier said that the Union Israelite Portuguese only offered help to its own members, while Ozer Dalim was founded to help the poor, and in its eight months of existence had done much good work and grown considerably.

A number of Sephardic clubs emerged in Chicago. *La America* announced in November 1917 the establishment of the Ladino American Club, which had a membership of twenty-six young men and women. Another club for young people was established, but both of these groups soon became inactive. On January 16, 1921, a new society with ninety-seven members, the Oriental Israelite Fraternity, was incorporated and took over the functions of the two previous societies.

The small community in Cincinnati, Ohio, began to organize itself in 1911. La Hermandad of Dardanelles Society of Cincinnati developed a constitution comprised of twenty-four paragraphs. Moise Gadol complimented the Sephardim of Cincinnati for their small and practical constitution, which could easily serve as a guide for all other new Sephardic societies in the United States. In 1913 the society had about seventy members, and charged five cents a week dues. It had a treasury of $600 and provided help to its members. The society continued to expand and was incorporated as the Spanish Hebrew Congregation in 1914. As the community grew, other organizations were established. In August 1916 *La America* announced the founding of the Salonika Social Club and a new Bikur Holim Society.

In a 1913 study of the Sephardic colony in Cincinnati, Maurice Hexter counted 219 members. Among them were twenty-seven American-born children and three Russian-Jewish wives. Most of the community derived from Dardanelles and some were from Salonika. The immigrants were not yet assimilated into American society. Hexter found that the Sephardim were at the bottom of the economic ladder, working as peddlers, salesmen, unskilled workers, shoemakers, tailors, and waiters. Of the fifty Sephardic families in Cincinnati, forty-three lived in tenement buildings. Many took in boarders or lodgers to supplement their meagre incomes. Hexter found that, as in New York City, the Sephardim of Cincinnati frequented their own coffeehouses.

La America reported from time to time about the Sephardic community of Indianapolis, Indiana. In the issue of January 25, 1918, it was reported that the Zionist Federation of Monastir was founded. Later that year, the lack of unity in the community was called to the attention of the public. There was not a Talmud Torah at this time. Gadol urged the Sephardim of Indianapolis to unite.

SEPHARDIC COMMUNITIES IN THE SOUTH

The Sephardic community of Atlanta, Georgia, numbered fifty members in 1912, according to *La America*. There was a Sephardic society of which Victor Avzaradel, Yitzhak Hazan, Menashe Capuano, and Rabeno Galante were officers. The members of the society complained to Gadol that the committee of officers was not giving them a full accounting of the society's treasury. Gadol recommended that a public meeting be called to present a full report and accounting, and he suggested that the society should tighten its rules of organization, provide religious services, care for the sick and needy, and make other overall improvements. This conflict between the officers and members of the Atlanta society continued to arouse emotions. Gadol suggested that if the president did not give a full accounting, he would undermine the members' confidence in him and in the society.

In August 1912 *La America* reported the case of a Sephardic man in Atlanta who was hospitalized and in need of money. Some members of the community helped him but others not only did not contribute but tried to convince others not to. As the ill man had been a constructive member of the Sephardic community and had devoted much time helping individuals find jobs, this crisis further intensified the dissension within the community. Another issue of *La America* indicated that when the society had been asked to contribute something in order to help the hospitalized man, an officer of the society claimed that its treasury was depleted. Gadol urged the Sephardic community in Atlanta to establish a regular society with a name, a committee, and a charter. However, all was not as it appeared: the hospitalized man sent a letter to *La America* (October 11, 1912) stating that the officer of the society who had been criticized for not helping financially had, in fact, been quite helpful. He had visited the hospital on several occasions and had offered assistance. In an editorial note, Gadol said that in the future he would not pay attention to critical letters unless the facts were first verified. However, the bitterness of this case is indicative of the underlying tensions that existed in the Sephardic community of Atlanta.

By 1914 it was reported that there were about 150 Sephardim of diverse origins in the city of Atlanta. They made honest livings, helped each other, and were "the best supporters of our journal." Gadol praised his former correspondent, Rabeno Galante, and his newly appointed correspondent, Bohor Habib.

The Sephardim of Atlanta had two societies: Or Hahayyim, comprised of Turkish Jews; and Ahavath Shalom, established by Jews from the Island of Rhodes. Both societies shared the same goals, but neither had a constitution or a cemetery. The Sephardim of Atlanta relied on an Ashkenazic rabbi for religious ceremonies and were buried in the Ashkenazic cemetery. Gadol thought it a pity that the 150 Sephardim of Atlanta were not united into one society.

La America of July 31, 1914, included correspondence from Bohor Habib. He said that the two societies did not want to unite because Or Hahayyim refused to relinquish its name. This seemingly trivial objection is indicative of the pride and tenacity of the immigrants. After a period of negotiation and discussion, the two societies finally united on August 9, 1914, under the name Or Veshalom. This merger was highly commended by Gadol.

With this union the community began to progress. A very successful Simhat Torah celebration was held in 1914. It opened with the singing of "Ha-tikvah," and included a number of speeches by community dignitaries, followed by a banquet. *La America* noted in December 1916 that Or Veshalom was about to buy a synagogue at 234 Central Avenue for $3,200 and that the community sponsored a Talmud Torah for the young. On April 23, 1922, a new club was founded for young people, the Young Sepharadim Progress Club.

The community in Atlanta had close ties with the Sephardim of Montgomery, Alabama, as many from both communities were from the Island of Rhodes. In the issue of February 23, 1912, *La America* reported the formation of a new society of Sephardim in Montgomery, which had $200 in the bank. The Montgomery community was appreciated by Gadol since *La America*'s correspondents, B. Mizrahi and the Treves brothers, were helpful in obtaining subscriptions to the newspaper. The Sephardim of Montgomery were organized into a society known as Ets Hahayyim, which had a women's division. Not long after its establishment, the society split into two factions over a minor difference of opinion. By October 1915 the group was in the process of reorganizing. A general meeting was held that featured eloquent speeches calling for unity, and the society reunited.

SEPHARDIC COMMUNITIES IN THE WEST

La America reported in 1912 that there were forty to fifty Turkish Sephardim living in Los Angeles, California. This population, many of whom were involved in the importing and exporting trade with Mexico, had begun to settle in this region in the first decade of the twentieth century. Some of the immigrants worked as peddlers, grocers, or fruit vendors. There were a few Sephardim who were described as having "serious culture." No societies had been established because the Sephardim stemmed from various parts of Turkey and would not come together to form a united organization. With Sephardic migration to Los Angeles on the increase, the need for a society became more and more apparent. Jacob Hayyim wrote a letter to *La America* (June 14, 1912) describing Los Angeles as a marvelous city with more than 300,000 inhabitants. He said that Turkish Jews had arrived in California during the San Francisco Exposition of 1890 but had not remained there. The first permanent group settled in 1905. Hayyim wrote that Sephardim were involved in a variety of occupations and that most were married. The head of the community was Abraham Caraso, originally of Bursa, Turkey. Sephardim did belong to B'nai B'rith.

When it came time for the High Holy Days in 1912, the Sephardim of Los Angeles followed the pattern evident in Sephardic communities throughout the country; they intended to have a number of small congregations rather than form one large group. In the pages of *La America*, Gadol urged them to unite, to gain strength from being together. The issue of October 4, 1912, reports that the Sephardim of Los Angeles followed *La America*'s advice and had rented one hall for the holidays and formed a society known as Ahavath Shalom.

In February 1915 *La America* reported that there were now about 160 Sephardim in Los Angeles. Some young people had founded a new society known as Ahduth, and called on all the Sephardim of Los Angeles to unite in this one organization. But union was not easily accomplished: the community continued to be plagued with discord and antagonisms. The Ahavath Shalom Society of Los Angeles finally disbanded in 1920 due to disunity and infighting among its members.

In April 1920 *La America* reported that the Sephardim of Los Angeles formed a committee whose goal was to establish a united Sephardic community. It seems, though, that this attempt was short-lived. The Sephardic community of Los Angeles continued to grow. In April 1921 *La America* noted the establishment of the Los Angeles Sephardic Club, which sponsored a successful ball. In 1923 it was reported that Los Angeles had a Sephardic population of between 250 and 300 people.

Another Sephardic community existed in San Francisco, California. Writing in the February 23, 1912, issue of *La America,* a correspondent from San Francisco stated that the first Sephardic Jew to arrive in San Francisco had come some twenty-five years earlier. He had made a fortune but the earthquake of 1906 had ruined the greater part of his property. Other Sephardim had arrived in the last few years of the nineteenth century and now owned clothing stores, jewelry stores, and other such businesses. Most of the Sephardim were from Baghdad or Aleppo, Syria. Of the ten Turkish Sephardim in San Francisco, four had become very successful businessmen. Most of the Sephardic men had married Ashkenazic women. The San Francisco Sephardic community was criticized in *La America* (January 26, 1912) because its members tended to assimilate into the non-Jewish society and were quick to abandon their religious traditions and culture.

Portland, Oregon, had a small Sephardic community numbering about eighty in 1912. Most were from the Island of Rhodes, with smaller groups from the Island of Marmara and from the village of Tekirdag in Turkey. Most of the Sephardim in Portland had moved there from Seattle in 1908. They established a café and a kosher restaurant, where they gathered during their free time, preferring their own places to those established by non-Jewish Greeks.

The Portland Sephardim met for religious services only on the High Holy Days. One generous Jew provided space for the services and conducted them himself. The immigrants worked as shoe-shiners and in other such occupations and earned enough to live on. By living economically, a few had been able to amass considerable capital. But even this tiny community was troubled by internal disunity and dissension. In March 1912 *La America* noted that the Sephardic society in Portland was reorganizing itself and Gadol hoped that it would be characterized by harmony and union.

The new society in Portland was known as Hesed Israel Anshei Rodes, and Yitzhak Berro was elected president. Berro wrote a letter to Gadol saying that the credit for organizing this group was due entirely to Gadol and *La America*. Berro praised Gadol, stating that other societies have been formed or reorganized in other communities thanks to *La America*. "People like you, Mr. Gadol, help us very much. You know how to inculcate the masses with the spirit of solidarity."

But this harmonious mood was not to last. *La America* reported in July 1915 that the Portland colony was again in dissension. During the holidays, the Sephardim had raised about $120. Two men held the money and wanted to buy a Torah scroll with it. The rest of the community objected, saying that they had neither a synagogue nor a *hazzan*, so it was premature to buy a Torah scroll.

A letter from Portland to *La America* (April 27, 1917) indicated that there were then fifty or sixty Sephardic men in Portland as well as Sephardic women and children. The Rhodes society had folded, since most of the committee members had left Portland for Seattle or Los Angeles. At the end of 1916 a new society was formed—Ahavath Shalom—and it was hoped that this society would fare better than its predecessor. The writer of the letter asked Gadol for advice on how to organize the community in Portland.

The Sephardic community in Seattle, Washington, which dates back to the first years of the twentieth century, was the largest Sephardic community outside of New York before World War I. By 1912 there were more than eight hundred Turkish Jews in the city.

The first Turkish Jew to arrive in Seattle was David Levy, who had come in 1900. The early Sephardic settlers worked in the fish business and were hard-working people. They first lived on Jackson, Maine, and King streets between Tenth and Fourteenth avenues. The Sephardim of Seattle were very poor but were known for their generosity.

Hayyim Leon, the correspondent to *La America* from Seattle, wrote in December 1911 that the disorganization within Seattle's colony was lamentable. The leaders of the community had misused funds entrusted to them by the members. Gadol called on the leaders in Seattle to unite to form one society and offered to help.

The Seattle community was divided by the geographic origins of the members. There was an organization known as Ahavat Ahim composed of Sephardim from the Island of Marmara, which had a treasury of $450. There was also a society of Jews from the Island of Rhodes. A tiny society of Jews from Constantinople had a treasury of $35. The Jews of Tekirdag had a society with a treasury of $400, which by 1912 had dwindled to $80. The other $320 was the source of scandal and community dissension. Gadol urged the societies to place their money in banks and to give a full accounting to their members. "Brothers! It is time that you see that your precious money is well used." Gadol called on the little societies of Seattle to merge into a larger one.

In March 1912 *La America* reported that due to the proddings of the newspaper, the Jews from Rhodes in Seattle had in fact reorganized themselves. Gadol praised Hayyim Leon for his help to *La America* and for his leadership in the Sephardic community of Seattle. "His name will be engraved in gold letters in the history of our journal." However, later that year Gadol had occasion to write: "The news coming from Seattle always revolts us." This large Sephardic colony was not succeeding in uniting because of the jealousies of its members and because of inadequate leadership and guidance. The Sephardim did not have their own cemetery space and had not yet provided a Talmud Torah for their children. Moreover, there was much internal strife among leaders of the community and the pages of *La America* frequently reflected their hostilities, claims, and counterclaims. One individual who had received no satisfaction from *La America* wrote a letter to the

Judeo-Spanish newspaper in Constantinople, *El Tiempo,* in which he condemned Gadol and *La America.* In response, Gadol wrote that the letter was not worthy of a serious response: "It would be against our dignity to enter into a discussion with a nothing like you and to respond to a dirty letter filled with the most infamous of calumnies."

With all the communal turmoil, yet another Sephardic group established itself in Seattle. In August 1912 *La America* noted that the few Gallipoli Jews in Seattle had formed their own society. The Jews from Rhodes organized their own society in Seattle known as Ezra Bessaroth, which was incorporated on June 30, 1914. The group had a women's division and planned to build its own synagogue building.

La America of October 18, 1912, announced the establishment of a welfare society known as Yetomim Ve-Almanot. The president of this group was Shemuel Morhaim and members of its committee were Joseph Caston, Marco Cordova, and Marco Romey (the author's grandfather). Its goal was to help the Jews in Tekirdag as well as its own members in Seattle. They had a capital of $500 gained from dues of ten cents a week plus donations. As of July 22, 1914, the Tekirdag group had 111 members. They decided to establish their own synagogue as well as a Talmud Torah. The group came to be known as the Bikur Holim.

While the individual societies and groups within Seattle were struggling to organize themselves, a communitywide sentiment for a chief rabbi slowly emerged. It was felt that a rabbi would be able to serve the religious needs of the Sephardim and also be able to unite the various factions. In August 1915 La America reported that the community had invited Rabbi Aharon Benezra from New York to visit their community to determine whether he would take the position. Gadol, who was friendly with Benezra, wrote that Seattle could not have made a better choice: Benezra was young, intelligent, and energetic. Gadol believed that if the community could organize around one chief rabbi, it could ultimately have one synagogue and one Talmud Torah. Benezra was, it seemed, appointed rabbi and head of the Talmud Torah. Gadol believed that Benezra's first task should be to bring the different Sephardic groups together. The two major groups, Ezra Bessaroth and Bikur

Holim, already had their own buildings, but it was hoped that these two organizations would merge into one strong community. Gadol suggested that five members from each group should form a general committee to determine the best way to bring about unity. The two synagogues could remain separate, but have one administration.

Gadol was optimistic about Benezra's ability to lead the Sephardim of Seattle. Benezra's main responsibility was in the area of the Talmud Torah. The Bikur Holim made three rooms available at no charge for a Talmud Torah. Gadol wrote that October 5, 1915, would be a noted date in Seattle's history because that was the day the first Talmud Torah was to open. A great celebration took place in honor of the opening of the school and people contributed generously to the new project. The Talmud Torah grew under the direction of Rabbi Benezra. A Hanukkah celebration was held with more than 250 people attending. Eight students of the school put on a play dealing with the meaning of Hanukkah, and six students put on a comedy using Hanukkah characters as the heroes.

While progress was being made in the area of education, the Sephardim of Seattle still lacked a central self-help organization. A crisis brought this problem to everyone's attention: Rabbi Benezra wrote a letter to *La America* in February 1916, which stated that four young Sephardim had been killed in a fire and it had taken some time for the community to raise the necessary three hundred dollars for the funerals. Benezra called for the establishment of an Ozer Dalim society to care for the poor and to provide funds for such emergencies. This letter by Benezra sparked a new dispute. A man in the community, Shabbatai Naon, responded in *La America* that the prime need of the Seattle Sephardim was a cemetery, not an Ozer Dalim. Naon believed that the existing societies already provided well enough for their needy members, but that it was shameful that the Sephardim had to rely on the Ashkenazim for cemetery space. Several weeks later, Benezra responded to Naon's criticisms in *La America,* claiming that Naon's statements were unfair and that the funds available for the poor were inadequate. He felt that the need for an Ozer Dalim was obvious. He agreed with Naon that there was also a need for a Sephardic cemetery but this did not mean that an Ozer Dalim too was not necessary.

Things went from bad to worse. Naon responded to Benezra

in a letter to *La America,* sharply criticizing Benezra for referring to himself as the rabbi of Seattle. Naon stated that Benezra was not in fact a rabbi and had not been hired as one, in spite of the general impression created in *La America.* He was employed merely as a teacher of children—the community had thought of hiring him as a rabbi but chose not to do so. Naon then chided Gadol for having recommended Benezra to serve as rabbi in Seattle. Naon was very caustic: "When we need his [Benezra's] advice, we know his address." Although hurt by this attack, Benezra continued to serve the school in Seattle, as well as to speak out on other community matters. But the antagonism in the community was so great that he soon left Seattle and returned to New York.

The rivalry between the Ezra Bessaroth and the Bikur Holim continued unabated. *La America* of November 24, 1916, noted that the Bikur Holim had 103 members. At elections held on November 12, Joseph Caston was elected president and Marco Romey was elected vice-president. In the issue of August 31, 1917, it was reported that the Ezra Bessaroth had begun to build a synagogue building, which would cost over $10,000, for which it had, in one night alone, raised $3,000. There were many calls for unity but none had any real effect. The Ezra Bessaroth built its building on Fifteenth Avenue and East Fir Street and the Bikur Holim was located on Twentieth Avenue and East Fir Street.

A number of clubs emerged among the Sephardim of Seattle. There was the Young Hebrew Prosperity Club, founded by some Sephardic young people as a "musical and gymnastic club." On October 9, 1921, the Young Hebrew Literary Club was established to teach English to new Sephardic immigrants as well as to help poor Sephardim in Seattle, Europe, and Asia Minor.

Theater among the American Sephardim may have reached its highest level in Seattle. The best-known producer of Judeo-Spanish plays in Seattle was Leon Behar. Most of the plays produced in Seattle were performed in Washington Hall, located at Fourteenth Avenue and East Fir Street. The actors were always attired in elaborate costumes. Having a flair for drama, Behar would rent costumes for his actors rather than have them use homemade outfits. Since he took his hobby seriously, he expected his actors and his audience to do likewise.

These glimpses of Sephardic communities throughout the United States culled from the pages of *La America* provide interesting snatches of history. They reveal the unique experience of each community, while at the same time demonstrating the universal condition of Sephardic immigrants in the United States during the early twentieth century.

11

The Next Generations

Speaking in 1941 at a gathering of the Sephardic Center of the Bronx, Albert Matarasso told his audience: "I pray that some day something spectacular may come to pass to enable the Sephardim to maintain their identity and their name in this country." He was speaking at a time when the Judeo-Spanish language was still widely used, when the Judeo-Spanish newspaper *La Vara* was still popular, and when the American-born generations had not yet come to dominate Sephardic life. Yet, Matarasso spoke from despair. He believed that the culture of the Sephardim was slipping away and would ultimately be lost altogether. He wondered whether Sephardim had the ability to maintain their specific identity.

Obviously, the problem of survival for any ethnic group in the United States causes anxiety for their leaders. Historically, there has been a general erosion of ethnic cultures in this country, and the overwhelming pressure to adapt to American social standards has been pervasive. Even with the recent revival in ethnic pride, the forces of assimilation are enormous. It is extremely problematic for any small ethnic group not to be affected by patterns of American society at large.

All Jews have had to struggle courageously to maintain their religious and communal identity. The temptation of a minority culture to assimilate into the majority society has been powerful.

The sociological differences between the immigrant generation of Jews and subsequent generations not only have been documented in many studies but are evident to most Jews from their own personal experience.

But if all Jews face the problem of assimilation and loss of cultural identity, the situation for the Sephardim has been even more intense. The Sephardim are a minority group within the minority Jewish community. They not only have had to worry about avoiding assimilation into American society, but they also have had to be concerned about being assimilated into the Ashkenazic Jewish society. Since the group is so small, it can afford few defections if it hopes to maintain its communal cohesiveness. How have the Sephardim attempted to insure their cultural survival?

In the first issue of the *Sephardic Bulletin* (November 1928), David de Sola Pool noted: "Perhaps the basic problem which faces the Sephardim in their adjustment to American life is that of the Jewish education of their children. It is transparently clear that unless our children are trained in the traditions of their fathers there can be no future for Sephardic Jewry in America. . . . They will not be Sephardic Jews or any kind of Jews unless we make an active and positive effort to train them." While Pool's analysis was correct, the reality was that most Sephardic children were receiving far from adequate religious education. They attended poorly run and poorly staffed religious schools in the afternoons following their attendance at public schools. It is not surprising that the children who were educated in such schools grew up with little formal knowledge of Judaism.

The pity was that so much faith was invested in these schools. Although a culture can be transmitted only through education, the means of transmitting the Sephardic culture were radically different in the United States from how it was done in the old country. While many Sephardic immigrants had received only minimal formal Jewish education in Turkey or other countries, they had absorbed a great deal just from living in an intensely Jewish environment. In the old country, life was very much influenced by the authority of the synagogue and religious observances. However, in the United States, the children of immigrants no longer could readily learn religious values and teachings from the people around them. Social and economic pressures broke down the older patterns of life. Children needed formal Jewish education not only to teach them facts and skills, but to transmit the values and teachings that their parents and the general society could no longer convey naturally. The schools simply were not able to handle this responsibility.

With the breakdown of religious education, there also came a breakdown in religious observance. Sabbath observance, kashruth, synagogue attendance—and so many other religious observances—were compromised or cast aside altogether. A sociological survey of American-born Sephardim, conducted in 1972, indicates the broad decline in religious observance and religious education over the past several generations. There has been a steady increase in the number of Sephardic children who receive little or no Jewish education. But, on the other hand, with the rise of the Jewish day school movement, there are now more Sephardic children receiving better Jewish educations than their parents or grandparents had. This is especially true in Seattle, New York, Los Angeles, and Atlanta.

Moise Gadol had recognized the inevitable alienation that would develop between the immigrant generation and their American-raised children. As the children became more educated and assimilated, their immigrant parents seemed to them more ignorant and old-fashioned. The youngsters wanted to speak English, not Judeo-Spanish. They attended American schools, and had little respect for the Sephardic religious schools. Gadol had urged parents to see to it that their children received good religious instruction, training in the Judeo-Spanish language, and an appreciation of Jewish laws and traditions. Through religion and culture, Gadol thought, the generation gap could be bridged. However, the harsh realities of the period made such idealistic proposals seem empty.

Even the most traditional and old-fashioned Sephardim recognized that Americanization was obviously a desired goal for them and their children. But at the same time, they recognized it as a clear threat to group ethnic identity. Gadol and others encouraged Sephardim to become American citizens, to learn English, and to adapt to the conditions in the new land, yet not to abandon their Sephardic identity.

In order to bolster ethnic and religious identity among the new generation of Sephardim, several communal efforts were made. In 1924, a group of New York Sephardim established a central communal institution known as the Sephardic Jewish Community of New York, Inc. In structure, it resembled its forerunner, the Federation of Oriental Jews. It was based on the existing local societies rather than on the community as a whole. A number of societies affiliated themselves with the Community and assigned a certain number of delegates to the board. Louis Hacker, writing in 1926, noted that the Community had approximately $6,000 in its treasury but had no definite program for which to spend the money. David de Sola Pool, however, referred to the organization as "stable and responsible." By 1927, the Sephardic Community had purchased a community house at 40 West 115 Street, which offered a variety of social services and other activities. It included a synagogue with a capacity of about four hundred.

Recognizing the problems of a central organization based on affiliated societies, there was a movement to broaden the Sephardic community. In 1931, the minutes of the group included "tentative clauses arrived at towards the unity of all Sephardic mutual organizations." The first three clauses called for all the societies to turn over to the new organization all their assets; all the societies to drop their names; and the membership of all the societies to become the membership of the new organization. The remaining clauses described the benefits of membership. The ninth clause of this manifesto made a concession to the pride and self-respect of the individual societies. "Each society will be considered a branch and will be entitled to elect a delegate for every fifty members to a board of delegates that shall meet at least once a year. These delegates will add to themselves ten more delegates-at-large from the Sephardic colony, and altogether they are to elect a board of directors composed of fifteen, five of which shall be among the delegates of the Sephardic colony at large." This clause, while giving some recognition to the autonomy of the societies, generally attempted to transfer power to the new Sephardic Community. Although these goals were desirable, they were not implemented in practice, because each society tenaciously clung to its own autonomy.

The minutes of the Community running through February 22, 1933, reflect many problems. The organization never received proper financial backing. Meetings were often poorly attended. Clashes of personalities and societies erupted from time to time. The organization in its early stages did not have the full trust and recognition of the general Sephardic and Jewish communities. When Congregation Shearith Israel affiliated with the Community in April 1928, "this notice was received with the greatest possible enthusiasm by the members." Henry S. Hendricks and David de Sola Pool had worked to involve Shearith Israel officially with the Community. It was believed that with the involvement of the prestigious and well-established Congregation Shearith Israel, the Sephardic Community would achieve a greater degree of respect and credibility. Yet, many Sephardic societies still abstained from affiliating with it.

The Sephardic Community of New York sponsored clubs in its community house building. In the early stages, these clubs were successful and meetings were well attended. The Community primarily served the Sephardic Jews of Harlem, but often spoke of establishing a building downtown for the benefit of the Sephardim of the Lower East Side. The latter project never materialized.

Among the leaders of the organization were John Hezekiah Levy, Maurice Amado, Albert Valensi, Henry S. Hendricks, Simon Nessim, Robert Franco, and Victor Tarry. These men worked tirelessly in order to win the support of the various Sephardic societies as well as to gain the allegiance of the nonaffiliated Sephardim. The minutes of the meetings reflect the anguish of the board caused by the lack of enthusiastic support by the Sephardim of New York. From time to time societies would withdraw their membership and would have to be approached all over again in order to be convinced to rejoin. Questions of inadequate financial support were constantly on the agenda of the meetings. The lack of success of the programs offered by the Sephardic Community was much lamented.

With all its problems, the Sephardic Community of New York did provide professional social services to troubled and needy Sephardim. According to Victor Tarry, who served as executive secretary of the Sephardic Community beginning January 8, 1930, the social service department was one of its most active and important agencies. Its goal was to assist Sephardic immigrants to adjust to American life. The Community became the liaison and referral agency between the Sephardim and the Jewish social service agencies. It opened an office in one of the Sephardic synagogues on the Lower East Side and Victor Tarry spent several days a week there.

The Sephardic Jewish Community of New York issued the *Sephardic Bulletin,* which it billed as "a Bulletin for every Sephardic home." Volume one, number one, was dated November 1928. The purpose of the bulletin was to keep members informed of the activities of the Community, as well as to serve as a way of communicating with nonmembers. It was believed that once people read about the activities of the Community, they would see the merit of its work and would financially assist the effort. The *Sephardic Bulletin* was published monthly for a short while and no longer appeared after June 1930. Each issue featured three pages in English and one page in Judeo-Spanish. The *Sephardic Bulletin* served a useful purpose, but was unable to stem the decline of the Community.

The early 1930s witnessed a shift in population, with many of the Sephardim of Harlem moving to other areas, notably the Bronx. As a result, the Sephardic Community's building was no longer in a center of Sephardic life. Financial problems and inadequate involvement of the masses of the Sephardim in the project led to its ultimate failure. By 1933, the Sephardic Jewish Community of New York had ceased all activity. Its building was sold to a Pentecostal Puerto Rican congregation and the monies received from the sale were distributed among the societies that had originally advanced funds to the Community. The officers of record at the time of the dissolution were Simon S. Nessim, president; Henry S. Hendricks, treasurer; and Victor Tarry, secretary.

In the late 1920s, while the Sephardic Jewish Community was still operating, David de Sola Pool attempted to establish a national Sephardic organization that would serve the spiritual needs of Sephardim in New York and throughout the country. One of the problems of the time was the lack of a unified synagogue ritual: there were a variety of Sephardic prayer books, and even within one synagogue, worshipers might be using different prayer books. It was difficult for the American-born generation—which had received inadequate Hebrew training—to follow synagogue services. Moreover, there were no satisfactory prayer books that included a proper English translation.

Aside from the prayerbook difficulties, there were other problems: the lack of trained religious guides and the lack of a learned Sephardic lay leadership. Pool envisioned the establishment of a union of Sephardic congregations as a means of dealing with the spiritual and religious issues confronting the Sephardic synagogues in this country. Representatives of Congregation Shearith Israel of New York met with leaders of Congregation Mikveh Israel of Philadelphia and Shearith Israel of Montreal in 1928. Together, these three historic congregations took the lead in founding the Union of Sephardic Congregations.

The Union of Sephardic Congregations sponsored several national conventions. Although serious issues were discussed and debated, few constructive actions emerged from them. Attendance was often disappointing. At the May 1949 convention held at Shearith Israel in New York, Pool deplored the failure of so many New York congregations to send delegates. At that meeting, resolutions were passed encouraging communities to find promising young men who might be trained for the rabbinate. It was agreed that Jewish education should be supported in Sephardic community life and that the Sephardic synagogues should adopt a uniform ritual.

The Union of Sephardic Congregations was not successful in attaining all its goals, but it did make a major contribution to Sephardic religious life with the publication of the Sephardic prayer books translated and edited by David de Sola Pool. These are still used in many congregations throughout North America and in other English-speaking countries throughout the world. By the 1950s, the Union of Sephardic Congregations had become relatively inactive in all matters outside of the publication of prayer books.

Another attempt to unite the Sephardim was made in the early 1940s. A group of Sephardic businessmen in New York organized a Sephardic men's club, which developed into the Central Sephardic Jewish Community of America, Inc. This organization was launched through the efforts of Rabbi Nissim J. Ovadia, a recognized scholar and Sephardic leader who had been born in Turkey. Shortly after his arrival in the United States in 1941, he began to call for the

American Sephardim to establish a central Sephardic Jewish Community. Sephardim of all language backgrounds sent representatives to a meeting held in May 1941, and the new Community was founded. Although the organization was concerned mainly with New York City, its membership included Sephardim of other cities as well. Ovadia served as chief rabbi of the Central Sephardic Jewish Community until his death in August 1942 at the age of fifty-two. Rabbi David Jessurun Cardozo, then assistant minister of Shearith Israel, began to serve the Community and helped to organize a women's division, with the cooperation of Mazal Ovadia and Lucy Touriel. Rabbi Isaac Alcalay became the Community's chief rabbi.

The Central Sephardic Jewish Community of America set itself fine goals. It hoped to maintain Sephardic traditions in synagogue worship; to give proper religious education to the young; to assist Sephardic immigrants; to Americanize Sephardic immigrants as quickly as possible; to find employment for needy Sephardim; to provide social welfare services; and to create a Sephardic rabbinical court. The Community also saw itself as a cultural and social center for Sephardic Jews.

The Central Sephardic Jewish Community seemed to have a genuine possibility of succeeding. In September 1943 it issued a bulletin, *The Sephardi,* whose purpose—as stated in its first issue—was "to awaken the Sephardic masses to the necessity of a united Sephardic community throughout the Western Hemisphere." This bulletin appeared intermittently until 1957. In December 1944, Joseph M. Papo, a trained social worker, was appointed to serve as the Community's executive director. This was seen as a constructive move since it was felt that the Community required trained and dedicated personnel if it hoped to succeed. John J. Karpeles was hired as director of youth activities. In 1946, the Community's youth league had four operating chapters: in the Bronx, the Lower East Side, New Lots, and Sheepshead Bay.

The leadership of the Central Sephardic Jewish Community of America was composed of dedicated Sephardim, many of whom had proven to be successful financially and professionally. Most were educated in New York and were equipped intellectually and emotionally to develop an organized Sephardic Community. Henry

J. Perahia, then president of the Community, wrote in the *Sephardi* of September 1946: "As surely as water wears the stone, we are confident that we shall in time arrive at that utopia when all Sephardim will regard a unified community, with all its orderly processes, as the first essential in their life in America."

This ambitious effort of American-trained Sephardim manifested the struggles and conflicts of a culture in transition. While the leadership was strongly identified with the Sephardic tradition, they still had made accommodations to American life. The minutes of their meetings were written in English. Their publications were entirely in English. Although they all could speak Judeo-Spanish, most of their children had much less fluency in that language. While the leaders were emotionally attached to the Sephardic past and were committed to perpetuating Sephardic traditions, they had great difficulty in training their young people in these traditions.

The dismal situation of Jewish education among Sephardic youth in New York has been pointed out from the earliest years of Sephardic immigration. In *The Sephardi* of September 1946, Joseph Papo reported: "The number of Sephardic children attending Hebrew school is very small ... most of them do not attend Talmud Torah long enough to acquire a real knowledge of Jewish subjects which constitute our Jewish heritage. It is most unfortunate that a large number of our children are growing up without any Jewish education. It is no secret that many boys, upon approaching their thirteenth birthday, spend just a few weeks in preparation for their Bar Mitzvah." Papo's survey of the Sephardic religious schools in Brooklyn, the Bronx, and Manhattan revealed that only a total of 624 Sephardic children were enrolled, 491 of whom were boys. Interestingly, the two largest schools were those of the Syrian Sephardim, not of the Judeo-Spanish-speaking Sephardim.

Although the condition of Jewish education for young Sephardim was often lamented, little was done in a practical way to ameliorate the situation. It is instructive to consider the five main points of the platform of the new administration of the Central Sephardic Jewish Community of America, as reported in *The Sephardi* of August 1953. The aims of the Community were to provide a center for all information regarding Sephardic activities and needs; to perpetuate Sephardic tradition; to serve as a clearinghouse for all Sephardic activities; to gain recognition and prestige for Sephardic tradition and Sephardic Jews at large; and to set up a fund for scholarships for Sephardic students—to assist and further their education through college. None of these points deals directly with the religious education of Sephardic youth. In sum, they represent a desire for public acceptance for Sephardim, but offer no specific plan for perpetuation of Sephardic traditions.

There were a few voices, however, that did argue forcefully for Jewish education among the young Sephardim. Aaron Ben Elias, a native of Jerusalem, who had received his doctorate from the University of Berlin and had served several years as a rabbi in Chicago before coming to New York in 1932, as the executive director of the Pro-Palestine Federation of America, was one such intellectual. In the pages of *The Sephardi,* he argued for "a life-line for Sephardic culture." He wrote in November 1953: "The survival of our specific Sephardic culture and traditions depends upon our ability and readiness to supply the means needed to create and maintain proper educational institutions. Knowledge of our Sephardic background is the life-line that will insure the continuity of Sephardic Jewish life. As matters stand now, the religious and educational needs of the rising Sephardic generation are poorly provided for."

Elias made a practical suggestion: "It is incumbent upon us to immediately embark upon an educational campaign aiming at securing the means for the establishment of an American Sephardi Seminary to train urgently needed rabbis and teachers for Sephardic communities in the Western Hemisphere. . . . It is a task the realization of which will establish a solidly anchored life-line which will save Sephardic religious and cultural values and will inspire our youth to treasure our traditions and to strengthen the ties that bind us to a great and glorious past." He further pursued this theme in the December 1953 issue of *The Sephardi.* "The life interests of Sephardic Jewry depend on the speedy spiritual and cultural rehabilitation of its adolescent youth. Without active participation of our rising generation in our communal life there can be no hope for a Sephardic renaissance. . . . A Sephardic Institute for Jewish Studies, featuring our Sephardic background, is the crying need of the hour."

A front-page article in *The Sephardi* (January 1954) also called for a Sephardic institute for Jewish studies. "We must afford our Sephardi youth an opportunity to gain the knowledge that will instill in them the love and esteem for their spiritual and cultural heritage. A Sephardi Institute for Jewish Studies is the only effective answer to this deeply felt need to meet the educational problem facing our Sephardi youth. . . . The rehabilitation of our Sephardi youth is our foremost task. . . . Let us then rise to the occasion and fulfill our duty towards our rising generation, thus further developing and preserving our sacred heritage!" In spite of these articles, no such Sephardic institute was created. The Community was able to mobilize its resources to establish a Sephardic home for the aged, but was unable to mobilize itself to organize a Sephardic institute for young people.

Although the Central Sephardic Jewish Community of America did not provide a substantial educational program, it did try to involve the Sephardic community of New York in national and international Sephardic and Jewish affairs. In this way, it hoped to win the involvement of all Sephardim, young and old. In December 1944 it founded the World Federation of Sephardi Communities. Already in 1941, the Pan American Union of Sephardic Communities had been organized under the leadership of Nissim Ovadia. At the founding meeting of the World Federation of Sephardi Communities in New York, there were six delegates from Latin America, seven from Europe, three from Africa, and a number from the United States. This organization proposed to cooperate with the Ashkenazim in the realization of a Jewish commonwealth in Palestine; act as the representative body for Sephardim worldwide and seek proper representation in various Jewish organizations; assist Sephardic groups desirous of settling in Palestine; foster and promote Jewish religious and cultural education among Sephardim; assist in the establishment of Hebrew schools and yeshivot; encourage Sephardic youth to serve as rabbis, teachers, and communal leaders; and extend moral and material assistance to all Sephardic communities that suffered as a result of World War II. The organization had the warm blessings of the Sephardic chief rabbi of Palestine, Benzion Meir Hai Ouziel, and other international Sephardic figures. The organization was headed by Simon

Nessim, president; Rabbi David Jessurun Cardozo, secretary; and Isaac Shalom, treasurer. Henry V. Besso served as executive director. The organization gained a number of affiliates from throughout the Sephardic world and managed to have a number of meetings and gatherings to discuss issues of vital concern to the Sephardim.

In spite of the progress, the organization was constantly plagued by lack of adequate financial support and by the apathy of the Sephardic masses. The original leaders of the Central Sephardic Jewish Community of America were idealistic and dedicated. However, they were unable to convey their sense of dedication or idealism to the American-born generation in matters concerning Sephardic Jewish life. The active members of the organization continued to grow older without replenishing the ranks with younger leadership. Consequently, the Central Sephardic Jewish Community of America gradually became inactive. By the 1960s, only the women's division continued with any vitality, and it too has been unsuccessful in attracting younger leadership.

In 1951, the American branch of the World Sephardi Federation was formed. Its goals were "to promote religious and cultural interests of Sephardic communities throughout the world; to assist them morally and materially; to assist Sephardim who wish to settle in Israel." Simon S. Nessim served as president and Aaron Ben Elias as executive director. The organization issued a bulletin, which was issued irregularly, called *World Sephardi*. Its first number appeared in January 1959. The United States Council of the World Sephardi Federation set as its goals the establishment of close ties between Sephardic communities in the United States, the propagation of the ideals of the World Sephardi Federation, the stimulation of Sephardic life, and the publication of a bulletin to keep all members informed of the aspirations and progress of the group.

In 1959, Isaac Moyal of the World Sephardi Federation visited Sephardic communities in the United States. He found that the Sephardi spirit among American Sephardim "is strong, and the lay leaders in most places are able and willing to preserve it." Moyal suggested that the World Sephardi Federation send representatives from time to time to the various Sephardic communities in order to encourage their work. He cautioned, however, that the religious emissaries "must be people of the world; they must have contemporary education and wide knowledge with deep understanding of local problems and capable of grasping quickly local conditions, especially for the sake of the second generation of Americans, who constitute the majority of the Sephardi population. The leadership in the various congregations is slowly but surely passing into their hands." Moyal also indicated: "The situation of religious leadership in the United States is very serious. Although the tension caused in the Jewish community due to the different religious ideologies is still not very marked in the Sephardi group, bitterness is beginning to be felt. . . . It is therefore essential to influence the present Sephardi rabbis and ministers to form a country-wide organization and to attempt to open a Sephardi Yeshiba in the United States or at least influence one of the big Ashkenazi seminaries to open a Sephardi branch." Moyal's recommendations were not implemented. In fact, this organization, too, was unsuccessful in gaining support and gradually grew dormant.

In 1972 there was an attempt to reestablish the American branch of the World Sephardi Federation, and a founding convention was held at Congregation Shearith Israel in February 1973. The Jewish Agency provided office space as well as an executive director to organize the activities of this group. Within several years the organization reconstituted itself as the American Sephardi Federation and set as its goals the fostering of Sephardic Jewish life in the United States, serving Sephardic youth, and working for Sephardic involvement on behalf of the State of Israel. Although the American Sephardi Federation has had some success, it has not been able to gain the status of a genuine Sephardic Community. It has derived strength from newer Sephardic immigrants who have come to the United States from North Africa during the 1950s and 1960s. The younger American-born element has not been overwhelmingly involved in the organization, except in the youth movement.

The dream of Moise Gadol for a united Sephardic Community was never realized. It seems, now, an unlikely prospect for the future. The American-born generations of Sephardim have drifted away from the ideals of establishing a Sephardic Community, preferring to deal with their Sephardic background individually or through their synagogues, rather than through general Sephardic communal organizations.

12

Epilogue

American Sephardim of Judeo-Spanish origin have undergone a profound cultural metamorphosis during the past several generations. The world of their grandparents—the world in which Moise Gadol lived—is by now only a distant memory, a source of nostalgia.

The Sephardim of the immigrant generation, though adapting to American life, still carried with them much of the culture of the old world. Their language of communication was Judeo-Spanish; they had large families; they tended to live in ghettos; their cuisine and folklore reflected their Sephardic origins. But two generations later, the patterns are significantly different. The birthrate has dropped sharply among Sephardim, reflecting changing ideas and acceptance of American middle-class values. The influence of the extended family, which had been so pronounced in the immigrant generation, is now diminished because of the mobility of American Sephardim. It is rare to find families with parents, grandparents, children, uncles, aunts, and cousins all living within walking distance of each other. On the contrary, families are now scattered, some members living in a city, others in suburbia, and yet others living in different communities throughout the country.

Judeo-Spanish is little used as a language of communication among third-generation American Sephardim. Even those who still know the language generally employ it infrequently and only in specific ritual contexts, such as the reading of the Passover Haggadah. Hearing Judeo-Spanish songs may evoke fond memories of parents and grandparents, but in few cases are the songs a regular part of life.

The assimilation of American Sephardim of Judeo-Spanish background into American society has been pervasive. Whether from the standpoint of religious observance or cultural behavior or language of communication, there is a chasm that separates third- and fourth-generation American-born Sephardim from their immigrant forebears. Aside from the Americanization process, Sephardim have also been significantly influenced by their far more numerous Ashkenazic coreligionists. Almost all of the Jewish day schools and yeshivot in the United States are run by Ashkenazim, and these schools exert little effort to make Sephardic youngsters understand anything about their own specific heritage. Ashkenazic foods and Yiddish phrases have found their way into the life of Sephardim.

Another important factor to consider in any analysis of Sephardic life in this country is the marriage pattern. During the immigrant generation, most Sephardim had Sephardic spouses. Husband and wife spoke the same language and shared the same cultural background. But American-born Sephardim often chose to marry Ashkenazic mates. Although in the first decades of this century, Sephardic-Ashkenazic "intermarriage" created something of a scandal for the families involved, such marriages soon became accepted by both groups. Presently, about 75 percent of Sephardic young people of Judeo-Spanish origin marry Ashkenazic partners. Such marriages obviously require compromises from both, and the children of such couples may or may not identify strongly as Sephardim. While many Sephardic-Ashkenazic couples become involved in Sephardic synagogue and community life and attempt to perpetuate some Sephardic customs, there are many others who are only tangentially involved in Sephardic life. There can be no doubt at all that in the future Sephardic culture in the United States will largely depend on individuals who are of mixed Sephardic-Ashkenazic background.

None of this would have surprised Moise Gadol. Indeed, he foresaw these cultural changes and forewarned his readers. But there are other phenomena in American Sephardic life that might have surprised Gadol.

He would probably be pleased to find that there is an interest among third- and fourth-generation American Sephardim to preserve the vestiges of the Judeo-Spanish language. A number of Sephardic synagogues have incorporated Judeo-Spanish translations of prayers in their religious services. On the High Holy Days, in particular, it is not uncommon to find congregations chanting hymns in Judeo-Spanish, with the younger congregants singing along with their parents and grandparents. Increasingly, younger Sephardim have tried to include the use of Judeo-Spanish in the Passover Haggadah services in their homes. If only for nostalgic reasons, this practice does serve to keep some ties between the new and old generations. There is a general unwillingness to let the language slip away entirely. There has also been a revival of interest in Judeo-Spanish folk music. This is manifested not only in the significant increase in recordings by popular singers, but by the emergence of local groups and individual performers who specialize in Judeo-Spanish music.

American Sephardim have shown an increasing interest in their own cultural background, just as other ethnic groups in America have felt the need to search for their roots. Many third- and fourth-generation American-born Sephardim still have vivid recollections of older relatives who were living repositories of Sephardic culture. Customs, songs, foods, and even superstitions, which once seemed of no significance at all, now gain a new importance among the younger generations. They serve as bridges between an individual and his or her own past.

Those American Sephardim who are trying to deepen their self-awareness have opportunities that Moise Gadol could never have dreamed of. The growing interest in Sephardic studies on a worldwide basis has provided opportunities for study as well as the pride that comes with recognition. In the United States, major universities—Columbia, Harvard, Princeton, the University of Washington, to name a few—offer courses in Sephardic history and culture. Yeshiva University established a Sephardic Studies Program in 1964. In Israel, the Misgav Yerushalayim—affiliated with the Hebrew University—is a center for Sephardic research. The Ben

Zvi Institute in Jerusalem has developed an impressive collection of works dealing with all aspects of the Sephardic experience.

Spain itself has shown a profound interest in the Sephardim. The Supreme Council for Scientific Studies of Spain established the Instituto Arias Montana de Estudios Hebraicos in Madrid in 1939. The institute publishes a quarterly journal, *Sefarad,* devoted to Sephardic history and culture. During the 1960s the universities of Madrid, Barcelona, and Granada established chairs in the Hebrew language, in Jewish history, and in Jewish literature. An institute of Sephardic studies was established in Madrid. In 1954, a Sephardic center was created in Toledo.

Recent years have seen a significant increase in publications of Sephardic value. Scholarly books and articles dealing with aspects of Sephardic life are issued regularly. An interesting phenomenon is the revival of interest in the *Me-am Lo'ez,* the classic Judeo-Spanish biblical commentary, the first volume of which was published in Constantinople in 1730. The *Me-am Lo'ez* is a vast work of encyclopedic scope, originated by Rabbi Jacob Huli. Some Sephardic immigrants came to the United States early this century with copies of the *Me-am Lo'ez* with them. This set of books was sometimes used for study sessions in the synagogues, as well as for private home study among Sephardic families. It is a repository of the folk religious culture of Judeo-Spanish-speaking Sephardim. While the *Me-am Lo'ez* enjoyed some popularity among the Sephardic immigrants, the next generation tended to ignore it. But, then there was a revival. The Spanish scholars David Gonzalo Maeso and Pascual Recuero began to publish the *Me-am Lo'ez* in Latin letters. The first volume, the *Prolegomenos,* was published in Madrid in 1964 by Editorial Gredos. In 1967, a Hebrew translation appeared in Israel, translated by Shemuel Yerushalmi and published by Or Hadash in Jerusalem. In 1977, Maznaim Publishing Corporation issued its first volume of the *Me-am Lo'ez* translated into English by Rabbi Aryeh Kaplan. The series in English is published as *The Torah Anthology.* Also of interest is a volume compiled by David N. Barocas in 1970, which was published by the Foundation for the Advancement of Sephardic Studies and Culture. Entitled *In Search of Our Sephardic Roots,* the volume includes an essay about the *Me-am Lo'ez* by Professor Maír José Benardete, as well as some translations, and a discussion of the Hebrew aspects of this work by Rabbi Nissim Gambach. Thus it happens that a book that was a classic among Sephardic communities in Turkey and had almost become extinct in the American Sephardic community has enjoyed a remarkable worldwide revival. It has not only come back to the American Sephardim, but has been read with interest by Jews and non-Jews throughout the world.

The Sephardic reawakening has been stimulated by the activity of individual Sephardim and small Sephardic cultural committees. Through their efforts, classes and lectures are offered and materials of Sephardic interest are published. While most of these efforts have only local impact, they are indications of the Sephardic will to survive as a distinct culture.

The most important and successful current cultural effort is the Sephardic House, based at Congregation Shearith Israel in New York. Founded in 1978, Sephardic House offers a wide variety of classes on Sephardic and general Jewish topics, and also sponsors regular public programs on Sephardic themes. The public response has been encouraging, with hundreds of individuals attending the classes and thousands more attending the individual programs and events. Sephardic House has a publication program and issued its first book, *Studies in Sephardic Culture,* in 1980. This volume includes a Ladino-English dictionary, a bibliography on Judeo-Spanish proverbs, and other studies in the field of Judeo-Spanish literature and culture. In 1982, Sephardic House issued a new edition of *Hispanic Culture and Character of the Sephardic Jews,* by Maír José Benardete. Among the projects of Sephardic House are the development of curricular material for religious schools and day schools, an outreach program to communities outside the New York area, and the development of an archive center for material dealing with American Sephardic life. Sephardic House has a grow-ing national membership.

Although the American-born Sephardim have been unable or unwilling to create a viable Community, there is still hope that individually and collectively they will remain attached to their Sephardic culture. As we have seen, there are indications of cultural vitality as well as signs of assimilation and loss of cultural identity.

We can only speculate as to how Gadol would survey the

contemporary situation. Obviously, he would be struck by the many differences between contemporary Sephardic life and the early immigrant generation. He might be impressed with the notable economic progress of American Sephardim—their advancement in American society, their high level of secular education. He would marvel at some of the large Sephardic synagogue buildings that have been constructed around the country. He would be happy at the reawakening in Sephardic culture, and in particular he would applaud the efforts of Sephardim to promote and develop their own cultural traditions. But he would also be disappointed. He would still argue for the need to establish a central Sephardic Community, with its own administrative and religious leaders. He would resent the patronizing attitudes of many non-Sephardim who like to speak of the Sephardic heritage in exotic or romantic terms and too often ignore the Sephardic intellectual and literary traditions.

Gadol would be struck by the similarity in the position of intellectuals of Sephardic Jewry today and his own seventy years ago. Just as Gadol found himself as a lonely voice in the wilderness, so too do today's Sephardic cultural leaders have a sense of isolation and frustration. The masses of the Sephardic community were apathetic to Gadol's message, just as many Sephardim today remain indifferent to religious and cultural stimulation. Gadol suffered because the wealthy Sephardim of his time did not support Sephardic communal and intellectual efforts. Yet, today the same tendency is evident. Although individual Sephardim of Judeo-Spanish background have supported a variety of institutions, their support of indigenous Sephardic cultural ventures has not been particularly noteworthy. They have rallied admirably to build and support a Sephardic home for the aged, but have made no similar commitment to a single day school, yeshiva, or cultural or communal organization. Successes in Sephardic cultural life have come from individuals who, like Gadol, are keenly aware of how alone they are in their work.

Gadol would view the material successes and spiritual failures of American Sephardim with some degree of anger. If only people had listened to him, if only he could have found a wider following for his ideas—perhaps things might have turned out differently. Looking to the future, Gadol might very well wonder whether the signs of cultural vitality will be sufficient to insure a flourishing Sephardic life in the United States. The forces against such an eventuality are enormous. The efforts to foster such a goal are relatively weak. Gadol might say, "What the Sephardim today need is a newspaper to unite them and encourage them. They need a paper like *La America!*"

Notes

CHAPTER 1

A description of the funeral of Moise Gadol was printed in *La Vara*, June 20, 1941, p. 7. The article includes some information about Gadol's life as well as a photograph of him. Biographical information about Gadol's background in Europe and his early activities in New York is given in *La America*, February 23, 1912, p. 1.

The experience of Yiddish-speaking Jews of the Lower East Side is the subject of Irving Howe's *World Of Our Fathers* (New York, 1976). Jeffrey Gurock's *When Harlem Was Jewish* (New York, 1979) describes Jewish life in the uptown section of Manhattan. However, he ignores the existence of Sephardim in Harlem, though that was an important area of Sephardic settlement in the city. Moses Rischin's *The Promised City* (Cambridge, Mass., 1977), describes Jewish life in New York City from 1870 to 1914. He makes only a few scattered references to the Sephardic immigrants whom he calls "Levantines" and even these few references contain errors.

CHAPTER 2

Albert Amateau prepared twenty-six typewritten pages of his reminiscences of Moise Gadol, at the request of Joseph Papo. I thank Mr. Papo for making this material available to me.

The reasons for Sephardic migration to the United States from the Levant are discussed in *La America*, December 29, 1911, p. 2, March 15,

1912, p. 1, and May 22, 1914, p. 2. Useful insights on this topic are found in Maír José Benardete, *Hispanic Culture and Character of the Sephardic Jews* (New York, 1952), p. 139; David de Sola Pool, "The Levantine Jews in the United States," *American Jewish Year Book,* vol. 15 (1913–14), pp. 209–10. The same volume, p. 431, describes the impact of the Balkan wars on the Sephardim. The minutes of the Hebrew Immigrant Aid Society (HIAS), available on microfilm at the YIVO Institute in New York, describe the situation in the Levant following World War I, in the minutes of February 10, 1920, p. 91, and July 28, 1920, p. 128.

In contrast to the difficulties faced by Sephardim in the Levant, the promise of a bright future in America was a strong inducement to migrate here. Gadol pointed out the many advantages of settling in the United States in *La America,* May 22, 1914, p. 2. In that article he referred to the United States as "the land of the dollars."

HIAS kept records of the number of Sephardim entering the United States. Louis M. Hacker, "The Communal Life of the Sephardic Jews in New York City," *Jewish Social Service Quarterly* 3 (December 1926): 34, reports the HIAS figures. Immigration statistics may also be found in David de Sola Pool's aforementioned article in the *American Jewish Year Book,* vol. 15, as well as in an article, "The Immigration of Levantine Jews into the United States", *Jewish Charities,* June 1914, pp. 12–27. Jack Farhi, writing in *La America,* August 9, 1912, p. 2, estimated that Turkish Jews in New York would soon number about thirty thousand. *La America* provided statistics, based on the information of HIAS, in its issues of January 31, 1913, p. 2, and February 20, 1914, p. 2. In its December 12, 1913, issue, p. 1, *La America* reported that more than two hundred Oriental Jews had arrived from Turkey and Macedonia during the previous week.

La America, March 8, 1912, featured a front-page article about Sephardic immigration to New York. The newspaper ran a picture of a ship, the Statue of Liberty, as well as a picture of a meeting at HIAS, with a caption that indicates the existence of the Oriental Bureau and its hours. Gadol regularly printed articles about HIAS in the pages of *La America,* generally with lavish praise for the work it was doing. He was extremely proud of the fact that he had founded the Oriental Bureau. Many issues of *La America* carried articles describing the kind of help being provided to specific immigrants. Articles dealing with the Oriental Bureau appeared in many issues of *La America,* including, December 22, 1911, p. 2, March 29, 1912, p. 1, May 31, 1912, p. 1, June 21, 1912, p. 1, September 20, 1912, p. 1, and February 7, 1913, p. 2. In *La America,* June 28, 1912, p. 1, Gadol recommended Jack Farhi for the post of secretary of the Oriental Bureau. In the issue of July 5, 1912, p. 1, there is an article about Farhi, where he is described as one of the most popular young men among the Sephardim. Articles relating to the closing and reopening of the Oriental Bureau are in *La America,* October 1, 1915, p. 2, December 24, 1915, p. 2, and August 18, 1916, p. 4.

HIAS minutes relating to the Oriental Bureau include entries dated February 11, 1913, p. 3, February 10, 1914, p. 3, February 15, 1914, p. 2, September 15, 1914, p. 3, April 13, 1915, p. 16, and December 13, 1921, p. 249. Concerning the Industrial Removal Office, see *La America*, February 7, 1913, p. 2.

Gadol continually printed articles concerning proposed immigration laws. For example, see *La America*, December 9, 1910, p. 3, March 1, 1912, p. 1, April 26, 1912, p. 3, May 3, 1912, p. 1, May 10, 1912, p. 1, May 24, 1912, p. 2, December 20, 1912, p. 4, February 6, 1914, p. 1, May 15, 1914, p. 5, January 22, 1915, p. 2, February 5, 1915, p. 2, February 2, 1917, p. 1, and February 9, 1917, p. 3.

The effects of the immigration quotas and the specific quotas per country are given in *La America*, June 3, 1921, p. 1, July 15, 1921, p. 1, and April 25, 1924, p. 2. During the summer of 1921, Gadol ran many articles dealing with the immigration laws and how they affected the Sephardim. In the issue of October 17, 1924, p. 2, he printed his article indicating that immigration of Sephardim to the United States had come to an end.

CHAPTER 3

Farhi's article appeared in *La America*, July 19, 1912, p. 3. In Dr. Pool's article in *Jewish Charities*, p. 16, and in his article in the *American Jewish Year Book*, vol. 15, p. 218, he roundly criticizes the Sephardic coffeehouses and characterizes them as places of idleness, gambling, and other undesirable activities. Joseph Gedelecia defended the coffeehouses in *Jewish Charities*, June 1914, p. 29. *La America*, May 23, 1913, p. 1, reports a fight in a café in which one man was hospitalized, and another was arrested. The article states that there had been other fights in the coffeehouses as well.

The poor quality of food in the Sephardic restaurants is reported in *La America*, August 9, 1912, p. 3. The problem of gambling in the coffeehouses and restaurants is discussed in *La America*, January 23, 1914, p. 1.

Some of the social problems confronting the community are reported in *La America*, July 12, 1912, p. 3, September 6, 1912, p. 2, August 22, 1913, p. 3, August 29, 1913, p. 1, February 13, 1914, p. 5, and August 17, 1917, p. 3. Concerning bombs on Chrystie Street, articles appeared in *La America*, August 16, 1912, p. 2, December 20, 1912, p. 4, and May 23, 1913, p. 1. The activities of con artists who exploited Sephardim are reported in *La America*, August 22, 1913, p. 5, and August 29, 1913, p. 6.

Nessim Behar seems to have been universally respected and loved. His incredible sincerity won the admiration of the entire community. Information about his life can be found in David N. Barocas, *Albert Matarasso and His Ladino* (New York, 1969), p. 56, published by the Foundation for the

Advancement of Sephardic Studies and Culture. Benardete, in his book *Hispanic Culture and Character of the Sephardic Jews* (New York, 1952), discusses Nessim Behar on pp. 169–70. Z. Szajkowski discusses Behar in "The Alliance Israélite Universelle in the United States 1860–1949," in *Publications of the American Jewish Historical Society* 39 (June 1950): 406–43. Behar is mentioned often in *La America*. An article on p. 2 of the February 13, 1914, issue reported that Behar had done much good work in Europe and had been well received by the pope in Rome. He also had had an audience with the king of Italy.

Information about the Sephardic societies and their leaders was drawn from the pages of *La America*. The issue of January 5, 1912, p. 2, lists eight New York Sephardic societies then in existence and gives some information about each of them. Articles about the Oriental Progressive Society appeared in *La America*, February 3, 1911, p. 2, and April 28, 1911, p. 2. An article about the Union and Peace Society appeared in the issue of February 3, 1911, p. 3. An article about Hebra Ahava Ve-Ahvah Janina appeared on November 25, 1910, p. 1. Articles about Ahavath Shalom of Monastir appeared in the issues of February 3, 1911, p. 3, and April 14, 1911, p. 2. An article about the Society of Jews from Rhodes appeared in the issue of January 19, 1912, p. 3, and an article about the Rodefei Tsedek appeared on February 2, 1912, p. 3; Tikvah Tovah is discussed on December 9, 1910, p. 2.

Events leading to the formation of the Ez Hahayyim of Salonika were described in *La America*, April 19, 1912, p. 2, and an announcement of the formation of the society appeared in the issue of May 3, 1912, p. 3. Information about Mekor Hayyim of Dardanelles appeared in *La America*, May 16, 1913, p. 1, and March 20, 1914, p. 2.

News items about the various societies appeared frequently in the pages of *La America*. Gadol attempted to keep his readers informed of all the latest developments within the Sephardic community.

La America of September 19, 1913, p. 6, lists the societies that were planning to sponsor services for the upcoming High Holy Days. Eight of the societies were located on the Lower East Side and two in Harlem. The societies and their addresses are:

Ahavath Shalom Monastir, 98 Forsyth Street
Hesed Ve-Emet Kastorialis, 79–81 Forsyth Street
Mekor Hayyim Dardanelles, 73 Allen Street
Hayyim Vahesed Gallipoli, 83 Forsyth Street
Tseror Hahayyim Constantinople, 98 Forsyth Street
Anshei Rhodes, 281 Grand Street
Ezrat Ahim, 63 Orchard Street
Keter Zion Angora, 1 Second Avenue
Shearith Israel of Turkey, 132 East 111th Street
Ez Hahayyim, 75–77 East 116th Street

Gadol lamented the disorganization of the Sephardic community and the proliferation of competing societies. Of special interest are articles on the subject that appeared in *La America* October 4, 1912, p. 2, June 27, 1913, p. 3, September 17, 1915, p. 2, December 8, 1916, p. 2, September 24, 1920, p. 2, and October 14, 1921, p. 2.

An article describing the need of founding a Talmud Torah appeared in *La America,* May 26, 1911, p. 3. The successes of the downtown Talmud Torah were described in the issues of December 13, 1912, p. 2, and March 28, 1913, p. 2. The reports of Benyunes are found in the minutes of the Oriental Committee of the Sisterhood of the Spanish and Portuguese Synagogue, January 28, 1914, p. 18, March 9, 1914, p. 29, November 16, 1914, p. 49, and January 24, 1916, pp. 79–80.

Efforts to establish a downtown Talmud Torah were described in *La America,* July 30, 1915, p. 2, January 19, 1917, p. 6, February 2, 1917, p. 4, and February 9, 1917, p. 3. The schools of Angora and Monastir are discussed in articles of August 30, 1918, p. 1, September 6, 1918, p. 3, November 15, 1918, p. 1, January 10, 1919, p. 5, and December 12, 1919, p. 4. Articles describing the need for union and the establishment of a larger school are in articles of January 3, 1919, p. 5, and December 19, 1919, p. 2.

Articles describing Talmud Torah education in Harlem are found in *La America,* October 11, 1912, p. 1, March 14, 1913, p. 2, November 17, 1916, p. 3, February 23, 1917, p. 4, July 20, 1917, p. 1, August 3, 1917, p. 1, August 10, 1917, p. 1, May 24, 1918, p. 2, September 6, 1918, p. 6, and February 21, 1919, p. 5.

Teacher problems are reported in the minutes of the Sisterhood's Oriental Committee, December 21, 1914, p. 53, January 26, 1915, p. 57, February 8, 1916, p. 82, and April 11, 1916, p. 86. The report of the Sephardic teachers' organization is in *La America* April 17, 1925, p. 2. Hacker's comments are found in his article in *Jewish Social Service Quarterly* 3 (December, 1926): 39.

Articles dealing with the need for a chief rabbi for the Sephardic community in New York appeared in *La America,* September 20, 1912, p. 2, July 25, 1913, p. 2, October 1, 1913, p. 2, December 26, 1913, p. 4, April 9, 1915, p. 5, October 27, 1916, p. 1, and in other issues as well.

CHAPTER 4

Angel Pulido's *Españoles sin patria* was published in Madrid in 1905. For a discussion of Spain's interest in Sephardim and Jewish culture, see Yosef Hayim Yerushalmi's review essay in *American Jewish Historical Quarterly* 62 (December 1972): 180–89. For a discussion of Sephardic community life and cultural background in the Ottoman Empire, see Maír José Benardete's volume, *Hispanic Culture and Character of the Sephardic Jews* (New York, 1952). See also Marc Angel, *The Jews of Rhodes: The History of a Sephardic Community* (New York, 1978). On the economic decline of the communities of Turkey, see Benardete, chap. 6. The chapter opens with a quotation of David Porter from *Constantinople And Its Environs* ... (New York, 1835), vol. 2, p. 167. The description of the poverty in Rhodes by Leon Semach is drawn from a letter he wrote, which is now in the archives of the Alliance Israélite Universelle in Paris. See also Angel on Rhodes, p. 53.

The Sephardic desire for independence was noted by many observers. Cyrus Adler's speech to the Sisterhood of the Spanish and Portuguese Synagogue on November 27, 1916, is included in the minute book of the Oriental Committee of the Sisterhood. Louis Hacker, in "The Communal Life of the Sephardic Jews in New York City," *Jewish Social Service Quarterly* 3 (December 1926): 33, perceives the Sephardim as a "people apart."

Gadol's sympathy for Turkey is reflected in *La America* articles of January 25, 1918, p. 2, and February 29, 1924, p. 1. Articles discussing assistance that American Sephardim gave to Sephardic communities abroad appeared in the issues of August 23, 1912, p. 3, August 30, 1912, p. 1, September 11, 1912, p. 2, August 16, 1918, p. 2, and February 16, 1923, p. 4.

Information about the reception for Ambassador Henry Morgenthau appeared in the issues of February 25, 1916, p. 4, March 3, 1916, p. 3, and April 28, 1916, p. 2.

Information about the dramatic productions put on by the various societies can be be found in *La America*, February 3, 1911, p. 3, August 23, 1912, p. 2, October 4, 1912, p. 1, December 27, 1912, p. 2, December 17, 1915, p. 1, March 10, 1916, p. 1, April 7, 1916, p. 1, December 22, 1916, p. 4, December 29, 1916, p. 3, and in other issues as well. An article by Joseph Alhadeff praising drama among the Sephardim appeared in *La America*, April 2, 1920, p. 4. An article critical of the Sephardic dramatic productions is found in the issue of January 27, 1922, p. 2. For an account of the Sephardic theater in Seattle see the article by Marc Angel "The Sephardic Theatre of Seattle", *American Jewish Archives*, November 1973, pp. 156–60.

Articles dealing with the status of women in the Sephardic community appeared in *La America*, April 14, 1911, p. 2, April 21, 1911, p. 3, February 7, 1913, p. 1, February 14, 1913, pp. 2–3, February 28, 1913, p. 2, March 28, 1913, p. 2, and December 5, 1913, p. 1. The letter from Rabbi Nahoum appeared in *La America*, June 21, 1912, p. 2. Articles dealing with morality appeared in the issues of June 19, 1914, p. 4, September 5, 1918, p. 2, and July 11, 1919, p. 3. The Jewish Business Agency was discussed in the issue of February 10, 1922, p. 4. An article of March 12, 1920, p. 6, describes a wedding of a Sephardic man to an Ashkenazic woman, which had taken place in the Ashkenazic style. Gadol felt that Sephardic weddings were much nicer and that with much less expense, Sephardim had a better time. He wished the couple well!

The debates about the viability of the Judeo-Spanish language in the United States appeared in the pages of *La America*, December 9, 1910, p. 1,

June 20, 1913, p. 3, November 20, 1914, p. 2, November 27, 1914, p. 2, and March 12, 1915, p. 2. The first article on this topic appeared in the issue of November 25, 1910, p. 2.

David N. Barocas in his pamphlet, *The Broome and Allen Boys,* published by the Foundation for the Advancement of Sephardic Studies and Culture (New York, 1969), describes the problems of the children of the first Sephardic settlers on the Lower East Side and the tensions created by the forces of assimilation versus the forces of traditionalism.

Gadol believed that the publication of *La America* would convince Ashkenazim that the Sephardim were really Jews. His article of March 29, 1912, p. 2, notes that the Ashkenazim did indeed come to consider the Sephardim as real Jews. The union between Sephardim and Ashkenazim in Turkey was discussed in an article on February 23, 1912, p. 2. From time to time, Gadol felt compelled to defend the honor of Sephardim against attacks by Ashkenazim. *La America,* November 11, 1910, p. 1, rebuts an article in the Yiddish newspaper *Varheit,* which claimed that the only reason Sephardim came to the United States from Turkey was to avoid the draft. *La America,* September 27, 1912, p. 2, notes that the New York *Tribune* published an article that maligned the Sephardim, and indicates that Gadol planned to mount a response.

The Kretchmer case is described in *La America,* February 9, 1912, p. 1, March 15, 1912, p. 2, and March 29, 1912, p. 2. Other instances when Gadol came to the defense of the honor of the Sephardim are found in *La America,* February 16, 1912, p. 1, and January 21, 1916, p. 4.

Articles praising Ashkenazim appeared in *La America,* November 25, 1910, p. 3, December 29, 1911, p. 1, and November 7, 1913, p. 1. Articles critical of the Sephardim themselves appeared in a number of issues. In *La America,* May 19, 1911, pp. 2–3, an article laments the fact that Sephardim are not recognized as Jews by the Ashkenazim, and that the Sephardim are losing their distinctive creativity. The article by "Yehudi" appeared in *La America* on November 14, 1913, p. 5, and continued in the November 21, 1913, issue, p. 5.

Gadol believed that it was important for Sephardim to be involved in general Jewish organizations. The New York Kehillah attracted his attention. For a history of the Kehillah, see Arthur Goren, *New York Jews and the Quest for Community* (New York, 1970). Articles about the Kehillah and its relationship with the Sephardic community appeared in *La America,* February 3, 1911, p. 2, April 12, 1912, p. 1, May 3, 1912, p. 2, January 10, 1913, p. 3, April 18, 1913, p. 2, and May 1, 1914, p. 2. An article of February 27, 1914, p. 5, called on Sephardim to be more involved in the support of the United Hebrew Charities. The leadership of the Federation of Oriental Jews in mobilizing the Jewish community to help the Jews of the Balkans and Turkey suffering due to the war was noteworthy. This effort is discussed in *La America,* November 22, 1912, p. 2, November 29, 1912, p. 3, December 20, 1912, p. 4, and March 7, 1913, p. 2.

The religious life of the Sephardim suffered in the process of Americanization. Gadol argued that it was important for Sephardim to maintain their Jewish identity. Articles on this subject appeared in *La America*, November 25, 1910, p. 2, and January 5, 1912, p. 3. Articles reflecting a decline in religious observance are found in the issues of March 29, 1912, p. 1, September 24, 1915, p. 6, and August 23, 1917, p. 1. The problem of the missionaries is discussed by Jack Farhi in the issue of May 31, 1912, p. 1.

CHAPTER 5

The establishment of the Federation of Oriental Jews was announced in *La America*, March 22, 1912, p. 1. Subsequent articles dealing with the Federation appeared in the issues of April 5, 1912, p. 1, April 12, 1912, p. 1, April 26, 1912, p. 1, and May 10, 1912, p. 1. Dr. Pool's election as honorary president was announced in *La America*, May 24, 1912, p. 1.

Reports on the meetings and activities of the Federation of Oriental Jews were printed regularly by Gadol. See the issues of June 21, 1912, p. 2, July 5, 1912, p. 6, August 9, 1912, p. 2, September 6, 1912, p. 2, November 8, 1912, p. 2, December 27, 1912, p. 2, January 17, 1913, p. 2, May 2, 1913, p. 2, March 28, 1913, p. 2, April 4, 1913, p. 2, and May 16, 1913, p. 2.

Gadol records his unhappiness with the progress of the Federation in the issue of June 20, 1913, p. 2. Albert Amateau attempted to win greater support for the Federation in articles of August 1, 1913, p. 2, and August 22, 1913, p. 3. The issue of October 17, 1913, p. 1, reports that the Federation pursued a rape case in the Sephardic community and had succeeded in having the criminal prosecuted.

Financial data about the Federation is recorded in *La America*, October 31, 1913, p. 4, and November 7, 1913, p. 5. Gadol's dissatisfaction with the Federation prompted him to try to establish the Oriental Jewish Community of the City of New York. Articles describing the formation of this Community and reports on its mass meetings are found in the issues of November 14, 1913, p. 2, November 21, 1913, p. 2, November 28, 1913, pp. 1 and 2, December 12, 1913, p. 2, and December 19, 1913, p. 2.

Prior to this effort, Gadol had attempted to found a Sephardic self-help society. This effort did not succeed. His plans for this society were reported in *La America*, February 2, 1912, p. 1, May 2, 1913, p. 1, and August 1, 1913, p. 4.

The conflict between the new Community and the Sisterhood of Shearith Israel is reflected in *La America*, December 26, 1913, p. 1, and January 9, 1914, p. 2. The *American Hebrew*, December 12, 1913, p. 190, and December 19, 1913, p. 220, included articles about the founding of the new Community. The article in the December 12 issue was particularly annoying to the Sisterhood, since it reported the resolution of the Oriental

Jews that no organizations or individuals—including the Sisterhood—had the right to collect funds on behalf of the Oriental Jews.

The issue of January 2, 1914, p. 2, records Gadol's optimism about the progress of the Community. The issue of February 27, 1914, p. 5, gives a financial report and also notes that the Community would not tolerate attacks on the honor of any of its members. Albert Amateau had been criticized by various individuals and a letter was issued in his defense signed by many individuals, the first being Moise Gadol. The issue of March 6, 1914, p. 6, suggested that people keep charity boxes in their homes with the aim of raising money for hiring a chief rabbi.

The activities of the Federation of Oriental Jews continued, even while the Community was operating. Information about the Federation during this period is found in the issues of June 12, 1914, pp. 1 and 2, and September 11, 1914, p. 5. Negotiations between the Federation of Oriental Jews and the New York Kehillah concerning a chief rabbi for the Sephardim are reported in the issues of January 1, 1915, p. 1, February 12, 1915, p. 5, and June 11, 1915, p. 3.

For background material about Abraham Galante, see Abraham El-maleh, *Ha-professor Abraham Galante* (Jerusalem, 1954). Galante's role in the Jewish education of the Jews of Rhodes is described in Marc Angel, *The Jews of Rhodes* (New York, 1978), pp. 78–79.

Amateau's description of the poor financial state of the Federation of Oriental Jews is found in *La America,* December 18, 1914, p. 2. Gadol's harsh criticism of the Federation is the subject of an editorial on p. 4 of the issue of June 11, 1915. The crisis of inadequate leadership is discussed by Aharon Ben Eliyahu in *La America,* November 20, 1914, p. 4.

Gadol's criticism of the Federation and its president appear in articles of June 18, 1915, pp. 4 and 5. The issue of October 22, 1915, p. 4, also criticizes Gedelecia.

Articles urging that *Oriental* be abandoned in favor of *Sephardic* appeared in the issues of June 18, 1915, p. 4, October 29, 1915, p. 2, October 13, 1916, p. 3, October 27, 1916, p. 2, and in articles on p. 2 of the four November 1916 issues. This issue was not easily resolved, and other articles on the same topic appeared in the issues of June 22, 1917, p. 2, and July 5, 1918, p. 4.

Gadol argued for the formation of a new Sephardic Community in the issue of June 25, 1915, p. 4. The issue of December 3, 1915, p. 5, announced that there would be an open meeting to establish a central and independent, Sephardic Community. The issue of December 17, 1915, pp. 2–3, included a long and impassioned article urging the establishment of a united Sephardic Community in New York. Other articles on the Community appeared in the issues of July 16, 1915, p. 2, December 10, 1915, p. 2, and January 14, 1916, p. 2. The conflict between the Federation of Oriental Jews and the idea of a Sephardic Community is evidenced in articles of February 18, 1916, p. 6, March 10, 1916, p. 2, March 17, 1916, pp. 2–3, May 5, 1916, p. 4, and June 2, 1916, p. 1.

The effort to unite the Bikur Holim and the Ozer Dalim is reported in the issues of January 21, 1916, p. 2, February 11, 1916, p. 2, and February 25, 1916, p. 5.

The correspondence between Gadol and Magnes is recorded in *La America,* June 2, 1916, p. 4, and June 9, 1916, p. 2.

The decline of the Federation of Oriental Jews is noted in articles of June 16, 1916, p. 2, and December 1, 1916, p. 2. Agitation for the Community movement appeared in the issues of August 25, 1916, p. 2, and December 15, 1916, p. 2. Gadol's address to the Gallipoli Progressive Club in favor of a Sephardic Community was reported in *La America,* April 6, 1917, p. 3.

Articles concerning the establishment of a Sephardic Community appeared during the summer of 1917 in the issues of June 22, p. 6, July 6, pp. 1 and 2, July 13, p. 1, July 27, p. 5, August 3, p. 2, and August 17, p. 1.

Progress toward the establishment of a Sephardic Community was slow and the discussion dragged on for a number of years. Articles on this subject appeared in the issues of October 19, 1917, p. 2, May 3, 1918, p. 2, July 5, 1918, p. 3, January 9, 1920, p. 2, and January 23, 1920, p. 2. The issue of January 30, 1920, p. 2, announced that the Sephardic Community was actually formed.

The early development of the Community and reports of the meetings are described in articles of March 19, 1920, p. 2, and March 26, 1920, p. 2. The involvement of the Sisterhood of the Spanish and Portuguese Synagogue as well as of Henry S. Hendricks of Shearith Israel are referred to in articles of July 2, 1920, p. 4, and October 8, 1920, p. 4. The Berith Shalom became involved in the Community, as evidenced from an article of November 19, 1920, p. 6. The issue of March 11, 1921, pp. 2 and 3, contains a history of the movement toward the Sephardic Community and urges all Sephardic societies to affiliate.

Reports of the inner workings of the Community are found in the issues of April 8, 1921, p. 2, and April 22, 1921, p. 10. Dissatisfaction with the Community and demands for the establishment of yet another new Sephardic Community are discussed in *La America,* December 2, 1921, p. 3, and December 30, 1921, p. 2. In the issue of January 6, 1922, p. 2, an article by Albert Matarasso urged the establishment of a Central Sephardic organization.

Albert Amateau blamed Gadol for ruining the Federation of Oriental Jews. Gadol discusses this charge in the issue of January 27, 1922, p. 4.

Bohor Hanna's article in favor of a new Sephardic Community appeared in *La America,* February 23, 1923, p. 4. Other articles on this communal movement can be found in issues of March 2, 1923, p. 2, March 23, 1923, p. 4, April 27, 1923, pp. 1 and 2, May 9, 1923, p. 4, June 1, 1923, p. 2, May 2, 1924, p. 5, and in front-page articles of March 6 and March 27, 1925.

Louis Hacker, "The Communal Life of the Sephardic Jews in New York City," *Jewish Social Service Quarterly* 3 (December 1926): 36, stated that the Community had no definite program. David de Sola Pool thought the Community was stable and responsible and so stated in his "Report of the Committee on a Progressive Policy in the Congregation" (April 22, 1927), p. 7, a document in the possession of Congregation Shearith Israel. The *Shearith Israel Bulletin*, February 1927, p. 7, referred to the Community favorably.

CHAPTER 6

A discussion of Shearith Israel's relations with the new Sephardic immigrants appears in David and Tamar de Sola Pool, *An Old Faith in the New World* (New York, 1955), pp. 43 ff. See also Marc Angel, "The Sephardim of the United States," in the *American Jewish Year Book*, vol. 74 (1973), pp. 101–7. Pool delivered a sermon at Congregation Shearith Israel on March 9, 1912, urging his congregants to assist the newly arrived Sephardic immigrants. Entitled "The Numbering of the People," the sermon is included in *Rabbi David de Sola Pool: Selections from Six Decades of Sermons, Addresses and Writings,* ed. Marc Angel (New York, 1980), pp. 28–32.

The activities of the Oriental Committee of the Sisterhood of the Spanish and Portuguese Synagogue are reported in a minute book in the possession of the Sisterhood. The first entry is dated November 24, 1913. David de Sola Pool was then serving as chairman. The minute book runs through December 26, 1916. The minutes of the trustees of Congregation Shearith Israel, vols. 8 and 9—in the possession of Congregation Shearith Israel—contain a number of references to the Sephardic immigrants. The *Shearith Israel Bulletin* was published regularly in order to inform members of activities in the synagogue and community. A number of issues included articles relating to the Sephardic immigrants. In order to get a balanced picture of the relationship between Shearith Israel and the new Sephardic arrivals, it is necessary to study the source materials of Shearith Israel as well as *La America*. In this way, the attitudes and positions of both groups can be seen in context.

Gadol's initial admiration of Shearith Israel is recorded in his article of November 25, 1910, p. 4. David N. Barocas, in his pamphlet, *The Broome and Allen Boys*, pp. 8–9, describes the role of the Sisterhood of the Spanish and Portuguese Synagogue and its settlement houses on the Lower East Side.

The meeting of February 13, 1912, proved to be controversial. An account of the meeting and subsequent discussions concerning it are found in *La America*, February 16, 1912, p. 3, February 23, 1912, p. 1, and March 1, 1912, p. 1.

A description of the Sisterhood Purim celebration for the Oriental Jews is to be found in *La America*, March 1, 1912, p. 1, and March 8, 1912, p. 2. Other Sisterhood activities on behalf of the Oriental Jews are described in *La America*, April 12, 1912, p. 1, May 31, 1912, p. 1, June 28, 1912, p. 1, and July 12, 1912, p. 2.

Gadol's criticism of Shearith Israel's free High Holy Day services appears in the issue of September 27, 1912, p. 1, and again in the issue of October 17, 1913, p. 2. The Sisterhood Sukkot celebration is described in *La America*, October 4, 1912, p. 2.

The dedication of the synagogue at 86 Orchard Street is described in *La America*, December 5, 1913, p. 2. The minutes of the Sisterhood's Oriental Committee dealing with the dedication are from November 24, 1913, pp. 2–3, and December 11, 1913, pp. 5–7. At the latter meeting, Benyunes "expressed the belief that the Oriental colonies were in sympathy with the Sisterhood activities." The minutes of the trustees of Shearith Israel, vol. 8, December 2, 1913, p. 449, indicate that the board, upon receiving a communication from the Sisterhood, agreed to let the synagogue at 86 Orchard Street use two Torah scrolls and related items.

Correspondence between Mendes and Gadol appeared in *La America*, December 12, 1913, p. 4, and December 26, 1913, p. 2.

The idea of establishing a *kolel*—a union of Sephardim that would include Shearith Israel and the Oriental Jews—was discussed in *La America* of February 6, 1914, p. 1, and March 6, 1914, p. 2. In the minutes of the trustees of Shearith Israel, vol. 8, January 24, 1914, p. 455, Mayer Swaab, Jr., urged that Shearith Israel support the cause of a *kolel*, arguing that the need among "our Sephardic brethren from the Orient of recent immigration was so imperative that it was our duty to unite with them." The trustees resolved to join the *kolel* and to support it financially.

Gadol's anger at the takeover of the uptown Talmud Torah by the Sisterhood is recorded in the issue of March 20, 1914, p. 1. His attack on the Sisterhood's Purim party appeared in *La America*, March 20, 1914, p. 2. Mendes responded in a letter, *La America*, April 3, 1914, p. 2, which was followed by a refutation by Gadol.

Articles dealing with the activities of the Sisterhood appeared in the issues of January 30, 1914, p. 1, February 13, 1914, p. 2, July 24, 1914, p. 3, and August 21, 1914, p. 2.

Gadol's critique of the associate membership arrangement is recorded in *La America*, August 28, 1914, p. 4. This topic is considered in the minutes of the trustees of Shearith Israel, vol. 8, March 5, 1914, p. 459, March 16, 1914, p. 461, and April 7, 1914, p. 461. Benyunes's defense of the Sisterhood's settlement house is found in *La America*, September 4, 1914, p. 4. *La America*, September 18, 1914, p. 2, reports Gadol's opinions when the Sephardic Zionist organization was refused a room in the Sisterhood's settlement house. The minutes of the Oriental Committee of the Sisterhood, October 13, 1914, p. 45, mention this problem.

On the feud concerning the Talmud Torah, see *La America*, October

15, 1915, p. 6. The question of the Talmud Torah is also discussed in the minutes of the Sisterhood's Oriental Committee, December 17, 1913, pp. 9–11.

The continued progress of the Sisterhood's settlement house is reported in *La America,* March 24, 1916, p. 2. Praise of the synagogue services of Shearith Israel is given in the issue of October 10, 1916, p. 2.

The decision to buy 133 Eldridge Street is reported in the issue of February 15, 1918, p. 5. Contributions toward this project were reported in *La America,* March 8, 1918, p. 3. The dedication of the synagogue there was described in the issue of May 17, 1918, p. 2, while the text of the sermon given at the dedication of the synagogue by Rabbi Aharon Benezra appeared in the issues of May 24, 1918, p. 4, and May 31, 1918, p. 5. The steady progress and Gadol's own involvement are reflected in the issue of July 9, 1920, pp. 1 and 4. New tensions arose, as can be seen from *La America,* September 16, 1921, p. 2, February 3, 1922, p. 2, and October 17, 1924, p. 7. The following issue ran the refutations of Mortimer Menken and Joseph Benyunes. Pool's letter to Mortimer Menken is in the archives of Congregation Shearith Israel.

The deterioration in the relationship between Shearith Israel and Berith Shalom is reflected in the minutes of the joint meeting of the trustees of Shearith Israel, the Sisterhood of the Spanish and Portuguese Synagogue and the Berith Shalom held on December 2, 1924 in the trustee room of the Spanish and Portuguese Synagogue. Problems leading up to that meeting are recorded in the minutes of the trustees of Shearith Israel, vol. 9, October 23, 1924, p. 289, November 17, 1924, p. 291, and November 25, 1924, p. 296. The decision of the Berith Shalom to break formal ties with Shearith Israel is reported in the minutes of the trustees of Shearith Israel, vol. 9, June 3, 1925, p. 310.

CHAPTER 7

Gadol gives an account of how he founded *La America* in the issue of December 29, 1911, p. 2. The issue of September 11, 1912, p. 1, offers a glimpse of the publication record of *La America* since its inception.

Articles stressing the importance of this journal appeared on April 14, 1911, p. 1, April 21, 1911, p. 1, and May 12, 1911, p. 1. The latter issue also included a front-page article in Yiddish explaining what *La America* was. Gadol wanted the Ashkenazim to recognize the Jewishness of Sephardim.

The very first issue of *La America* contained an article on p. 2 describing the differences between the Democratic and Republican parties. On the bottom of p. 3, Gadol offers his readers an English lesson; in the issue of February 17, 1911, p. 1, he announced that he would publish English phrases and vocabulary that could be collected and made into a booklet in order to help one learn English. An article on the history of *La America* appeared on December 29, 1911, p. 3. An article on the importance of the home, by Jack Farhi, appeared on p. 2 of the issue of April 28, 1911. An anonymous author known only as Miss A. wrote a series of articles on various topics. The issue of February 16, 1912, p. 2, discussed the importance of willpower. The issue of April 26, 1912, p. 3, lists the questions asked on an examination to become an American citizen.

Gadol listed the names of his correspondents from time to time. See for example the issues of December 22, 1911, p. 1, June 14, 1912, p. 1, and October 24, 1913, p. 1. His agreement with Moise Solam to write humor for *La America* is reported in the issue of September 12, 1913, p. 1. Gadol's desire to gain popular support by changing the format of the journal is reported in *La America*, January 7, 1916, p. 1.

The financial problems of *La America* are reflected in the issues of November 18, 1910, p. 3, November 25, 1910, p. 1, and February 3, 1911, p. 1. In the issue of November 8, 1912, p. 1, Gadol assured contributors he was not making personal profits from the contributions to *La America*. A long article describing the financial difficulties since its inception appeared in the issue of October 11, 1912, p. 2. Pleas for support for *La America* appeared regularly, including the issues of May 24, 1912, p. 1, May 31, 1912, p. 1, July 12, 1912, p. 1, and October 18, 1912, p. 2. The financial distress of *La America* is described in the issues of November 22, 1912, p. 1, and December 6, 1912, pp. 1 and 2.

In spite of the progress being made in 1913, financial problems still weighed heavy on Gadol. On March 28, 1913, p. 1, he announced the doubling of subscription rates to three dollars per year in order to meet costs. On April 25, 1913, p. 1, he again offered a history of *La America* and stressed its present financial trouble. The issue of July 25, 1913, p. 2, indicated that the office of *La America* had been robbed, but the issue of August 1, 1913, p. 1, reported that the stolen machine had been returned. A review of the progress of *La America* during 1913 appeared in the issue of December 12, 1913, p. 1. Gadol claimed one thousand subscribers in the issue of November 12, 1915, p. 2.

Gadol's financial ventures aside from *La America* are indicated in the issues of July 19, 1912, p. 2, June 19, 1914, p. 3, July 3, 1914, p. 4, and August 28, 1914, p. 3. A book service was announced in the issue of April 21, 1911, p. 2. The project of publishing small pamphlets was announced in the issue of December 8, 1916, p. 3.

Gadol's confidence in the justness of his work is stated eloquently in an article of March 1, 1912, p. 3. His dissatisfaction with the low level of support received from Sephardim of New York is reported in the issue of December 13, 1912, p. 2.

Gadol's refusal to accept money in return for publication of articles is evident from articles of March 1, 1912, p. 3, and September 8, 1916, p. 3. Gadol's insistence on printing only the truth in spite of personal dangers is expressed in an article on p. 2 of the issue of July 11, 1913.

Gadol's feud with the Monastirlis can be traced through the issues of January 3, 1913, p. 2, January 10, 1913, p. 2, and January 17, 1913, p. 2.

Gadol's running dispute with *La Aguila* can be followed in the issues of *La America,* February 23, 1912, p. 3, March 1, 1912, p. 3, March 8, 1912, p. 3, March 22, 1912, p. 2, March 29, 1912, p. 3, and April 5, 1912, p. 3.

A discussion of *El Progresso,* later known as *La Boz del Pueblo,* appeared in *La America,* December 17, 1915, p. 3, and September 22, 1916, p. 5.

Gadol's efforts to strengthen the financial condition of *La America* are described in articles of February 20, 1920, p. 2, February 27, 1920, p. 2, March 5, 1920, p. 2, March 12, 1920, p. 2, January 7, 1921, p. 2, and February 16, 1923, p. 2.

Gadol struggled to form partnerships that would insure the viability of *La America;* but none succeeded for long. The Ladino Publishing Company is noted in *La America,* April 6, 1923, p. 8, and is discussed in the issue of March 30, 1923, p. 1. Other articles on the Ladino Publishing Company appear in the issues of April 20, 1923, p. 1, May 9, 1923, p. 3, May 11, 1923, p. 2, May 18, 1923, p. 1, and May 18, 1923, p. 3.

The failure of the partnership in the Ladino Publishing Company resulted in the suspension of *La America* for over four months. Discussion of the problems appeared in *La America* June 8, 1923, p. 1, and October 26, 1923, p. 2. That Gadol joined Covo and Varsano to form the La America Publishing Company is noted in the issue of November 16, 1923, p. 1. The breakdown of this partnership was announced on p. 1 of the issue of July 3, 1925. That was the last issue of *La America* ever to appear.

Material dealing with the struggle between *La America* and *La Vara,* and Gadol's battle with the Sephardic Brotherhood, is found in *La America* during 1922 in the issues of January 20, p. 2, August 15, p. 4, August 29, p. 4, October 6, p. 2, October 13, p. 4, October 27, p. 4, November 10, p. 4, and November 24, p. 4. In 1923, articles on this matter appeared in the issues of February 9, p. 4, May 4, p. 4, May 11, p. 3, May 25, p. 5, and June 8, p. 4. In 1925, *La America* dealt with this struggle in the issues of January 23, p. 2, February 6, p. 2, February 27, p. 2, March 13, p. 2, and March 20, p. 2. The transcript of the trial in 1925 is recorded in the issues of March 20, p. 5, March 27, p. 5, April 10, pp. 2 and 7, and May 1, p. 3. Later articles appeared in the issues of April 24, 1925, p. 5, May 8, 1925, p. 5, and May 22, 1925, p. 2.

La Vara printed inflammatory material and attacks on Gadol regularly during the time when the two newspapers were competing with each other. The item that finally led Gadol to take legal action appeared in *La Vara,* June 15, 1923 (number 42). The conclusion of the court battle was described in *La Vara,* May 15, 1925, p. 1.

The relevant minutes of the Sephardic Brotherhood on this dispute were made available by Marius Pilo. These are minutes of the meetings of

January 31, February 8, and March 3, 1925. Gadol's own account of the case is given in a pamphlet, *Christopher Columbus Was a Jew* (New York, 1941), p. 15. Albert Amateau also provided a one-page description of his memory of the case.

Information about Gadol's life following 1925 is drawn from *La Vara*, July 30, 1937, p. 9, August 13, 1937, p. 9, and in a letter he wrote to *La Vara*. This letter is in the possession of Joel Halio-Torres, grandson of Albert Torres, who made this letter available, together with his translation. Susan Halio also lent her cooperation. Notice of the death of Rachel Gadol appeared in *La Vara*, July 14, 1933. Gadol printed a short announcement in *La Vara*, September 30, 1938, p. 8. Articles by Gadol about Abraham Yehuda appeared in *La Vara*, in the issues of February 21, and February 28, 1941.

Amateau's account of the reasons for Gadol's failure are contained in the text of his reminiscences which he provided.

A file of letters typed by Gadol in 1938 and 1939 was found by Denise Gluck and Joseph Tarica in the archives of Shearith Israel. These letters demonstrate the despondency of Gadol as well as his emotional instability during the latter period of his life. He was a bitter man, believing he was right and almost everyone else was wrong.

CHAPTER 8

H. P. Mendes was one of the founders of the Zionist Organization of America and spent a year in the Holy Land. Pool lived in Palestine for several years following World War I. See David and Tamar de Sola Pool, *An Old Faith In The New World* (New York, 1955), pp. 405–8. Pool wrote an essay "Palestine And The Diaspora," which was originally published by the Federation of American Zionists in May 1913. It is reprinted in *Rabbi David de Sola Pool: Selections from Six Decades of Sermons, Addresses and Writings,* ed. Marc Angel (New York, 1980), pp. 167–80.

A Zionist mass rally is described in *La America,* November 18, 1910, p. 2. The issue of February 23, 1912, p. 2, notes the progress of the Zionist movement in Ruschuk.

Gadol's particular Zionist ideas are to be perceived in the issues of November 18, 1910, p. 2, March 1, 1912, p. 1, and April 5, 1912, p. 2. His opinion that Sephardim should not go to Spain but rather to the Holy Land is expressed in the issue of August 16, 1912, p. 2.

A mass rally for Zionism is the subject of articles on January 31, 1913, p. 1, and February 7, 1913, p. 2.

The Maccabee society is discussed in the issues of February 6, 1914, p. 2, and March 13, 1914, p. 2. The formation of the Zionist Sepharadim Society is recorded in *La America,* July 24, 1914, p. 1, July 31, 1914, p. 2; the success of its first meeting is recorded in the issue of August 7, 1914, p. 2.

More news about the group is found in *La America,* August 21, 1914, p. 5, August 28, 1914, p. 3, October 2, 1914, p. 1, October 9, 1914, p. 2, December 25, 1914, p. 2, January 1, 1915, p. 1, and January 8, 1915, pp. 1 and 5. The decline of this group is demonstrated in *La America,* May 7, 1915, p. 8, June 18, 1915, p. 1, August 13, 1915, p. 3, and March 10, 1916, p. 2.

The reorganization of the Maccabee Society of Sephardim is traced in the issues of May 5, 1916, p. 1, September 27, 1916, p. 3, October 20, 1916, p. 3, and December 29, 1916, p. 5. Gadol's antagonism to this group is evident in the issue of January 5, 1917, p. 2.

Gadol's unhappiness at the exclusion of Sephardim from general Zionist groups is expressed in an article of July 7, 1916, pp. 2–3.

Information about a Zionist Sephardic propaganda committee is found in *La America,* January 12, 1917, p. 1. An article praising Zionism appeared in the issue of April 27, 1917, p. 2.

Gadol's difference of opinion with the general Zionist movement is expressed in the issues of May 11, 1917, p. 2, and May 18, 1917, p. 3.

Efforts to gain the assistance of Spain on behalf of the Sephardim in the Holy Land are recorded in *La America,* May 25, 1917, p. 1, June 8, 1917, p. 1, and June 29, 1917, p. 6.

The success of the Zionist rally sponsored by Greek-speaking Jews is recorded in *La America,* November 15, 1918, pp. 2 and 6.

Articles urging active Sephardic participation in the Zionist movement and in their own Zionist societies appeared in *La America,* May 7, 1920, p. 2, May 28, 1920, p. 2, December 2, 1921, p. 2, and February 3, 1922, p. 4. On page 6 of the same issue it was announced that a Sephardic Zionist Maccabee Society was started in Harlem. Progress of that group appeared in articles of March 24, 1922, p. 1, January 19, 1923, p. 4, and February 23, 1923, p. 4.

Articles prodding Sephardim to move directly to the Holy Land appeared in the issues of April 4, 1913, p. 2, May 2, 1913, p. 1, and August 28, 1914, p. 2. Gadol's belief that Christians would accept a Jewish presence in the Holy Land is reflected in articles of February 17, 1911, pp. 1 and 2, and May 9, 1913, p. 2. Other articles dealing with Sephardic Zionism are found in the issues of August 29, 1913, pp. 2–3, November 13, 1914, p. 2, May 21, 1915, p. 5, and March 31, 1916, p. 6. In the issue of September 28, 1917, p. 3, Gadol reports that the Reform temples in New York made no reference at all to the idea of returning to the Holy Land.

The resolutions concerning the establishment of the State of Israel by the Union of Sephardic Congregations are included in a printed account of the convention, copies of which are in the possession of the Union of Sephardic Congregations, 8 West Seventieth Street, New York.

CHAPTER 9

Albert Matarasso (1890–1971) brought a new flair to Sephardic oratory in New York. Matarasso was born in Salonika and came to New York at the age of twenty-five. He was one of the few well-educated Sephardic immigrants. He was fluent in Hebrew and knew Turkish and French as well. His main love was Jewish education. David N. Barocas, in *Albert Matarasso and His Ladino*, published by the Foundation for the Advancement of Sephardic Studies and Culture (New York, 1969), states (p. 16): He [Matarasso] was endowed with the silver tongue of an accomplished orator. His Ladino and Hebrew eloquence attracted large audiences. Were there speakers invited to take part in a solemn memorial service, Matarasso was one of them to speak or to deliver a moving invocation. Was a bond rally to take place, he was there at the invitation of its sponsors to move the masses with patriotic oratory. His talks abounded in profound scholarship, in philosophical reflection and in humor."

Matarasso's description of the difficulty faced by a new Sephardic immigrant appears in the Barocas volume, pp. 30–31. The economic condition of Sephardic immigrants is described in an article, "A New Communal Need," *Jewish Charities*, March 29, 1913, pp. 11–12.

In the first issue of *La America*, November 11, 1910, p. 4, Gadol asked his readers who knew of available jobs to write to the editor and those who sought jobs were also asked to let the editor know. His hope was to print the information in the newspaper so that people could find employment. As it turned out, he did most of this work personally, not in the pages of *La America*.

Articles describing the poverty of Sephardim and their difficulty in finding jobs are found in *La America*, November 25, 1910, p. 2, and January 12, 1912, p. 2.

Articles dealing with the Schinasi brothers appeared in the issues of February 17, 1911, p. 3, January 23, 1914, p. 2, June 5, 1914, p. 5, and October 10, 1919, p. 5. Leon Schinasi's contribution to a Christmas fund was noted in *La America*, December 26, 1919.

An article of January 19, 1912, p. 2, indicates the positive qualities of Sephardic workers. Miss A's article on initiative and system appeared in *La America*, March 8, 1912, p. 3.

David Barocas described the effect of poverty on the Sephardic family in his pamphlet, *The Broome and Allen Boys*, pp. 6–7. Gadol's words to the Sephardic young ladies who were on strike are reported in *La America*, January 31, 1913, p. 2. The strike in the battery factories is reported in the issues of September 15, 1916, p. 2, and September 27, 1916, p. 5.

Economic progress among Sephardim and the establishment of thriving businesses are reported in *La America*, February 21, 1913, p. 1, January 21, 1916, p. 2, February 11, 1916, p. 3, May 19, 1916, p. 3, September 1, 1916, p. 3, October 27, 1916, p. 5, and August 6, 1920, p. 5. The announcement that Jack Hananiah received a dentist's diploma was reported in the issue of June 8, 1917, p. 4. The tragic circumstances concerning his death were reported in the issues of January 16, 1920, p. 1, and March 12, 1920, p. 1. Ely Hananiah became a dentist, as recorded in *La America,* June 17, 1921, p. 4. The appointment of Maír José Benardete to teach in a New York public school was announced in *La America,* December 1, 1916, p. 4.

The information about Louis Rousso was drawn from an interview with Rousso and his son Ely at the offices of Russ Togs, in February 1979.

Other information relating to the economic life of the Sephardim in New York is found in articles of August 8, 1922, p. 2, August 15, 1922, p. 4, March 23, 1923, p. 4, September 19, 1924, p. 2, and February 6, 1925, p. 3.

The significant economic and social progress made by the Sephardim is reported by Louis Hacker in his study, "The Communal Life of the Sephardic Jews in New York," *Jewish Social Service Quarterly* 3 (December 1926): 38.

CHAPTER 10

Pool's estimates of the number of Sephardim living in cities throughout the United States are found in his article in the *American Jewish Year Book* vol. 15 (1913–14), p. 212. Pool also discusses the efforts made to divert immigration from New York. This topic is discussed in the minutes of the Oriental Committee of the Sisterhood of the Spanish and Portuguese Synagogue, October 13, 1914, pp. 43–44, and December 11, 1916, p. 95. The role of HIAS in this matter is mentioned by Mark Wischnitzer, *Visas to Freedom* (New York, 1956), p. 68. The efforts of the New York Kehillah are noted by Arthur Goren, *New York Jews and the Quest for Community* (New York, 1970), p. 69. *La America,* January 12, 1912, p. 2, gives a listing of Sephardic communities outside New York City.

The Raritan community is noted in *La America,* May 24, 1912, p. 1. Information about the community in New Brunswick is found in the issues of October 15, 1915, p. 5, October 20, 1916, p. 5, and February 16, 1917, p. 6. The Philadelphia community is discussed in the issues of July 16, 1915, p. 4, and January 5, 1917, p. 4.

Articles and correspondence concerning the Sephardic community of Rochester appeared fairly often in the pages of *La America.* Articles of special interest are found in the issues of June 21, 1912, p. 3, July 5, 1912, p. 2, September 6, 1912, p. 2, July 25, 1913, p. 2, August 15, 1913, p. 3, January 16, 1914, p. 1, March 20, 1914, p. 1, June 26, 1914, p. 3, July 3, 1914, p. 1, July 17, 1914, p. 4, October 16, 1914, p. 6, January 1, 1915, p. 1, July 16, 1915, p. 3, July 23, 1915, p. 1, September 3, 1915, p. 4, September 8, 1916, p. 1, December 1,

1916, p. 2, January 19, 1917, p. 6, March 19, 1920, p. 6, and March 10, 1922, p. 2.

Articles dealing with the community in Chicago appeared on December 9, 1910, p. 2, June 21, 1912, p. 3, September 11, 1912, pp. 1–2, June 19, 1914, p. 3, July 21, 1916, p. 6, November 23, 1917, p. 2, and February 10, 1922, p. 2.

The Sephardim in Cincinnati are the subject of an article by Maurice Hexter, "The Dawn of a Problem," *Jewish Charities*, December 1913, pp. 2–5. Articles in *La America* referring to Cincinnati appeared in the issues of April 14, 1911, p. 3, May 17, 1912, p. 2, January 10, 1913, p. 1, September 5, 1913, p. 3, February 13, 1914, p. 1, August 4, 1916, p. 1, August 25, 1916, p. 4, and March 24, 1922, p. 2.

The Sephardim of Indianapolis are discussed in the issues of January 25, 1918, p. 3, and May 6, 1921, p. 2.

The history of the Sephardic community of Atlanta is discussed in an article written by Rabbi Joseph Cohen in *The Sephardi*, November 1954, pp. 2–3. *La America*, over the years, included much information about the community in Atlanta. Among the articles of interest are: in 1912, the issues of March 22, p. 2, May 24, p. 2, August 23, p. 2, September 6, p. 2, October 11, p. 2, and December 27, p. 3; in 1913, the issue of September 5, p. 3; in 1914, the issues of February 6, p. 1, July 10, p. 4, July 31, p. 4, September 11, p. 2, and October 30, p. 6. Other articles appeared on January 22, 1915, p. 6, December 22, 1916, p. 4, December 31, 1920, p. 4, and April 28, 1922, p. 4. See also Sol Beton, *Sephardim and a History of Congregation Or Veshalom* (Atlanta, 1981).

The history of the Sephardic community in Montgomery is recorded in a pamphlet by Rubin Hanan, *History of Etz Ahayem Congregation* (Montgomery, 1962). Articles dealing with the community in Montgomery appeared in *La America*, June 21, 1912, p. 3, March 21, 1913, p. 2, June 6, 1913, p. 2, and October 1, 1915, p. 6.

A history of the Jews from Rhodes in Los Angeles is provided in the *Dedication Book* of the Sephardic Hebrew Center of Los Angeles, 1967. Articles and correspondence dealing with the community in Los Angeles appeared fairly often in the pages of *La America* over the years. Articles of interest are to be found in the issues of March 22, 1912, p. 2, June 14, 1912, p. 2, September 11, 1912, p. 1, October 4, 1912, p. 2, November 21, 1913, p. 5, February 19, 1915, p. 6, December 15, 1916, p. 6, February 16, 1917, p. 5, June 14, 1918, p. 4, March 5, 1920, p. 6, April 2, 1920, p. 4, April 15, 1921, p. 6, and May 11, 1923, p. 1.

Articles about San Francisco appeared in the issues of February 23, 1912, p. 2, and January 26, 1912, p. 2.

News from the community in Portland appeared in the issues of March 1, 1912, p. 2, March 29, 1912, p. 3, April 12, 1912, p. 3, July 12, 1912, p. 2, July 23, 1915, p. 6, April 27, 1917, p. 5, and May 11, 1917, p. 4.

Information about the Sephardic community of Seattle is available in an article written by Rabbi William Greenberg, "History of Ezra Bessaroth," which appeared in the *Dedication Program of Ezra Bessaroth*, Seattle, 1970. See also Marc Angel, "Notes on the Early History of Seattle's Sephardic Community," *Western States Jewish Historical Quarterly*, October 1974, pp. 22–30. An important study of the community is the master's dissertation of Albert Adatto, "Sephardim and the Seattle Sephardic Community" (University of Washington, 1939). See also the articles by Marc Angel, "The Sephardic Theatre of Seattle," *American Jewish Archives*, November 1973, pp. 156–60, and "'Progress'—Seattle's Sephardic Monthly, 1934–35," *The American Sephardi*, Autumn 1971, pp. 91–95.

La America included many references to life in the Sephardic community of Seattle. Among them are the issues of December 22, 1911, p. 4, and in 1912, issues of January 12, p. 2, January 26, p. 2, February 2, p. 2, February 16, p. 2, March 1, p. 3, March 8, p. 2, March 22, p. 2, March 29, p. 3, May 10, p. 2, May 31, p. 1, June 21, p. 3, July 5, p. 6, August 2, pp. 2–3, August 16, pp. 2 and 3, August 30, p. 3, October 11, p. 2, October 18, p. 1, and December 20, p. 1. See also the issues of November 21, 1913, p. 1, and January 9, 1914, p. 2. In 1915, articles appeared in the issues of April 2, p. 6, April 23, p. 5, July 16, p. 4, August 6, p. 3, August 27, p. 6, September 24, p. 5, October 15, p. 5, November 5, p. 3, December 3, p. 3, and December 24, p. 5. In 1916, articles about the Sephardim of Seattle appeared in the issues of February 11, p. 4, March 3, p. 5, March 24, p. 5, April 14, p. 7, June 9, p. 3, June 23, p. 5, July 7, p. 4, and November 24, p. 6. Later articles about the community appeared in the issues of August 31, 1917, p. 6, September 7, 1917, p. 4, and November 2, 1917, p. 4. During 1918, articles appeared in the issues of February 22, p. 4, March 1, pp. 1 and 5, March 8, p. 5, March 15, p. 5, May 10, p. 3, July 19, p. 1, and August 16, p. 1. In 1919, articles appeared in the issues of February 14, p. 5, April 25, p. 5, and October 24, p. 6. Other articles appeared in the issues of June 3, 1921, p. 2, August 5, 1921, p. 4, February 17, 1922, p. 2, April 21, 1922, p. 2, and March 2, 1923, p. 3.

CHAPTER 11

Albert Matarasso's analysis of the situation of Sephardim in the United States and his prayer for a greater future are contained in David N. Barocas, *Albert Matarasso And His Ladino* (New York, 1969). The quotation that appears in the beginning of this chapter is from p. 71.

The Sephardic Bulletin, published monthly by the Sephardic Jewish Community of New York, beginning November 1928, listed itself as "a bulletin for every Sephardic home." It included a section in Judeo–Spanish.

A sociological survey of American-born Sephardim of Judeo-Spanish background is included in Marc Angel, "The Sephardim of the United

States: An Exploratory Study," in *American Jewish Year Book*, vol. 74 (1973), pp. 114–36.

David N. Barocas, in his pamphlet, *The Broome and Allen Boys* (New York, 1969), described the process of growing up on the Lower East Side as experienced by young Sephardic boys.

Information about the Sephardic Jewish Community of New York, Inc. was drawn from the minutes of the Community, now in the possession of Congregation Shearith Israel in New York. A comprehensive study of the Community is available in an article by Joseph M. Papo, "The Sephardic Jewish Community of New York," in *Studies in Sephardic Culture*, ed. Marc Angel (New York, 1980), pp. 65–94. Louis Hacker's comments about the Community appeared in his article, "The Communal Life of the Sephardic Jews in New York City," in *Jewish Social Service Quarterly* 3 (December 1926): 36. Pool's evaluation appeared in an unpublished document, "Report of the Committee on a Progressive Policy in the Congregation," April 22, 1927, p. 7. This document is in the possession of Congregation Shearith Israel.

The establishment of the Union of Sephardic Congregations can be traced in the minutes of the trustees of Congregation Shearith Israel, vol. 9, January 5, 1928, p. 411, April 3, 1928, p. 430, November 12, 1928, p. 462, and May 7, 1929, p. 487. The *Shearith Israel Bulletin* of May 2, 1929, p. 2, and May 25, 1930, p. 3, carried articles about the Union. In Pool's report to the congregation of April 22, 1927, p. 9, the idea of a union of Sephardic congregations is presented. The *Sephardic Bulletin* of May, 1929, carried a front-page article about the formation of the Union of Sephardic Congregations. The officers elected were: president, Dr. David de Sola Pool; vice-presidents, Dr. Solomon Solis-Cohen of Philadelphia, Captain Charles Montefiore of Montreal, Samuel Coen of New York; secretary, Simon S. Nessim; treasurer, Matthew Levy; directors: Dr. Cyrus Adler of Philadelphia, Reverend Charles Bender, Robert Franco, Henry S. Hendricks, Joseph Josephs, John H. Levy, Dr. Abraham A. Newman, Captain N. Taylor Phillips. At a meeting held on April 14, 1929, the following congregations were represented: Shearith Israel of New York, Kahl Kol Israel Synagogue of New York, Sephardic Jewish Community of New York, Sephardic Brotherhood of America, Light of Israel of Monastir of Rochester, Ahavath Shalom of Monastir, New York, Shearith Israel of Janina of New York, and Kehila Kadosha of Janina of New York. Out-of-town congregations that had already joined the Union were Mikveh Israel of Philadelphia and Shearith Israel of Montreal. The Union printed annual reports and reports of conventions irregularly.

The Central Sephardic Jewish Community of America is discussed in an article by Joseph Papo, "The Sephardic Community of America," *Reconstructionist* 12 (1946): 13–14. The history and activities of this organization can be traced through its bulletin, *The Sephardi*; a complete set is in the possession of Congregation Shearith Israel.

Information about the Pan American Union of Sephardic Communities and the World Federation of Sephardi Communities is drawn from correspondence and documents of the Central Sephardic Jewish Community of America, in the possession of Congregation Shearith Israel. Copies of the *World Sephardi*, published by the American branch of the World Sephardi Federation, are in the possession of Congregation Shearith Israel, as are other documents and correspondence.

CHAPTER 12

Information about the contemporary sociological status of American Sephardim is available in Marc Angel, "The Sephardim of the United States: An Exploratory Study," in *American Jewish Year Book*, vol. 74 (1973). See also Hayyim Cohen, "Sephardi Jews in the United States, Marriage with Ashkenazim," *Dispersion and Unity* 13–14 (1971–72): 151–60.

Other works relating to the sociology of American Sephardim—but that do not focus on Sephardim of Judeo-Spanish background— are Morris Gross, *Learning Readiness in Two Jewish Groups* (New York, 1967); and Victor Sanua, "A Study of Adjustment of Sephardic Jews in the New York Metropolitan Area," *Jewish Journal of Sociology* 9 (June 1967): 25–33. A book dealing with the Syrian Jewish community was written by Joseph Sutton, *Magic Carpet: Aleppo-in-Flatbush* (New York, 1979).

Bibliography

NEWSPAPERS

La America, all issues, 1910–25.
La Vara, selected issues, 1923–48.
American Hebrew, selected issues, 1908–13.

BULLETINS

Shearith Israel Bulletin, selected issues, 1912–31.
The Sephardic Bulletin, published by The Sephardic Jewish Community of
   New York, all issues, November 1928–June 1930.
The Sephardi, published by the Central Sephardic Jewish Community of
   America, all issues, 1943–57.
World Sephardi, published by the American Branch of the World Sephardi
   Federation, all issues, 1959–60.

MINUTES, CORRESPONDENCE, AND UNPUBLISHED MATERIALS

(all in the possession of Congregation Shearith Israel in New York, unless
otherwise stated)
Minute book of the Oriental Committee of The Sisterhood of the Spanish
   and Portuguese Synagogue, 1913–16.
Minutes of the trustees of Congregation Shearith Israel, vols. 8 and 9.

Minutes and correspondence of the Sephardic Jewish Community of New York, Inc., 1928–33.

Minutes of the Central Sephardic Jewish Community of America, 1941–45.

Minutes of the Sephardic Brotherhood, January 31, February 8, and March 3, 1925 (in possession of the Sephardic Brotherhood).

Minutes of HIAS, selected, 1912–21 (in the possession of YIVO Institute).

Address of Dr. Cyrus Adler to the Sisterhood of the Spanish and Portuguese Synagogue, November 27, 1916.

"Report of the Committee on a Progressive Policy in the Congregation," prepared by David de Sola Pool, April 22, 1927.

Letter of Dr. Pool to Mortimer Menken, November 25, 1924.

Files, records, and correspondence of Union of Sephardic Congregations, 1929–55.

Letters of Moise Gadol, 1938 and 1939.

INTERVIEWS

Victor Alhadeff, New York

Albert Amateau, Hollywood, California (a written record of reminiscences of Moise Gadol)

Sam Gadol, Santa Barbara, California (telephone conversation)

Rachel Pilosoff, New York

Eli Rousso, New York

Louie Rousso, New York

Victor Tarry, New York

Joseph and Lily Varsano, New York

OTHER WORKS CONSULTED

Adatto, Albert. "Sephardim and the Seattle Sephardic Community." Master's thesis, University of Washington, Seattle, 1939.

Angel, Marc. *The Jews of Rhodes: The History of a Sephardic Community.* New York, 1978.

———. "Notes on the Early History of Seattle's Sephardic Community." *Western States Jewish Historical Quarterly,* October 1974, pp. 22–30.

———. "'Progress'—Seattle's Sephardic Monthly, 1934–35." *The American Sephardi,* Autumn 1971, pp. 91–95.

———, ed. *Rabbi David de Sola Pool: Selections from Six Decades of Sermons, Addresses and Writings.* New York, 1980.

———. "The Sephardic Theatre of Seattle." *American Jewish Archives,* November 1973, pp. 156–60.

———. "The Sephardim of the United States: An Exploratory Study." In

American Jewish Year Book, vol. 74 (1973), pp. 77–138. New York and Philadelphia.

———, ed. *Studies in Sephardic Culture.* New York, 1980.

———. "Thoughts About Early American Jewry." *Tradition,* Fall 1976, pp. 16–23.

Barocas, David N. *Albert Matarasso and His Ladino.* New York, 1969.

———. *The Broome and Allen Boys.* New York, 1969.

Benardete, Maír José. *Hispanic Culture and Character of the Sephardic Jews.* New York, 1952; reprinted, 1982.

Beton, Sol. *Sephardim and a History of Congregation Or Veshalom.* Atlanta, 1981.

Cohen, Hayyim. "Sephardi Jews in the United States, Marriage with Ashkenazim." *Dispersion and Unity* 13–14 (1971–72): 151–60.

Elmaleh, Abraham. *Ha-Professor Abraham Galante.* Jerusalem, 1954.

Gadol, M. S. *Christopher Columbus Was a Jew.* New York, 1941.

Goren, Arthur. *New York Jews and the Quest for Community.* New York, 1970.

Greenberg, William. "History of Ezra Bessaroth." In *Dedication Program of Ezra Bessaroth,* Seattle, 1970.

Gross, Morris. *Learning Readiness in Two Jewish Groups.* New York, 1967.

Gurock, Jeffrey. *When Harlem Was Jewish.* New York, 1979.

Hacker, Louis M. "The Communal Life of the Sephardic Jews in New York City." *Jewish Social Service Quarterly* 3 (December 1926): 32–40.

Hanan, Rubin. *History of Etz Ahayem Congregation.* Montgomery, 1962.

Hexter, Maurice. "The Dawn of a Problem." *Jewish Charities,* December 1913, pp. 2–5.

Howe, Irving. *World of Our Fathers.* New York, 1976.

Papo, Joseph M. "The Sephardic Community of America." *Reconstructionist* 12 (1946): 12–18.

———. "The Sephardic Jewish Community of New York." In *Studies in Sephardic Culture,* ed. M. D. Angel, New York, 1980, pp. 65–94.

Pool, David de Sola. "The Immigration of Levantine Jews into the United States." *Jewish Charities,* June 1914, pp. 12–27.

———. "The Levantine Jews in the United States." In *American Jewish Year Book,* vol. 15 (1913–14), pp. 207–20. Philadelphia.

Pool, David and Tamar de Sola. *An Old Faith In The New World.* New York, 1955.

Porter, David. *Constantinople and Its Environs.* New York, 1835.

Pulido, Angel. *Españoles sin patria.* Madrid, 1905.

Rischin, Moses. *The Promised City.* Cambridge, Mass., 1977.

Sanua, Victor. "A Study of Adjustment of Sephardic Jews in the New York Metropolitan Area." *Jewish Journal of Sociology* 9 (June 1967): 25–33.

Shirazi, Helen. "The Communal Pluralism of Sephardi Jewry in the United States." *Le Judaisme Sephardi,* January 1966, pp. 23–25, 32.

Sutton, Joseph. *Magic Carpet: Aleppo-in-Flatbush.* New York, 1979.

Szajkowski, Z. "The Alliance Israélite Universelle in the United States 1860–1949." In *Publications of the American Jewish Historical Society* 39 (June 1950): 406–43.

Wischnitzer, Mark. *Visas to Freedom.* New York, 1956.

Yerushalmi, Yosef H. Review essay in *American Jewish Historical Quarterly* 62 (December 1972): 180–89.

Index

Abolafia, Joseph, 111
Adams Paper Company, 145
Adler, Cyrus, 42
Agudat Ahim, 151
Aguila, La, 55, 116–17
Ahavah Ve-Ahvah (New Brunswick, N.J.), 149–50
Ahavat Ahim, 159
Ahavath Shalom (Atlanta), 155
Ahavath Shalom (Portland, Oreg.), 158
Ahavath Shalom of Monastir, 28–29, 35, 62
Ahavath Shalom Society of Los Angeles, 157
Ahava Ve-Ahvah Janina, 27, 28, 64
Ahduth, 157
Ahduth Benei Israel, 30
Ahim Mevorakhim Society, 30
Albahari, David, 150
Albania, immigration from, 17
Alcalay, Isaac, 171
Alkalai, Yehudah, 129
Allen Street, 20, 27, 64, 112
Allen Street Religious School, 33
Alliance Israélite Universelle, 10, 25–26, 34, 41, 145
Alphonso XIII, king of Spain, 136

Alvo, Shelomo, 29
Amado, Maurice, 168
Amado, Raphael, 85
Amateau, Albert J., 5, 9–10, 16, 23, 24–25, 31, 70
    Federation of Oriental Jews and, 63, 67, 68–69, 70, 74, 75, 77, 85
    in *La Vera* feud, 119, 121–27
America, La, see La America
American Immigration Office, 13–14
American Sephardi Federation, 176
American Zionist Federation, 34
Angora Union Club, 30, 34, 35
Arabic-speaking Jews, 6, 29, 47, 64, 65, 96, 126, 148
Argentina, Sephardim in, 18
Ashkenazim, 3, 20, 23, 36, 40, 41, 50, 65, 66, 71, 77, 116, 133, 135, 140, 149, 150, 151, 152, 155, 157, 161, 174
    Sephardim vs., 15, 24, 34, 44–45, 52–58, 79, 81, 88–89, 98–99, 131–32, 136, 142, 146, 165, 178
assimilation, 49–52, 58–60, 105, 129, 152, 157, 164–66, 177–78
Atlanta, Sephardim in, 114, 149, 154–55, 166
Avzaradel, Victor, 154

Balkan countries:
immigration from, 6, 10, 12, 17–18, 20
see also Turkey; Turkinos
Balkan Wars, 58
Barcelona, University of, 180
Bar Kokhba, 133
Barocas, David N., 141, 180
Baron de Hirsch Fund, 16
Bazaravo, Abraham, 50–51
Behar, Leon, 162
Behar, Morris, 113
Behar, Nessim, 25–26, 33, 34, 44, 53, 54, 77, 81, 82, 134, 135, 145
Beit Hinukh Sephardi, 31
Beja, Joseph, 136
Benardete, Maír José, 23, 25–26, 38, 145, 180, 181
Benezra, Aharon, 99, 113, 160–62
Benguiat, Ephraim, 33, 67
Benjamin, Alfred, 149
Benveniste, Asher, 111
Benveniste, Morris, 132
Benyunes, Joseph, 34, 72, 82, 86, 95, 99, 102, 104
Ben Zvi Institute, 179–80
Berith Shalom Synagogue, 35, 82–83, 85, 86, 91, 95, 99–105
Berro, Yitzhak, 158
Besso, Henry V., 175
Besso, Jacob, 150
"Biblioteca del Pueblo, La," 113
Bikur Holim, 28, 78–79, 102
Bikur Holim (Cincinnati), 153
Bikur Holim (Seattle), 160–62
Bnei Zion, 58
Boz del Pueblo, La, 117–18
Brighton Leather and Finishings Company, 127
Bronx, Sephardim in, 146, 164, 169, 171, 172
Brotherhood Metal Workers Union, 142–43
Brotherhood of Rhodes, 24
Bulgaria:
immigration from, 12, 17, 18, 126
Jewish community in, 81
Bureau for the Placement of the Handicapped, 24

Caleb brothers, 145
Capouya, Joseph, 50
Capuano, Menashe, 154
Caraso, Abraham, 156
Carasso, David, 29, 65
Cardozo, David Jessurun, 171, 175
Carmel Hotel, 145
Caspi, Gabriel, 145
Caston, Joseph, 160, 162
Catskill Mountains, Sephardic hotels in, 145
Central Sephardic Jewish Community of America, 3, 170–74, 175
Chicago, Sephardim in, 139, 149, 152–53
Christian missionaries, 59, 66
Chrystie Street, 20, 21–22, 24, 28, 29, 34, 47, 63, 66, 75, 92, 112
Cincinnati, Sephardim in, 16, 139, 148, 153
Cleveland, Sephardim in, 16, 148
Cohen, Albert, 109
Cohen, Jack, 145
Cohen, Jacob, 145
Colchamiro, Leon, 27
Columbia University, 179
Columbus, Christopher, 4, 128
Columbus, Ohio, Sephardim in, 16, 148
Congress, U.S., immigration laws passed by, 16–18
Cordova, Marco, 160
Covo, Albert, 120, 121–22
Crespi, Eliah, 34, 144
Crespi, Jack, 144
Crudo, Albert, 31
Cuba, Sephardim in, 18

Dardanelles Social Club, 29–30
Democratic Party, 31
Diaspora, 129, 148–63

Educational Alliance, 132
Eikhah, 133
Eldridge Street, 20, 31, 34, 35, 82, 83, 91, 102, 134
Elias, Aaron Ben, 173, 175
Elias, Aharon, 109
Elias, Jack, 150

Eliyahu, Aharon Ben, 37, 109
Eliyahu, Delicia, 28
Ellis Island, 13–14, 16
Emanuel, Shelomo, 62, 101
England, immigration from, 17, 18
Ets Hahayyim, 156
Europe, eastern, immigration from, 5
Ez Hahayyim Society, 29, 64–65, 97
Ezra, 113
Ezra Bessaroth, 160, 162
Ezrat Ahim Society, 102

Farhi, Isaac, 111
Farhi, Jack, 15–16, 19, 22, 34, 44, 59, 66
Federation of Jewish Philanthropies, 128
Federation of Oriental Jews, 23, 24, 37, 44, 57, 58, 62–81, 85, 95, 112, 126, 167
Filo Center Club, 31, 85–86, 120
Forsyth Street, 20, 73
Foundation for the Advancement of Sephardic Studies and Culture, 180
France, Sephardim in, 18
Franco, Robert, 168
Fresco, David, 75

Gadol, Moise Salomon, 24, 25, 29–30, 32–35, 43–44, 48, 50, 51, 52–59, 140–46, 149–50, 153, 154–62, 176, 178, 182
   background of, 7, 130–31
   business ventures of, 107, 111, 112–13, 118, 127
   described, 8–9, 23
   as editor, 4–5, 7–8, 18, 21, 47, 107–27
   Federation of Oriental Jews and, 61–65, 67–81, 112
   finances of, 3–4, 15, 22, 57, 64–65, 86, 107, 110–14, 118, 124–28, 134
   funeral of, 3–4
   immigrants helped by, 14–17, 22–23, 108, 110, 122, 140
   La Vara vs., 118–28
   Oriental Bureau and, 14–15, 140

Gadol, Moise Salomon (continued)
   Sephardic Community and, 69–76, 81–87
   Spanish and Portuguese Synagogue and, 90, 92–94, 96–105
   as speaker, 23, 71–72, 142
   as Zionist, 100, 123, 126, 130–37
Gadol, Samuel, 150
Galante, Abraham, 75
Galante, Rabeno, 154, 155
Galicia, Jewish community in, 81
Gallipoli Jews, 30, 81, 160
Gallipoli Progressive Club, 30, 81
Gambach, Nissim, 181
Gary, Ind., Sephardim in, 16
Gattegnu, Morris, 119
Gedelecia, Joseph, 23–25, 34, 54, 84, 135
   Federation of Oriental Jews and, 23, 37, 44, 63, 66, 67, 70, 72–80
Germany, immigration from, 17, 18
Glenham, N.Y., Sephardim in, 148
Graciani, Shabatai, 113
Granada, University of, 180
Grand Handkerchief Manufacturing Company, 145
Grand Street, 28, 145
Gratz College, 150
Greece, immigration from, 6, 10, 12, 17
Greek-speaking Jews, 6, 27–28, 40, 47, 72, 126, 136, 148

Habib, Bohor, 155
Habib, Nissim, 132
Hacker, Louis, 36, 42, 105, 167
Halevi, Yehudah, 109
Halfon, Albert, 134
Hananiah, Eli, 111
Hananiah, Jack David, 145
Hanna, Bohor, 48–49, 85
Harlem, Sephardim in, 5, 31, 35–36, 67, 85–87, 101, 120, 136, 146, 167–69
Harvard University, 179
Haskalah Club, 30
Hasson, Raphael, 86, 103
"Ha-tikvah," 132, 137, 155
Hayyim, Jacob, 156

Hayyim Va-Hessed Gallipoli, 66
Hazan, Yitzhak, 154
Hebrah Hesed Ve-emet, 99
Hebrew Immigrant Aid Society (HIAS), 11, 13–16, 23, 58, 71, 140
Hebrew language, 50, 108, 130, 131, 132, 180
Hebrew Sephardi Club of Harlem, 36
Hebrew University, 179
Hendricks, Henry S., 82–84, 86, 103–4, 168, 169
Hermandad of Dardanelles Society, La, 153
Hesed Israel Anshei Rodes, 158
Hesed Ve-Emet, 28
Hevra Kadisha, 78
Hexter, Maurice, 153
Hispanic Culture and Character of the Sephardic Jews (Benardete), 181
Hispano-Jewish Publishing Company, 116
Howe, Irving, 6
Hugo, Victor, 109
Huli, Jacob, 180

immigrants, 5–6, 42, 61, 67, 91, 138
see also *individual nationalities*
immigration laws, 13–14, 16–17, 108
Independent Voters Political and Social Club, 30
Indianapolis, Sephardim in, 149, 153–54
Industrial Removal Office, 16, 148
In Search of Our Sephardic Roots (Barocas), 180
Instituto Arias Montana de Estudios Hebraicos, 180
Interstate Electric Battery Company, 142
Isaiah, 109, 113
Israel:
    creation of, *see* Palestine; Zionists
    Sephardic studies in, 179–80
Italian immigrants, 21–22
Italy, immigration from, 18

Janina Jews, 27–28, 64, 65, 73

Jewish Agency, 176
Jewish Agricultural and Industrial Aid Society, 148
Jewish Business Agency, 49
Jewish Friendship Circle, 99
Jewish Relief Committee, 81
Joint Distribution Committee, 44
Judeo-Spanish, 6, 39–40, 43, 49–51, 91, 126, 138, 148, 164, 166, 172, 177–78, 179, 181
Judeo-Spanish newspapers, 115–26
see also *individual titles*
judezmo, 40

Kaplan, Aryeh, 180
Karpeles, John J., 171
Kastoríalis, 27–28, 115
Kings County Hospital, 4
Kretchmer, A., 53–55

La America, 4–5, 7–8, 12, 20–23, 25, 37, 45, 50, 51, 52–59, 70, 81, 139–44
    competitors of, 115–26
    Federation of Oriental Jews and, 62–65, 68, 71–76, 78
    finances of, 7, 15, 32, 57, 64–65, 86, 107, 110–14, 118, 124–26, 134
    history of, 106–27
    on immigration, 13–14, 17–18
    La Vara vs., 118–27
    nationwide reporting of, 148–63
    Sephardic Community and, 81–87
    on Spanish and Portuguese Synagogue, 91, 92, 96–105
    on women's issues, 47–48
    on Zionism, 130–36
Ladino, *see* Judeo-Spanish
Ladino American Club, 153
Lastry, Joseph, 132
Legier, Leon, 152
Leon, Hayyim, 159
Levant, Jewish community in, 37, 41–42, 44–45, 46
Levantine Jews, 37, 44–45, 61–65, 82, 84, 150
    immigration of, 6, 10–12, 16–18
Levi, Preciado, 147

Levi, Zeharia, 27
Levy, Albert, 36, 118, 119, 120, 122
Levy, David, 159
Levy, John Hezekiah, 85, 86, 145, 168
Levy, Joseph B., 109
Levy, Raphael, 132
Los Angeles, Sephardim in, 149, 156–57, 166
Los Angeles Sephardic Club, 157
Lower East Side (New York):
    immigrants on, 5–6, 42, 61, 67, 91
    Sephardim on, 6–8, 9, 13, 19–22, 26, 61, 91, 99, 105, 139, 171
Luz, La, 31
Lyceum Hall, 134

Madrid, Sephardic studies in, 180
Maeso, David Gonzalo, 180
Magnes, Judah, 42, 57, 73, 74, 80, 97
Maimon, Sam, 43
Maimon, Stella, 47
Malakh, Salvadore, 30
Marmara, Island of, Sephardic immigrants from, 157, 159
Matarasso, Albert, 36, 138
Mayo, Benny, 145
Mayo, Bohor, 151
Mayo, Hannah, 28
Maznaim Publishing Corporation, 180
Me-am Lo'ez, 180
Mekor Hayyim Dardanelles, 29, 83
Mendes, Henry Pereira, 67, 88, 95, 96–97, 98, 101, 130
Menken, Alice, 33, 71, 72
Menken, Mortimer, 104
Mexico, Sephardim in, 18
Midwest, Sephardim in, 152–54
Mikveh Israel Congregation, 150, 170
Misérables, Les (Hugo), 109
Misgav Yerushalayim, 179
Mizrahi, Alfred, 54, 55, 116–17
Mizrahi, B., 156
Mizrahi, Moise, 145
Monastir Jews, 28, 35, 62, 115, 146, 150–51
Montgomery, Ala., Sephardim in, 114, 149, 155–56

Montreal, Sephardim in, 170
Morgenthau, Henry, 44
Morhaim, Shemuel, 160
Moroccan Jews, 131, 152
Mount Sinai Hospital, 71
Moyal, Isaac, 175–76

Nahmias, David, 124–25
Nahoum, Hayyim, 15, 48, 83
Naon, Shabbatai, 161–62
Naon, Vitale, 29
National Spanish Hebrew Society, 149
Nehama, Yaacov, 97
Nessim, Simon, 85–86, 168, 169, 174–75
New Brunswick, N.J., Sephardim in, 149–50
New Jersey, Sephardim in, 148–50
New Lots, Brooklyn, Sephardim in, 31, 146, 171
New York City, Sephardim in, see individual neighborhoods and streets
New York Kehillah, 23, 27, 34, 37, 42, 57–58, 66, 73, 74–75, 97, 126
New York Public Library, 4
New York Shoe Polish Manufacturing Company, 113
New York State, Sephardim in, see specific cities
Nissim Morris, 30, 34, 117
Novedades, Las, 131

Ohio, Sephardim in, 16, 139, 148, 153
Orchard Street Synagogue and Religious School, 34, 91, 95, 99–105
Or Hadash, 180
Or Hahayyim, 155
"Oriental," 76, 77, 79
Oriental American Civic Club, 30
Oriental Brotherhood Society of Raritan, N.J., 149
Oriental Bureau, 14–16, 71, 140, 142
Oriental Federation and Socialist Education Society, 30
Oriental Hebrew Association, 30
Oriental Israelite Fraternity, 153

Oriental Jewish Club, 151
Oriental Jewish Community of the City of New York, 69–76, 81
Oriental Jewish Maccabee Organization, 132, 134–36
Oriental Jewish Young Women's Social Club, 47
Oriental Printing and Publishing Company, 107, 111
Oriental Progressive Society, 27, 53–54, 116
Or Israel, 150–51
Or Veshalom, 155
Ottoman Empire, 40–41, 50, 128, 131
Ouziel, Benzion Meir Hai, 174
Ouziel, Binyamin, 29
Ovadia, Mazal, 171
Ovadia, Nissim, 3, 170–71, 174
Ozer Dalim, 28, 78
Ozer Dalim (Chicago), 152–53
Ozer Dalim (Seattle), 161

Palestine:
  Jewish state proposed in, 131, 135–37, 174
  Sephardim in, 18, 131
Pan American Union of Sephardic Communities, 174
Papo, Joseph M., 171, 172
Pardo, Barukh, 109
Perahia, Henry J., 171–72
Philadelphia, Sephardim in, 139, 150, 170
Phillips, N. Taylor, 92, 95
Pilosoff, Rachel, 3–4, 5
Poland:
  immigration from, 17, 18
  Jewish community in, 81
Pool, David de Sola, 13, 27, 33, 37, 53, 57, 63, 64, 67, 87, 88, 91, 92, 95, 97, 104–5, 128, 130, 135, 148, 165, 167, 168, 169, 170
Portland, Ore., Sephardim in, 149, 157–58
Portuguese Jews, 34, 73, 96, 152
Princeton University, 179
Progresso, El, 117

Prolegomenos, 180
Pro-Palestine Federation of America, 173
Pulido, Angel, 39

Raritan, N.J., Sephardim in, 148, 149
Rashi script, 108
Recuero, Pascual, 180
Reform Jews, 129, 143
Rhodes, Island of:
  Jewish community on, 41
  Sephardic immigrants from, 24, 29, 155, 157, 159, 160
Rivington Street, 92, 112
Rochester, N.Y., Sephardim in, 115, 149, 150–51
Rodefei, Tsedek, 29, 64
Romania, immigration from, 17
Romanian Jews, 152
Romey, Marco, 160, 162
Rosenberg, H., 106
Rousso, Louie, 30
Rousso, Louis, 146
Russia, immigration from, 5, 17, 18
Russian Jews, 135
Russo brothers, 145
Russ Togs, 146

Salonika Brotherhood, see Sephardic Brotherhood
Salonikan Jews, 29, 30, 44, 84–86, 109, 149
Salonika Social Club, 153
San Francisco, Sephardim in, 149, 157
Satan, El, 109
Schneider, Mr., 124
Seattle, Sephardim in, 16, 139, 148, 149, 157, 158–61, 166
Sefarad, 180
Seff, Mr., 53–55
Semach, Leon, 41
Sephardi, The, 171, 172–74
"Sephardic," 76, 77, 79
Sephardic Brotherhood, 30, 84–86
  La Vara published by, 118–26
Sephardic Bulletin, 165, 169
Sephardic Center of the Bronx, 164
Sephardic Community, 81–87, 96, 120

Sephardic Democratic Club, 31
Sephardic Home for the Aged, 5
Sephardic House, 181
Sephardic Jewish Community of New York, 167–69
Sephardic Liberty Loan Committee, 31
Sephardic Union of New Lots, 31
Sephardic Zionist Union, 100, 132–36
Sephardim:
    Ashkenazim vs., 15, 24, 34, 44–45, 52–58, 79, 81, 88–89, 98–99, 131–32, 136, 142, 146, 165, 178
    customs of, 45–46
    defined, 6, 51–52
    economic life of, 138–47
    immigration of, 10–18, 26, 89, 138–39
    origin of, 39–40
Sepharedim Social Club, 31
Serbia, Jewish community in, 81
Shabati, Aaron and Sarah, 127
Shaltiel, Joseph, 78
Shearith Israel, see Spanish and Portuguese Synagogue of New York City
Shearith Israel Bulletin, 89, 90–91
Shearith Israel of Montreal, 170
Shinasi, Leon, 143–44
Shinasi, M., 73–74
Shinasi, Shelomo, 143–44
Shinasi brothers, 27, 139, 141, 143–44
Sitton, Selom, 132
Solam, Moise, 109
Soulam, Moise, 30, 118, 119, 122
Spain:
    Jews expelled from, 39, 50, 131
    Palestinian intervention of, 136
    Sephardic immigration to, 18, 131
    Sephardic studies in, 180
Spanish and Portuguese Synagogue of New York City, 27, 31, 33–34, 53, 63, 64, 67–68, 71–73, 82, 88–105, 126, 130, 168, 170, 176, 181
    congregation of, 88–89
    Sisterhood of, 34–35, 36, 42, 66, 67, 71–72, 82–83, 90–103

Spanish Hebrew Congregation, 153
Spanish Jewish Printing and Publishing Company, 118
Spanish language, see Judeo-Spanish
Spanish-speaking Jews, 28, 29, 47, 71, 73, 83, 103
State Department, U.S., 136
Studies in Sephardic Culture, 181
Sunshine Battery Company, 144
Sunshine Table Manufacturing Company, 145
Supreme Council for Scientific Studies of Spain, 180
Syria, immigration from, 6, 10
Syrian Jews, 29, 157, 172

Taggeblatt, 55
Talmudei Torah, 33–36, 62, 64, 67–68, 71–73, 77, 87, 92, 95–102, 151, 155, 161, 165–66, 172
Tarry, Victor, 168–69
Tiempo, El, 75, 160
Tikva Tovah Society, 28, 64
Tobacco Produce Company, 143
Toledano, Pinhas, 101
Toledano, Rachel, 63, 71–72, 101
Toledo, Ohio, Sephardim in, 16, 148
Toledo, Spain, Sephardic studies in, 180
Torah Anthology, The, 180
Torres, Albert, 4
Touriel, Lucy, 171
Treves brothers, 156
Turkey:
    immigration from, 6, 10, 11–14, 17–18
    life in, 39–40, 47, 51, 53, 55, 58, 81
    Zionism feared by, 75, 126, 131, 133, 135–37
Turkinos, 20, 21, 27, 29, 30, 37, 39–45, 57, 66, 68, 94, 98, 101, 126, 132, 139, 142, 144, 152, 155, 156, 157, 158–59

Union and Peace Society, 27
Union Israelite Portuguese, 152
Union of Orthodox Jewish Congregations of America, 23

Union of Sephardic Congregations, 137, 170
unions, 141–43
United Nations, 137
United States Socialist Party, 30
Universal Electric Novelty Company, 145

Valensi, Albert, 168
Valensi, Edward, 74, 75–76, 87, 121
Vara, La, 4, 118–28, 164
Varsano, Joseph, 5, 23, 109, 113, 120, 121
Varsano, Lily, 5

Washington, University of, 179
Washington Hall, 162
Wise, Stephen, 143
women:
    abuse of, 21, 46, 141–42
    activist, 141–42, 151, 171, 175
    opportunities for, 13, 47–48
    see also Spanish and Portuguese Synagogue of New York City, Sisterhood of
World Federation of Sephardi Communities, 174–75
World of Our Fathers (Howe), 6
World Sephardi, 175
World Sephardi Federation, 175–76
World Trading Company, 113
World War I, 12–13, 43, 81, 133, 135–36
World War II, 174

Yahuda, Abraham S., 136
Yahya, Samuel, 145
Yerushalmi, Shemuel, 180
Yeshiva University, 179
Yeshuah Verahamim, 29
Yetomin Ve-Almanot, 160
Yiddish, 6, 42, 50, 53, 65, 108, 116, 140
Yiddish newspapers, 55, 98, 106–7, 140
Yiddish-speaking Jews, 6, 27, 47
Young Hebrew Literary Club, 162
Young Hebrew Prosperity Club, 162
Young Men's Sephardic Association of Rochester, 151
Young Men's Sepharedim Association, 31, 35–36
Young Sephardim Progress Club, 155
Young Turks, 11
Yugoslavia, immigration from, 12, 17

Zadok, Aaron, 113
Zionist Congress, 135
Zionist Federation of America, 132, 135
Zionist Federation of Monastir, 153–54
Zionists, 51, 100, 123, 129–37
    opposition to, 75, 126
Zionist Sephardim Society of New York, see Sephardic Zionist Union
Zion Memorial Chapel, 3

Angel, Marc.

La America

DEMCO